Creating Life

The Aesthetic Utopia
of Russian Modernism

Creating Life

The Aesthetic Utopia
of Russian Modernism

EDITED BY

Irina Paperno and
Joan Delaney Grossman

STANFORD UNIVERSITY PRESS
Stanford, California 1994

Stanford University Press
Stanford, California
© 1994 by the Board of Trustees of the
Leland Stanford Junior University
Printed in the United States of America

CIP data appear at the end of the book

Stanford University Press publications are
distributed exclusively by Stanford University
Press within the United States, Canada, and
Mexico; they are distributed exclusively by
Cambridge University Press throughout
the rest of the world.

Preface

The transliteration system throughout the volume is that used by the Library of Congress, adopting the traditional -sky and -y for personal name endings. An appendix at the end of the volume provides the original Russian texts of quotations from primary sources given in English translation. In the essays and the Appendix, contributors' omissions of material from cited passages are indicated by spaced ellipsis points (. . .); ellipses present in the original texts are indicated by suspension points without spaces (...).

Alexander Lavrov's essay in this volume is a revised and enlarged version of his article "Mifotvorchestvo argonavtov," which appeared in *Mif-fol'klor-literatura* (Leningrad, 1978). It is published here by permission of Nauka publishers. The translation from the Russian is by Joan Delaney Grossman.

In preparing this volume the editors relied on financial support from the Center for Slavic and East European Studies and the Committee on Research at the University of California at Berkeley. Irina Paperno wishes to acknowledge support from the Kennan Institute for Advanced Russian Studies. We are grateful to our graduate research assistants Margherita DiCeglie, Russell Valentino, and Glen Worthey.

I.P., J.G.

Contents

Contributors

JOAN DELANEY GROSSMAN is Professor Emeritus of Slavic Languages and Literatures at the University of California, Berkeley. She is the author of *Edgar Allan Poe in Russia: A Study in Legend and Literary Influence* (Wurzburg, 1973) and *Valery Bryusov and the Riddle of Russian Decadence* (Berkeley, Calif., 1985).

IRINA GUTKIN is Assistant Professor of Slavic Languages and Literatures at the University of California, Los Angeles. Her dissertation is entitled "The Socialist Realist Novel as a Phenomenon of Literary Evolution" (University of California, Berkeley, 1989).

ALEXANDER LAVROV is a Senior Research Fellow at the Institute of Russian Literature (Pushkinsky Dom), Academy of Sciences, St. Petersburg. He has written numerous articles and prepared the publication of archival documents concerning the history of Russian Symbolism. Scholarly editions of the major Symbolist texts appeared under his editorship, including Andrei Bely's memoirs—*At the Turn of the Century* (*Na rubezhe dvukh stoletii*), *The Beginning of the Century* (*Nachalo veka*), and *Between the Two Revolutions* (*Mezhdu dvukh revoliutsii*) (Moscow, 1989–90)—and Bely's *Symphonies* (Leningrad, 1991).

IRENE MASING-DELIC is Associate Professor of Slavic Languages and Literatures at Ohio State University. She is the author of *A. Blok's "The Snow Mask." An Interpretation* (Stockholm, 1970) and *Abolishing Death: A Salvation Myth of Twentieth-Century Russian Literature* (Stanford, Calif., 1993).

OLGA MATICH is Professor of Slavic Languages and Literatures at the University of California, Berkeley. She is the author of *Paradox in the Religious Poetry of Zinaida Gippius* (Munich, 1972) and coeditor (with Michael Heim) of *The Third Wave: Russian Literature in Emigration* (Ann Arbor, Mich., 1983).

IRINA PAPERNO is Professor of Slavic Languages and Literatures at the University of California, Berkeley. She is the author of *Chernyshevsky and the Age of Realism: A Study in the Semiotics of Behavior* (Stanford, Calif., 1988) and coeditor (with Boris Gasparov and Robert P. Hughes) of *Cultural Mythologies of Russian Modernism: From the Golden Age to the Silver Age* (Berkeley, Calif., 1992).

MICHAEL WACHTEL is Assistant Professor of Slavic Languages and Literatures at Princeton University. His dissertation is entitled "Goethe and Novalis in the Life and Work of Vyacheslav Ivanov" (Harvard University, 1990).

Creating Life

The Aesthetic Utopia
of Russian Modernism

Introduction

IRINA PAPERNO

This study takes its departure from one of the "accursed questions" in modern Russian culture—the relations of art and life. A cornerstone of romantic aesthetics, an issue of ideological importance for the mid–nineteenth-century positivist realists and their contemporaries, the problem was central to the creators of Symbolism, the movement (1890's–1910's) that launched modernism in Russia.

Following romanticism, the Symbolists aspired to merge the antitheses of art and life into a unity. Art was proclaimed to be a force capable of, and destined for, the "creation of life" (*tvorchestvo zhizni*), while "life" was viewed as an object of artistic creation or as a creative act. In this sense, art turned into "real life" and "life" turned into art; they became one. For the artist no separation existed between the "man" and the "poet," between personal life (*zhizn'*) and artistic (creative) activity (*tvorchestvo*).

In a retrospective glance at the movement, the Symbolists' younger contemporary Vladislav Khodasevich described this concern as central to Symbolism:

Symbolism did not want to be merely an artistic school, a literary movement. It continually strove to become a life-creating method, and in this was its most profound, perhaps unembodiable truth. Its entire history was in essence spent in yearning after that truth. It was a series of attempts, at times truly heroic, to find a fusion of life and art, as it were, the philosopher's stone of art.[1]

The principle of fusing art and life as practiced by Russian Symbolists is generally known as *zhiznetvorchestvo*.[2] The word itself is untranslatable. In Russian, it leaves room for multiple interpretations: *tvorchestvo* refers to artistic creation; when combined with the word *zhizn'* ("life"), it suggests both the creation of life and a synthesis of the two elements—creation and life.[3]

Zhiznetvorchestvo has been associated with highly publicized episodes from the artists' private lives that acquired the status of significant cultural events, such as the love relations involving Andrei Bely, Alexander Blok, and Liubov' Dmitrievna Blok[4] and the relations between Bely, Valery Briusov, and Nina Petrovskaia. All these episodes were self-conscious in a way suggesting deliberate aesthetic organization of behavior. In semiotic terms, the artist's life was treated as a text, constructed and "read" by a method similar to that used in art.[5] Contemporary critics mostly use the concept *zhiznetvorchestvo* to mean aesthetic organization of behavior.[6] This view is prompted by the association of the Russian phenomenon with the aestheticism of European Decadence, such as attitudes and forms of behavior of which Oscar Wilde became a symbol. In the Russian context, this interpretation of *zhiznetvorchestvo* can be traced to Khodasevich, who, in the essay "The End of Renata" ("Konets Renaty," 1928), derived his much quoted formulations of the Symbolist "method" from his reflections on the story of Petrovskaia, described as an "artist" who created a "poem" out of her own life and as "a true victim of Decadence."[7]

Looking back at the Russian "Decadents and Symbolists" of the 1900's, Khodasevich attempted to outline the mechanism by which a merger of art and life was effected:

They attempted to transform art into real life and real life into art. The events of life were never experienced as merely and solely life's events; instead, because of the lack of clarity and the instability of the boundary lines that outlined reality for these people, the events of life immediately became a part of the internal world, a piece of creation. Conversely, something written by any member of the circle became real, an event of life for all. In this manner, both life and literature were created, as it were, by joint, sometimes hostile, but still united, forces of all who found themselves in this extraordinary life, in this "symbolist dimension." This was, it seems, a true instance of collective creation.[8]

According to Khodasevich, the Symbolists did not find "the philosopher's stone of art." "The history of the Symbolists," wrote Khodasevich, "turned into a history of ruined lives"; at the same time, part of their creative energy, having "leaked" into the sphere of life, failed to become fully embodied.[9] For Khodasevich, Nina Petrovskaia, an artist merely in life and a woman whose unhappy life ended in suicide (in 1928), stands as a tragic symbol of the age.

Is the case of *zhiznetvorchestvo* closed?

That the principle of fusing art and life left a powerful imprint on the Russian culture, reaching from the turn of the century into the 1920's and 1930's and from literature into "real life," is undeniable. It is the purpose of this study to reevaluate it by exploring some of its crucial manifestations in the context of the metaphysical system of Russian modernism. Viewed in this perspective, deliberate organization of behavior appears as a part of what we call a Russian "aesthetic utopia."

Summing up an array of intellectual and artistic trends that developed in Western European cultures, and in Russia, at the turn of the century and lasted into the 1930's, the concept of "modernism" suggests a certain generalized new "consciousness," or "mentality," holding that the accepted model of reality, or the world itself, is up for rearrangement. This mentality drew its strength from a characteristic feeling: the apocalyptic sense that humankind was living at the "breaking point" of history, destined for totally novel times and a new world.[10] Modernism has been frequently described as a reaction against positivism and realism (or naturalism). Indeed, a major dynamic force behind modernist movements across Europe was a rejection of the positivistic mode of cognition that relied on the surface reality of empirical facts, subject to realistic representation. The notion of

the empirically given, objectively existing fact was questioned in
many areas of knowledge—philosophy, physics, psychology, art.
Primacy was given to the creative principle—the spontaneous,
as in Bergsonian creative evolution, or the deliberate. In the
framework of the latter, Nietzsche called man to self-creation,
an aesthetic process; the neo-Kantians placed their faith in con-
ceptualizing consciousness. A powerful trend in modernism was
inspired by a distrust of "nature" (as it was modeled by positivistic science). Those who shared in this distrust questioned the
validity and value of life that was allowed to run its "natural"
course. This attitude sustained a sense that "reality" is essentially
an object of deliberate creative activities.

There are varieties of modernism, each arising from the spe-
cifics of a national context. Russia had a long-lasting tradition of
apocalyptic thinking, which was closely intertwined with a tradition of philosophical and social utopianism. In the second part of
the nineteenth century, Russian culture went through a period
of positivistic realism, with its cult of "reality" (material reality
or sensual experience) and "action" (social activism, mostly of a
socialist bend), a movement that matured in the 1860's, in the
era of large-scale social and cultural change accompanying the
so-called Great Reforms. Although realism construed itself as a
radical rejection of the past, of romanticism, idealism, and the
Christian religion itself, it can be argued that romantic (idealistic and mystical) consciousness remained a tangible—though
denied—presence in the consciousness of the realist.[11]

The spirit of Russian modernism evolved in this context,
propelled by established patterns. The writings of modernists
abound in declarations of war on "realism." Positivism was rejected in favor of a new idealism, mysticism, and "the new religious consciousness." These statements have been echoed by
many critics and intellectual historians. Yet a case can be made
for continuity concomitant with the clearly marked, "apocalyptic" ruptures. The idealism and mysticism of Russian modernists
rested on a solid positivistic substratum.

Mechanisms of continuity can be illustrated with a case of

"recycled" metaphors. The radical "realists" of the 1860's drew the metaphors of reformation from the Christian tradition and adapted them for the use within the context of positivism. The central word of the day was "the new man" (or woman) who had shaken off "the old Adam." These metaphors were codified in Nikolai Chernyshevsky's social utopia, a novel entitled *What Is to Be Done? From the Tales About the New People* (*Chto delat'? Iz rasskazov o novykh liudiakh*, 1863), in which the conception of the transformation, or "transfiguration," of man was carefully encoded in the language of science and social theory.

Prompted by the apocalyptic sense of living at the great divide characteristic for the turn of the century, Russian modernists (along with Western European modernists) operated with the New Testament metaphors of renewal. They resorted, again, to the metaphors of "the new man" and "the new woman," which were "contaminated" by their previous use.[12]

The pattern of cultural development that accounted for the mixing of historical styles also revealed itself in the ways Russian culture, at various stages in its development, assimilated Western European influence. Western cultural paradigms were freely (but not necessarily consciously) rearranged to fit into a new context; they were alloyed with ideas and images specifically Russian. Russian modernism blended Nietzschean categories with the conceptions of Russian realism and Orthodox theology; Decadence existed side by side with utopianism, aestheticism with social concerns. In the final analysis, the "new man" of Russian modernism was an amalgam of the Pauline "new man," Chernyshevskian "new man," and Nietzschean superman.

The life-creating aspirations of the Russian Symbolists—the "shock troops of Modernism"[13]—can be traced to the ideas of two Russian philosophers, Vladimir Solov'ev (1853–1900) and Nikolai Fedorov (1828?–1903). Both Solov'ev and Fedorov developed their aesthetic ideas within the framework of Christianity and in close association with the apocalyptic doctrine; both worked in a context in which concepts of Orthodox theology coexisted with positivist mentality. A striking quality that they share is a type of utopianism that Fedorov called "projectivism"—concern with advancing coherent plans of action that would endow human thought with objective reality and send the world forth on the road to the practical realization of Christian ideals.

Solov'ev's influence was eagerly acknowledged by the Symbolists, who accepted him, along with Nietzsche, as a major prophet of the new apocalyptic times. Fedorov's influence, though undeniable, is hard to pinpoint. Though his works remained unpublished until 1907, he was known to such people as Dostoevsky, Tolstoy, and Solov'ev through personal contacts and correspondence; at the early stages in the development of Symbolism his ideas spread by word of mouth.[14] He is a powerful presence in the writings of Solov'ev, the Symbolists, and the post-Symbolists.

Fedorov sees man as a creator, acting in emulation of the divine creator and destined "to create in himself the new man" (the words of the Apostle Paul). He clearly associated divine and aesthetic creation: "Man is not merely a product of nature; he is also a work or creation of art. The final act of divine creation was the first act of human art." [15] The world is also meant to be re-created by man. "Regulated" by human reason, this new world would be freed from the forces of "blind nature" (most importantly, matter and death). This included rejection of sexual, procreative love. The most essential component of *imitatio Christi* was striving for personal immortality and for the total resurrection of the past generations here on earth. Resurrection, achieved with the help of science, would replace procreation. Fedorov deliberately merged Christian mysticism with positivism: "The doctrine of resurrection is true positivism, positivism in relation to action . . . the sort of positivism that eliminates any possibility of agnosticism, i.e., of anything that cannot be known." [16] His philosophy (known as the "philosophy of the common cause") is a "project" aimed at transforming the existing world into a controllable world, which would be exempt from mortality, through the collective efforts of human beings equipped with a powerful creative force—a synthesis of religion, science, and art. In this way word turns into deed, theoretical reason into practical reason, art into life. The notion is mediated by rhetorical operations. In Fedorov's terms, with "word" (*slovo*, or *Logos*) turned into "deed" (*deistvie*, or *ergon*), "theology" (*bogoslovie*) turns into "theurgy" (*bogodeistvo*).[17] Art should change from "art of like-nesses" (*iskusstvo podobii*) into "art of real life" (*iskusstvo deistvi-tel'nosti*); its task is not "representation of life" (*vosproizvedenie zhizni*) but "[re]construction of life" (*[vos]sozdanie zhizni*).[18] In this context life itself appears as a "project," a "common cause."

For Solov'ev, as for Fedorov, the key to salvation lies in the creative potential of human beings, manifested in two areas of human activity, art and love. According to Solov'ev, in art as well as in love the spiritual and the material are united. Thus, the aesthetic and the erotic operate, so to speak, "in the image and likeness of Christ." Endowed with a power to transform and im-mortalize the human being by reuniting the spirit and the flesh, the feminine and the masculine, Eros is not an instrument of procreation but a vehicle of divine action. Like love, art also is a divine action, or "theurgy"; artistic creation is an equivalent of divine creation.[19] The goal of theurgic art is self-creation in imi-tation of Christ as well as the "organization of reality" through "man's realization of the divine principle in empirical reality, or nature."[20] Thus art is destined to bring about a real change. The "task" of art is not mimesis but metamorphosis, not reflection but transfiguration of man and the world.[21]

In this idea the mystical merged with the positive or social. A contemporary, Evgeny Trubetskoy wrote: "Educated Russians have always expected the transfiguration of life from ideas and from artistic creations. In this spirit such antipodes as Pisarev, with his utilitarian view of art, and Dostoevsky, with his slogan, 'beauty will save the world,' come together." In this Trubetskoy saw the meaning of the aesthetic program of Fedorov, Solov'ev, and the Symbolists.[22] (Solov'ev's theories on art and love are treated in more detail below in Chapters 1 and 2.)

It was in this cultural environment that the Symbolists de-veloped their views on art's relation to life and the notion of "life-creation." Deliberate aesthetic organization of behavior was a part of a general utopian project of the total reorganization and divinization of the world and man, starting with human person-ality, interpersonal relations, and the human body. The destiny of human beings is, in Zinaida Gippius's words, "to create life collectively." Gippius described how, in refusing to accept marriage as "the first, natural, and the most practical solution," a member of the Symbolist generation "began to 'cogitate' upon the 'question of sex.'"[23] Art was to play a special, if not the leading, role in this project. Many a Symbolist author hastened to make a statement to that effect. Viacheslav Ivanov proclaimed that artistic creation is not the creation of images ("icons") but the creation of life itself (*ne ikonotvorchestvo, a zhiznetvorchestvo*).[24] "Art is the creation of life," affirmed Bely.[25] Equally important were the definitions of life, worded to fit the formula *zhiznetvorchestvo*. "Life itself is creation," wrote Bely.[26] "It is life, that is, movement forward, the growth of ever newer events—only life itself—is creation," echoed Gippius. She opposed this notion to that of quotidian life (*byt*), which is nothing but "crystallization" of dead matter.[27] "The art of our days affirms life as a creative process," wrote Fedor Sologub. He added, "It does not accept life ossified in the fetters of *byt*."[28]

Once art has fulfilled its function of a life-giving force, it will disappear as an independent ontological category. Art serves life to the point where it totally dissolves in life because it becomes life itself. This idea found its expression in the metaphor of "the artist as Pygmalion," which became a building block of the Symbolist myth of the artist. Reflecting on what the future might bring (in 1907, soon after the revolution of 1905), Bely chose to express this idea in terms of the Marxist theory of social revolution:

Art is a temporary measure: it is a tactical device in man's struggle with *fatum*. Just as for the liquidation of class society a sort of dictatorship of the class (proletariat) is necessary, it is necessary to proclaim the dead form [of art] as a banner in the abrogation of nonexistent, dead, fatal life. . . . But perhaps all of our life, subject to *fatum*, should be blown up, disappear, cease to be? Then the new art would merge with the new life.[29]

After the revolution of 1917, under the dictatorship of the proletariat, Symbolist theories were revitalized by the social developments and intellectual trends of the new era. Alexander

Bogdanov advanced his "universal organizational science," or "techtology" (from the Greek *tecton*, "builder"), created under the direct influence of Fedorov. It is the proletarian culture in a proletarian state, claimed Bogdanov, that is uniquely equipped for the global [re]organization of life, in all its aspects, from economic relations to bodily functions. And the problem of mortality can be finally brought to resolution.[30] The theoreticians of "the Left Front of Art" (*Levyi front iskusstv*, or *Lef*), which included members of the prerevolutionary Futurist avant-garde, modified the Symbolist notion of "life-creation" (*zhiznetvorchestvo*) into "life-building" (*zhiznestroenie*), a concept with social and technical connotations. Categories of Solov'evian aesthetic utopianism were integrated into the theory of socialist realism. In the years following the revolution, utopian visions of transforming the world through aesthetic creation informed social and technological utopianism, including the utopian projects of the state.[31] It is no accident that commentators as diverse as the émigré Symbolist Fedor Stepun, the repentant revolutionary Nikolai Valentinov, and Nadezhda Mandelshtam came to see Symbolist "life-creation" as contributing to an atmosphere that allowed the totalitarian control imposed by Stalin.[32]

This volume attempts to provide a comprehensive, but not an exhaustive, treatment of the modernist aesthetic utopia. Each essay takes up a specific dimension of the phenomenon and employs a specific set of techniques and approaches.

In Chapter 1, Irina Paperno offers a close look at the evolution of the theme of art and life in the theoretical writings of Vladimir Solov'ev and the Symbolists (Bely, Ivanov, and Briusov). She demonstrates that Symbolist theories are organized by a set of metaphors derived from Christian theology. Unfolding the logic of these metaphors, she traces the fusion of positivism with mysticism and the idiosyncratic combination of Nietzscheanism with Orthodox Christianity.

In Chapter 2, Olga Matich examines a series of Symbolist (and post-Symbolist) attempts to reconceptualize sexual love, in theory (beginning with Solov'ev) and in practice. Experimenting with human relations, character, and body, the Symbolists focused on a search for creative alternatives to biological procreation, seeking to break the cycle of birth and death by creating an immortal androgynous human being. Matich's analysis suggests that debates on sexuality and gender in early-twentieth-century Russia undertook a metaphysical and epistemological, rather than a social, cause. They articulated concern with such issues as the antithesis of matter and spirit, transience, and the creation of unity out of difference or division.

In Chapter 3, Irene Masing-Delic offers a different cross-section of the material: she traces the motif of Pygmalion and Galatea in Russian literature, from romanticism, through realism, to Symbolism. Her analysis shows how life-creation, an aesthetic principle, was encoded in the artistic reworkings of the myth. The motif reveals the relationship of continuity between realism and modernism.

In Chapter 4, Alexander Lavrov undertakes the investigation of yet another aspect of the phenomenon. *Zhiznetvorchestvo* was mediated by an institution of sorts—the circle of the "Argonauts" centered around Andrei Bely, with its peculiar "social structure," rituals, and private mythology. Lavrov has reconstructed the life of the circle on the basis of archival materials that to this day remain largely unpublished.

In Chapter 5, Joan Delaney Grossman reevaluates one of the central "life texts" of Russian Symbolism, the Petrovskaia-Bely-Briusov relationship. She reveals another source of Symbolist life-creation—the writings of Stanislaw Przybyszewski. Focusing on episodes from Briusov's life text rather than his writings, Grossman brings to light an alternative stance in Symbolist aesthetics. What emerges dramatically in his relationship with Petrovskaia as analyzed by Grossman is Briusov's principled opposition to utopian thinking. His position construes an alternative to the Solov'evian mystical brand of Symbolism practiced by Gippius, Dmitry Merezhkovsky, Bely, Blok, and Ivanov.

In Chapter 6, Michael Wachtel explores the life and work of Viacheslav Ivanov. He shows Ivanov seeking a "formula" for the fusion of art and life as he appropriated the heritage of the German romantics. In the course of translating Novalis's poetry into Russian, Ivanov "translated" German romanticism into Russian Symbolism and theory into biographical practice. Wachtel shows how symbols penetrated "real-life" experience, including that of Ivanov's recorded dreams and visions.

In conclusion, in Chapter 7, Irina Gutkin traces the transformations of the conception of life-creation in the post-Symbolist era, from Futurism to early Soviet culture to high Stalinism, revealing the continuous development and complex modifications of the idea.

Throughout the volume we advance two arguments concerning the historical evolution of the Russian literary and cultural tradition: that modernism, ostensibly reacting against positivism and realism, actually assimilated some of the fundamental principles of its archenemy; and that there is an essential continuity between modernist aesthetics originating at the turn of the century and Soviet culture in the 1920's and 1930's.

In emulation of the Symbolist principle of "collective creation," this project was undertaken by a group of authors who worked in close collaboration. Besides those whose essays appear in this volume, the group included several members who provided creative energy that was not embodied in texts but contributed substantially to the "common cause." They are Boris Gasparov, Robert P. Hughes, and Olga Raevsky-Hughes.

One

The Meaning of Art:
Symbolist Theories

IRINA PAPERNO

Symbolist theories of art are informed by the ideas of Vladimir Solov'ev, in whose works aesthetics is interwoven with theology. Solov'ev posits the notion of dualism as the foundation of his system. For him, the world is composed of antagonistic entities—heavenly and earthly, material and spiritual, ideal and real—and antagonistic realms—"inward reality" (the inner world of the individual) and "outward" (objective) reality. The destiny of man is the consolidation and "complete mutual penetration" of these antithetical entities and realms.[1] Art (or beauty), along with love, serves as a major vehicle of synthesis.

Solov'ev consistently describes the nature of art in terms of two theological metaphors: incarnation (*voploshchenie*) and transfiguration (*preobrazhenie*). They define the two complementary mechanisms of the aesthetic process: the materialization of spirit (incarnation) and the spiritualization of matter (transfiguration).[2] In "Beauty in Nature" ("Krasota v prirode," 1889) beauty is described as "the transfiguration of matter through the incarnation of another, nonmaterial element in it."[3] The main example is the

transformation of coal into a diamond. In their material ingre-
dients, their chemical elements, the two substances are identical.
Therefore, the beauty of the diamond does not lie in its material
nature; it is produced by the refraction of light in the crystalline
structure of the gem. Beauty is produced neither by the material body of the diamond nor by the light refracted in it, but
by the "distinct and inseparable [*nesliiannyi i nerazdel'nyi*] union
of the substance and light."[4] The "task" of art, claimed Solov'ev
in "The General Meaning of Art" ("Obshchii smysl iskusstva,"
1890) is "the transformation of physical life into its spiritual
counterpart, which . . . is capable of internally transfiguring,
spiritualizing matter or truly becoming embodied in it."[5] Art is
essentially a synthesis of the material and the spiritual.

The most important implication of the aesthetic process is
that, through participation in the spiritual achieved in art, the
physical world becomes a party to the immortality characterizing
the spiritual world: "with the immediate and indivisible union
in beauty of spiritual content and sensory expression, with their
complete mutual penetration, the material phenomenon, which
in reality has become beautiful, that is to say, actually has embodied in itself the idea, must become as permanent and immortal as the idea itself."[6] In this Solov'ev saw the difference between
his aesthetics and Romantic, Hegelian aesthetics:

According to Hegelian aesthetics, beauty is the embodiment of the universal and eternal idea in particular and transient phenomena; moreover, they remain transient and disappear like individual waves in the
flow of the material process, only for a moment reflecting the radiance of
the eternal idea. But this is possible only with an impersonal, indifferent
relationship between a spiritual principle and a material phenomenon.
For real and perfect beauty, expressing complete solidarity and mutual
interpenetration of these two elements, must necessarily make one of
them privy to the immortality of the other.[7]

Of no less importance is the quality of "reality" given to the
ideal. In "Beauty in Nature" Solov'ev argues that the embodiment of beauty "is no less real and considerably more significant
(in a cosmogonical sense) than those material elements in which
it is embodied."[8] From this it follows that art is a force capable of

bringing about the real transformation of the world. Opposing the Platonic notion of beauty as a "shadow" of the idea, accepted by "idealistic" romantic aesthetics, he claimed that beauty "must lead to *a real improvement of reality.*"[9] Georgy Chulkov quoted this definition in his "On Mystical Anarchism" ("O misticheskom anarkhizme," 1906), in which he presented art as a force capable of bringing about *social* transformation.[10]

In propagating this idea, with its obvious mystical overtones, Solov'ev found an ally in the positivist Nikolai Chernyshevsky, whose *The Aesthetic Relations of Art to Reality* (*Esteticheskie otnosheniia iskusstva k deistvitel'nosti*), when it appeared in 1853, became a manifesto of the new positivistic aesthetics in Russia—realism. In 1894 Solov'ev reviewed the new edition of Chernyshevsky's treatise. In his treatise Chernyshevsky reversed the romantic hierarchy in which art, as pertaining to the sphere of the ideal, was superior to life. He proclaimed reality superior to the ideal, real life superior to art. A philosophical category traditionally associated with art, the beautiful, was to be found not in art but in real life: "The beautiful is life" (*prekrasnoe est' zhizn'*). According to Solov'ev, with this idea Chernyshevsky became the first aesthetician to affirm "the reality of beauty."[11]

It appears that in Solov'ev's thinking positivist "realism" (a belief in the reality of the material world) was compounded with mystical "realism"—a belief in the objective reality of ideas. A synthesis of positivism and mysticism, his aesthetic theory took the theological doctrine of Logos as its main model. Solov'ev's notion of the "inseparable unity" and "total mutual penetration" of the spiritual and the material principles in art is an application of the Christological doctrine in aesthetics. The theological formulas that define the relations between the two natures of Christ (the inseparable union of the divine and the human; two natures united yet distinct and autonomous) are recognizable in his aesthetic formulations. He relies on the Christological notion of the transformation of the flesh through the incarnation of the immutable and impassible Logos (the means of conferring impassibility on man).[12]

Indeed, Solov'ev's aesthetic works complement his theological treatise, *Readings on Godmanhood* (*Chteniia o bogochelovechestve*, 1877–81). The theological concept of *bogochelovechestvo*, in the broadest sense, refers to the union of God and man in Christ. Solov'ev uses "godmanhood" as a universal paradigm of synthesis. While in *Readings on Godmanhood* Solov'ev argued that man's striving for the reconciliation of opposites in the unity of God and man is the ultimate goal of the historical process, in his aesthetic studies he declared that aesthetic activity, a force uniting the spiritual and the material, is destined to play a major role in that same process. Moreover, at the present stage in history, art is a prefigurement of the future eternal life. In "The General Meaning of Art" Solov'ev defined "real art" (*deistvitel'noe iskusstvo*) as "the palpable representation of any object or phenomenon from the point of view of its ultimate state, or in the light of the future world." [13]

From this point of view Solov'ev, in his "First Speech on Dostoevsky" ("Pervaia rech' o Dostoevskom," 1881), evaluated different aesthetic systems: while "pure" (idealistic) art (a thing of the past) "lifted man above the earth," contemporary realism returns man to earth, inspiring him with love and compassion for this world. This, however, should lead not to total immersion in the earthly life, but to renovation of this world. The art of the future, a religious art (prefigured in Dostoevsky), will attract heavenly forces to this world and achieve reconciliation of heaven and earth. [14] In this Solov'ev saw the "general meaning of art."

Solov'ev's philosophy of art, as well as his rhetorical strategies, was adopted by the Symbolists; his ideas and images are echoed in the writings of Dmitry Merezhkovsky, Zinaida Gippius, Andrei Bely, Viacheslav Ivanov, Valery Briusov, Fedor Sologub, and others. It was Bely who, taking Solov'ev as a starting point, worked out a complex (though by no means consistent) theory unifying art and life. [15]

In constructing the aesthetics of Symbolism, Bely follows Solov'ev's strategy of creating metaphors from theological concepts and applying them to aesthetic problems. Central to Bely's aesthetics is his thesis "art is the creation of life" (*iskusstvo est' tvorchestvo zhizni*). He argues that artistic creation inevitably takes on a religious quality. [16] In arguing this point Bely adopted Solov'ev's

concept of theurgy (divine action): "creativity, carried to its conclusion, directly turns into religious creativity—theurgy."[17] The
task of Symbolist, theurgic art is creation in the artist (and in
man as such) of the image of the "new man," that is, deification.[18] In Bely's "Symbolism as World Understanding" ("Simvolizm kak miroponimanie," 1903) the word "theurgy" refers to
the "indwelling of God in the human personality."[19] Although
these ideas focused on the metaphor of the artist as "the new
man," with its obvious New Testament connotations, the Pauline
phraseology and Solov'ev's religious aestheticism are not the only
sources of Bely's theory. In Bely's "new man" the New Testament
symbolism merged with Nietzschean images, primarily with the
doctrine of the superman. Bely claimed, "Nietzsche's doctrine
of the individual is an aesthetics"; Nietzsche's superman ("the
contemporary new man") is "an artistic image of personality."[20]
But, at the same time, he treated Nietzscheanism as a religious
system, a modernized Christianity.

In his famous 1886 preface to *The Birth of Tragedy* Nietzsche
claimed that the aesthetic view of the world implied attributing "a kind of divinity" to the world process, with God viewed
as "the supreme artist." Yet this view involved a conception of
creation as an essentially amoral act, with God, the "supreme
artist," "realizing himself indifferently in whatever he does or un-
does." Moreover, Nietzsche emphasized that his purely aesthetic
interpretation and justification of the world put his doctrine "at
the opposite pole from Christian doctrine, a doctrine entirely
moral in purport."[21] To Russians, particularly to Solov'ev and
Nikolai Fedorov, who were obviously fascinated with Nietzsche,
such insistence on the anti-Christian nature of his doctrine was
unacceptable. Solov'ev, in "Literature or truth" ("Slovesnost' ili
istina"), an essay in *Sunday letters* (*Voskresnye pis'ma*, 1897–98),
reproached Nietzsche for substituting "philology" for religion
in his approach to life. In Nietzsche's insistence on seeing life
as a purely aesthetic phenomenon (i.e., as a text), Solov'ev saw
a view of life devoid of any mystical component, the triumph
of "superphilology" over true "supermanhood."[22] The latter he
considered attainable only within the framework of Christianity.

Striving to resolve the contradiction between aestheticism and

Christian doctrine, Bely and Ivanov too reinterpreted Nietzsche along the lines suggested to them by Solov'ev's critique: Nietzschean aestheticism they read as Christian mysticism.

Bely saw no contradiction between "philological" and religious approaches to life in Nietzscheanism; he read *literally* Nietzsche's metaphor "God as supreme artist," and understood the Nietzschean concept of aesthetic creation in life as mystical activity akin to the creation of the world. In Bely's synthetic system, Nietzschean and Christian concepts are interchangeable: Nietzsche's superman *is* the Pauline new man.

Following Fedorov and Solov'ev, Bely included the issue of personal immortality in his view of art. In the article "Art" ("Iskusstvo," 1903) he elaborates: when applied to life, art extends life into eternity; in this way art becomes the creation of personal immortality.[23] Bely and other Symbolists saw immortality as one of the most important components in the thinking of their predecessors. According to Bely, Nietzsche in *Zarathustra* offered a practical strategy for the "bodily transfiguration of man"—a step toward physical immortality ("Friedrich Nietzsche" ["Fridrikh Nitsshe," 1907]).[24] Viacheslav Ivanov saw "the problem of victory over death" as the focus of Solov'ev's godmanhood, a concept that Ivanov described in Nietzschean terms as the "true supermanhood" (*istinnoe sverkhchelovechestvo*).[25]

An essential part of the theory of life-creation is establishing Symbolism's place in the historical succession of creative styles. In his programmatic essay "Symbolism" ("Simvolism," 1908, published in *Lug zelenyi*) Bely describes the relation of the poet's creative consciousness to "nature" (the outward world) from the point of view of different artistic systems. He acknowledges two artistic methods in the art of the past. In the first system, the artist re-creates the forms of visible nature (the "real world"), which he understands as true images, or symbols, of the "true" world. The metaphor of this artistic strategy is the Sun (or the sun god, Helios), who illuminates the images of this world to reveal them with ultimate clarity. Bely calls this method "classicism" and names Goethe as its representative. In the second system, the artist derives his images not from the exterior world but from internal reality, or his own soul, which reveals the "true" world. The result is a world of fantastic images taken from the artist's imagination. This method is "fantastic romanticism," exemplified by Milton. Having created his own world, the artist may discover that the external world (nature) is actually created in the image and likeness of his world (that is, of art). This is, according to Bely, the strategy of realistic romanticism, or "romanticism of reality," exemplified by Gogol. The metaphor of this type of creativity is Orpheus, who draws the ghost into the world of reality. The third method, propagated by Bely as the strategy of Symbolism, is based on a synthesis of the first two. The image, which is a creation of the artist's consciousness, receives embodiment, that is, physical manifestation, in the real world, and thus *becomes the real world*. In this way art is merged with reality, the inward (subjective) with the outward (objective); the image is fused with the "reality" that it denotes. Bely's metaphor of this type of creation is "the Word become flesh" and, by implication, Christ. Bely uses the metaphor to describe not only the aesthetic process but also the artist himself. The artist is a true incarnated Logos, the Word made flesh. The act of incarnation overcomes the separation between "poet" and "man." Like the divine creator in the act of incarnation, the poet himself creates his human nature, or his life. Bely argues: "the artist should become his own artistic form: his natural 'I' should merge with his art; his life should become artistic. He himself is 'the word made flesh.' "[26]

In order to fully understand Bely's view, we turn now to an earlier Symbolist attempt to deal with the relations between art and life as that attempt evolved historically, Briusov's article "The Sacred Sacrifice" ("Sviashchennaia zhertva," 1905).[27] According to Briusov, the task of Symbolism is to merge life and art. This synthesis can be achieved by further developing the aesthetic principles of realism, which came to replace romantic aesthetics. Romanticism limited the sphere of art to the "beautiful" and "sublime." As a result, only some elements of the poet's life could be turned into poetry. Realism extended the realm of the beautiful by including the whole world in all of its manifestations. Realism opened all of life for inclusion in the sphere of art, thus erasing the borders between the poet's art and his life. In Briusov's view, the realist and the Symbolist both "embody" life in art. But while the realist turns the external world into art, the Symbolist creates by embodying his inner self: "Like realists we recognize life itself as the only thing that is to be incarnated in art. But while they were looking for it [life] outside of themselves, we turn our gaze inward." Thus, the artist in his entirety is turned into art. From this it follows that the goal of the artist is to make his life into an art form: "Let the poet create not his books, but his life."[28]

The connection between Bely's theory and Briusov's article is obvious. Both Briusov and Bely view Symbolism as a synthesis of the romantic and a different, "objective" artistic method. But "objectivity," which Briusov describes as the method of realism, Bely attributes to "classicism." Both authors use Solov'ev's metaphor of incarnation for the description of the artistic process. But while Briusov, who would not subscribe to the Solov'evian dualist worldview, ignores the mystical connotations of the concept and uses the term purely as a metaphor for the concrete expression of an idea, Bely restores its original theological and mystical significance; his metaphors are "real."

These ideas, metaphors, and strategies of reasoning are shared by another major proponent of Symbolist aesthetics, Viacheslav Ivanov. The notion of art as transfiguration of reality informs the thematics of much of his early poetry. "Vozzovi/Preobrazhenie Vselennoi" ("Call forth/the Transfiguration of the Universe"), Ivanov orders the artist in his early programmatic poem "Creativity" ("Tvorchestvo," in the collection *Kormchie zvezdy*, 1903). Similarly, Ivanov's poetry repeatedly uses Solov'ev's image of the transformation of coal into a diamond. It appears in "Diamond" ("Almaz," in the collection *Prozrachnost'*, 1904), "Dispute" ("Spor," in *Cor Ardens*, 1911), "Language" ("Iazyk," 1927, in *Svet vechernii*).[29] Like Bely, Ivanov employs the theological concept of incarnation as a metaphor for artistic creation. However, Ivanov focuses not on the nature of the relation between "man" and "poet" but on the nature of the poetic word (a question that also interested Bely).[30] For the Symbolists, argues Ivanov in his "Testaments of Symbolism" ("Zavety simvolizma," 1910), the poetic word is essentially different from the general linguistic sign: it is "a symbol"; that is, it must be understood as was the word in general in medieval realism—as a total, mystical equivalent of the "reality" that it signifies. The prototype for such a word is the divine Logos. In Ivanov's terms, the symbol is not a dead image (or idol) of reality but its "living" image, "the Word striving to become flesh." In this sense, Symbolist poetry, which operates in word symbols, is an art that strives to merge with reality, to become reality itself.

According to Ivanov, in this lies the difference between Symbolism (a religious, "theurgic" art) and romanticism. While romanticism evokes visions of the "other world," Symbolism embodies those visions in reality. In conclusion to these arguments, which are based on realizing the metaphor "word become flesh," Ivanov affirms that poetry (Symbolist poetry) is by its very nature an art that is "not contemplative, but active"; "art is not the creation of images, but the creation of life" (*ne ikonotvorchestvo, a zhiznetvorchestvo*).[31]

I now return to the Symbolists' theories to clarify the logic of their reasoning.

Solov'evian Symbolism adopted the romantic, Neoplatonic notion of the dualism of "this world" and "the other world," or *Jenseits* (the duality of real and ideal, flesh and soul, matter and spirit, human and divine, outer and inner, objective and subjective, object and idea). Kant posited the basic polarity as that of the world of the object and the world of human consciousness, in which the objects are known. From this followed the romantic separation between art and life, with art seen as a realm of "the ideal" and thus superior to life. In the romantic context, attempts at overcoming the separation between art and life and between the two worlds involved the following conceptual operation: "life" was proclaimed to be consubstantial with art; reality was projected into the realm of the ideal. Life then became a legitimate object of creative activity, a sphere of application of aesthetic principles. However, in the course of this projection, a "residue" remained. Whole spheres of "life"—"the empirically low" (such as physiological processes and trivial details of daily existence) were excluded from art; they were regarded as material suitable neither for artistic creation nor for aesthetization in real-life creation. And, in a mystical key, not the whole of the earthly life could inherit "life eternal."

Russian Symbolists saw their attempts to merge art and life as a revival of romanticism. However, they operated in the culture that had passed through and responded to the experience of realism. Realism was worked into their aesthetics.

Symbolism aspired to effect a total coincidence between the two planes or the two worlds. While romanticism saw the other world as the "true" world, Symbolism adopted the realistic notion of the ultimate "truth," or reality, and superior aesthetic value of this world and of life. In their view Chernyshevsky's famous thesis "the beautiful is life" implied that real life in its entirety could become a domain of the beautiful and, therefore, a sphere of artistic creation. Life as a whole, without any "residue," can be transformed into art. In a mystical key, the whole of "this world" can be transformed into "the world beyond."[32] Thus, romantic striving for *Jenseits* was replaced with the desire to bring the *Jenseits* into this, "real," world.

The model for the total consolidation of the two domains was found in Christian theology. For Solov'ev, who laid the foundations of Symbolist aesthetics, the notions of transfiguration and incarnation, used in conjunction, provide the paradigm for the aesthetic process. His followers, the Symbolists, privilege incarnation over transfiguration because, by making the spiritual material, incarnation gives them access to "reality."[33] The Christological doctrine provides the paradigm for the union of the man and the poet, life and art.[34] In place of the dichotomy "art and life" (*zhizn' i tvorchestvo*) Symbolism offers a unity of art-lifehood, or *zhiznetvorchestvo*, a direct parallel to godmanhood, or *bogochelovechestvo*. The opposition between "word" and "thing" is resolved by advancing a concept of "symbol," a total equivalent of the "essence" it connotes, that is constructed by analogy with divine Logos.

Merging theology and aesthetics, the Symbolists appeared to have reconciled the world's tragic dichotomies; moreover, they resolved the conflict between the secular and the religious that had plagued Russian culture throughout its modern history. Viewed in this context, "life-creation" in daily life means much more than organizing life aesthetically, as if it were a literary text. By projecting principles used to construct verbal texts into life the Symbolists realized the metaphor "the incarnation of the Word." Thus, ironically, aestheticization of life is an expression of the yearning for "reality." For the Symbolist, only life created by art, that is, life as a product of the incarnation of the spirit, was "the living life" (Bely, using Dostoevsky's phrase).[35] "Symbolism is real" insisted Bely. "In this," he added, "lies the meaning of Vladimir Solov'ev's views on art."[36] Concrete attempts at an aesthetic organization of personal life had far-reaching mystical implications. Transformed through art, life was capable of becoming "life eternal." Aestheticization of life was a way to achieve deification and to gain the kingdom of heaven, including the "realistic" kingdom of heaven on earth: the social utopia and Fedorovian personal immortality in the flesh. Viewed in this light, "life-creation" appears as a manifestation of utopianism inspired by the atmosphere of apocalyptic forebodings and nurtured by the amalgamation of mysticism and positivism in turn-of-the-century culture.

TWO

The Symbolist Meaning of Love:
Theory and Practice

OLGA MATICH

The self-conscious construction of one's life according to a philosophical, social, or literary model was begun not by the Symbolists but by literary forebears who set wide-ranging precedents for Symbolist behavior: first the romantics of the Decembrist era, then the men of the 1840's, and then the "new men" of the 1860's. For these several generations of Russians, "living ideas," so typical of Dostoevsky's heroes, became a life strategy. The tendency to turn philosophy into praxis and abstract ideas into a strategy for living had European sources as well as Russian; one of these, for the generation of the 1860's, was L. A. Feuerbach's anti-idealism, which privileged the senses and the immediacy of lived experience at the expense of pure ideas. At the end of the century, Nietzsche reinforced the emphasis on praxis by rejecting abstract theory in favor of a philosophy of life, a move that captured the imagination of the Symbolist generation.

The Symbolists' immediate Russian predecessor in the sphere of life-creation was, of course, Vladimir Solov'ev. In keeping with the emphasis on an experiential rather than an abstract philosophy, he began the process of translating key religious and aesthetic concepts into a life strategy. Solov'ev's ideas, which incorporated Platonism, Christian mysticism, Hegelianism, and positivism, became a way of life for the Symbolists, believing as they did in the sacramental transubstantiation of "the word"— that it could become flesh and blood.

The ultimate goal of the men and women at the turn of the century was a total transformation of life resulting in earthly immortality. In this they were inspired by Solov'ev's Christological model of godmanhood as based on the union of flesh and spirit, as well as Nietzche's godlike superman, who, they believed, would transcend death by giving birth to himself; Nikolai Fedorov's project of resurrecting dead ancestors in the flesh; and Nikolai Chernyshevsky's "new men and women." Love played a seminal role in these utopian projects. For Solov'ev love was even more powerful than art in that it had real-life potential to bring about the actual end of history and transform material reality.

Building on the ideas of Feuerbach and French Christian socialists, nineteenth-century Russian utopian thought in the 1860's commonly combined militant atheism, Christian theological terminology, and asceticism in private life. Solov'evian romantic *life-creation*, adopted by the Symbolists, reinstated the centrality of religion. Reappropriating it from the hidden underside of the utopian culture of Russian radicals and the metaphoric discourse to which they had relegated it, Solov'ev fused religion and eros in his theory of love. That theory was closely linked with his theory of art, described in the preceding chapter.

Seeking transcendence and immortality through love, the Symbolist new man and woman, inspired by Solov'ev, were driven by the eschatological impulse toward rebirth or resurrection, not procreation. Premised on the continuous cycle of birth and death, procreation was rejected; hence the common preoccupation with abstinence in the here and now and with conquering death by a higher form of love that rechanneled erotic energy away from the biological drive to reproduce.[1] In their search for these higher forms, the Symbolists offered a variety of erotic practices as alternatives to the traditional family. Among them

were Platonic love for a soul twin, Dionysian eros, new versions of
the romantic triangle, homoerotic love, narcissism, and romantic
love for an unattainable object. These models were frequently
intertwined, reflecting the eclectic, syncretic spirit of the time.
In its cultural sources, the Symbolist ethos brought together ancient Greek life practice (in the Platonic, or Apollonian, sense,
and in the Dionysian as defined by Nietzsche); elements of Gnostic mysticism; the ideal of courtly love filtered through German
romanticism; the Slavophile notion of collectivity; and aspects of
Russian radical ideology of the 1860's.[2]

The Solov'evian Erotic Utopia

Vladimir Solov'ev in his seminal work "The Meaning of Love"
("Smysl liubvi," 1892–94) presented a program of action for an
"erotic utopia,"[3] which had a profound influence on the Symbolist generation's mythology of love. Solov'ev envisioned eros,
which, he believed, was the only sign of divinity in the material world, as having transformative power, not a procreative
function. Its goal was the creation of the new man who would
transcend death by reclaiming divine androgyny. According to
Solov'ev, the meaning of love emerged from a synthesis of opposites—the feminine and masculine and the spiritual and material. His summons to recover the union of the spirit and flesh
in love, as well as in art, paved the way for the later Symbolist
attempts to combine Greek paganism and Christianity.

Eros was to be retrieved from the dustbin to which Christian
life practice had discarded it and reunited with the spirit in the
new man: "False spirituality is the negation of the flesh; true
spirituality represents its transformation, salvation, rebirth."[4]
This, however, did not connote the physical consummation of
passion by historical men and women, but the transubstantiation
of the flesh. Like his followers, Solov'ev was both ambivalent and
ambiguous about the physiology of love. It may be that he intended a collective physical union of all humanity to mark the
end of history and the emergence of the new man; before the
coming of that time the consummation of passion would be pro-

scribed because it resulted in the disintegration of humanity and death. Conflating the spirit and flesh, as if in an erotic retort, the androgynous godman could be re-created only by mankind as a whole, not by individuals. (Like Fedorov and other Russian utopians before and after, Solov'ev insisted on the Slavophile principle of communality [*sobornost'*].)

In keeping with nineteenth-century utopian discourse, he associated the transformation of life with the notion of task (*delo liubvi*), connoting activity and process. Moreover, the task of love was intertwined with the task of Logos (*delo slova*); their common goal was the creation of the new man. In the words of Evgeny Trubetskoy, "for [Solov'ev] Godmanhood . . . is . . . that unique *task* which man is called upon to accomplish on this earth. The calling of man is first of all *theurgy*, i.e. the fulfillment of God's *task* . . . both in private and public life."[5]

Solov'ev's theory of love, premised on unconsummated eros and an antiprocreative bias, had its basis in Plato. Emphasizing the experiential, personal character of Plato's erotic philosophy, the Russian thinker explored its potential to transcend abstract thought. The title of his most extensive essay on Plato, "Plato's Life Drama" ("Zhiznennaia drama Platona," 1898), emphasizes the philosopher's personal history and life practice at the expense of pure philosophy. Written against the background of Russian nineteenth-century utopian thought, Hegelianism, and Nietzsche, Solov'ev's "The Meaning of Love" was, first of all, a response to Plato's *Symposium* (translated into Russian as *Pirshestvo*, or *Pir*). In the words of Viacheslav Ivanov, "Perhaps no one since Plato has said anything so deep and vital about love and sex . . . as Solov'ev, crowning the former and restoring the latter's human dignity and goal of godmanhood."[6] Plato was the source of Solov'ev's ideas of unconsummated divine love and divine androgyny.[7] Created in the image and likeness of God, Solov'ev's androgyne reclaims the original wholeness that reinstates immortality. But in contrast to Plato, whose androgyne exists only in the realm of forms, Solov'ev awaited its actual materialization in the future.

Solov'ev's mythology of love took as its starting point the distinction between earthly and divine love described in the *Symposium*. Plato represented them by Aphrodite Pandemos and Aphrodite Urania. The former, who is younger than her heavenly counterpart, was born of the union of male and female and is the patron of physical love. Spiritual love is associated with Aphrodite Urania, who is older and "springs entirely from the male," according to Pausanias in the *Symposium*; "those who are inspired by this Love are attracted toward the male sex."[8] Describing the higher form of love, Socrates says that those "whose creative desire is of the soul, and who long to beget spiritually, not physically," beget wisdom and virtue. This he associates with sublimated love between male friends. Socrates' teacher of eros, Diotima, posits a third and higher form of love, which is linked to philosophy and involves the transcendence of the sensible world. Divine love in the Platonic sense is a pilgrimage that starts with the love of male physical beauty, moves to love of spiritual and moral beauty, proceeds to love of the beauty of knowledge and truth, and finally attains to the contemplation of absolute beauty (*Symposium*, p. 94). Mystical light illuminates the end of this path from ordinary physical love to Platonic eros.

In distinguishing between the two Aphrodites, Solov'ev, unlike his Athenian predecessor, did not draw a sharp line between them, although his preference was for the celestial goddess. Nor did Solov'ev associate her with homoerotic love. For Solov'ev, Aphrodite Urania was the emblem of the eternal feminine, whom he described as the woman clothed in the sun (*zhena oblechennaia v solntse*), an image from *The Revelation of St. John*:

The woman clothed in the sun is already suffering birth pains: she must reveal the truth, give birth to the word, but the ancient serpent is gathering his last forces against her . . . in the end Eternal beauty will be fertile, and from her will emerge the world's salvation, when her deceptive physical likeness has disappeared, as that sea foam which gave birth to Aphrodite Pandemos. My poems do not serve *her*, not with a single word.[9]

Juxtaposing images from the Apocalypse, Old Testament, Plato, and Greek mythology, Solov'ev imitated Plato's method of "the midwifery of thought" by using metaphors of love that were pointedly procreative. Despite a disdain for physical progeny, paradoxically, both Plato and Solov'ev appropriated the imagery of birth and fecundity to describe divine love. Solov'ev depicts eternal beauty as *fertile*, out of which will emerge salvation (in the sense of rebirth), but not till the disappearance of beauty's physical form. The image that he proposes is that of a woman enveloped by the sun and in the throes of childbirth, giving birth to Logos.

However, in contrast to Plato, who put ideas above praxis, Solov'ev adapted the Platonic discourse of love to a utopian ideal and to the Russian tradition of turning ideas into life practice. Like Chernyshevsky and Fedorov—his nineteenth-century utopian predecessors in Russia—he emphasized the transformative power of eros, whose goal is the transfiguration of human nature: "Plato had not mastered the eternal power of Eros to perform the real task of the *rebirth* of physical nature, his and another's," although he had already begun transforming erotic philosophy into a life strategy.[10] According to Solov'ev, the three most important aspects of active love existed in Plato's philosophy in embryonic form: "the concepts of androgyny, spiritual corporeality, and godmanhood . . . [t]he first—in the myth put into the mouth of Aristophanes (*Symposium*), the second—in the definition of beauty (*Phaedrus*), and the third—in the very concept of eros as a mediating force between God and mortal nature (the speech of Diotima in the *Symposium*)" ("Zhiznennaia," p. 235). These three manifestations of eros were for Solov'ev the goal of the transformation of life. For Plato, however, they remained in the realm of fantasy: "He did not tie them together and put them at the real basis of life's journey," wrote Solov'ev, "and for this reason the end of the journey, [which was] the resurrection of mortal nature to eternal life, remained hidden from him, although logically it followed from his own ideas. . . . Plato's Eros did not fulfill its goal, did not unite heaven with earth and the underworld, did not build between them any actual bridge, and, empty-handed, flitted away indifferently to the world of ideal speculation" (ibid., p. 235).

As this passage so clearly illustrates, Solov'ev, like one of his other teachers, Fedorov, believed in the creation of a *real* bridge between heaven and earth, what he called *pontifex*, and in the *actual* rebirth of mortal human nature. Modeled on the resurrection of Christ, the prototypical godman, the transfiguration of mortal flesh that is mediated by love's winged eros is the path to immortality: "Our personal task . . . [and] the common task of the whole world . . . [is] to spiritualize matter. It is being prepared by the cosmic process in the natural world, being continued and reified in the historical process of mankind." [11] This path is associated with divine androgyny and the union of spirit and flesh. Identified as the triad of divine love, androgyny, sanctified flesh, and godmanhood became Solov'ev's life task.

Like Fedorov, whose philosophy of the "common task" rejected consummated, procreative love in favor of an active, redemptive love that resurrects the dead fathers, Solov'ev seems to have considered tampering with nature. He suggested the actual physical transfiguration of man, especially since Adam the procreator would become obsolete with the advent of androgyny. (Reproduction, after all, is premised on the polarization of male and female.) Resembling Fedorov's, as well as positivist, utopian visions of the scientific transformation of nature, his description of man's rebirth borrowed terms from the physical sciences: "Only this, so to speak, chemical fusion of two beings of the same kind and significance, but throughout different in form, can render possible (both in the natural and the spiritual order) the creation of a new man, the actual realization of the true human individuality." [12] This new man was to be an androgyne, representing the free union of the masculine and feminine principles, whose androgynous wholeness will reestablish in him the image and likeness of God:

In empirical reality there is no man *as such*—he exists only in a one-sided and limited form as a masculine or a feminine individual. . . . The true human being . . . cannot be merely a man or merely a woman, but must be the higher unity of the two. To realize this unity or to create the true human being as the free unity of the masculine and the feminine elements, which preserve their formal separateness but overcome their essential disparity and disruption, is the direct *task* of love.[13]

Although Solov'ev does not actually name Fedorov, "The Meaning of Love" concludes with Fedorov's ideas about the internalization of sexual energy that transcends procreation: love's task is "the transformation or the *turning inwards* of the creative power which in nature, being turned outwards, produces the bad infinity of the physical reproduction of organisms." This will be accomplished by the release, or liberation, of "spiritual-material currents [*dukhovno-telesnye toki*], which will gradually gain possession of the material environment," resulting in the birth of the "living and eternal likeness of absolute humanity." [14]

Solov'ev's images of the physical transfiguration of the body and his call for androgyny and the fusion of spirit and flesh were to remain on the plane of discourse until the advent of Symbolist discussions about life-creation. One of the examples of the Symbolist attempt to translate Solov'evian theory into practice was the debate in the Merezhkovsky circle about new forms of sexuality that circumvent procreation. (In 1900, the circle included Vasily Rozanov, Alexander Benois, Leon Bakst, Dmitry Filosofov, Pavel Pertsov, Vladimir Gippius, Walter Nuvel', and Sergei Diaghilev.) According to Zinaida Gippius, they were all preoccupied with "the unsolved mystery of sex," its relation to God, and possible alternatives to the biological sex act. Unlike some of the others, Gippius proposed that it be abolished altogether: "The abolition of procreation abolishes the [sex] act, of its own accord—not by any law, but because of its having become . . . an unlawful state. . . . Conversely we must . . . assert the phenomenal . . . transfiguration of the flesh here." [15] In contrast to his wife, Dmitry Merezhkovsky, like Solov'ev, seems to have toyed with ideas that prefigure genetic engineering. Both he and Filosofov believed that the procreative sex act would be replaced "by some other common single act . . . , equally powerful in its sensation of union and corporeality"; but Gippius saw in this vestiges of the animal law and old procreative psychology. [16]

Among the Symbolist followers of Solov'ev, there was a broad range of erotic ideology. The Merezhkovskys attempted to reify his ideas about the transfiguration of the body. Alexander Blok and Andrei Bely borrowed Solov'ev's romantic form of Platonic

love, which had distinct courtly connotations and which the philosopher had projected onto the Gnostic image of Sophia. Gippius also appropriated the myth of divine androgyny and conse-
crated flesh. The bolder Viacheslav Ivanov and especially Mikhail
Kuzmin experimented with Platonic love in its original, homoerotic sense. In many cases, these elements of Platonism and
Neoplatonic, neoromantic, and Christian mysticism were inter-
laced with vestiges of the preceding Russian tradition of radical
utopianism formed in the 1860's.

Homoerotic Love

An alternative to procreation was homoerotic love, celebrated
in European artistic and intellectual circles at the turn of the
century. According to Foucault and his followers, male homosexuality was a late–nineteenth-century cultural construct, which
permeated the Decadent ethos. According to Elaine Showalter,
the homoerotic discourse of the 1890's reflected the emergence
of two different kinds of homosexual identity. One was the *fin de
siècle* model of sexual intermediacy, characterized by liminality
and border-crossing in the sphere of gender. The other emphasized sexual polarization, or heightened forms of masculinity
and femininity.[17] Whatever the differences, both life strategies
were opposed to the subordination of erotic love to procreation.
The adoption of the second type as an elitist cultural model
was part of a general revival of ancient Greek culture and Platonic thought at the end of the century, which also characterized
Russian cultural development. Reclaiming the spirit of classical antiquity, with its cult of sensual beauty, the post-Victorian
and post-Nietzschean generation rebelled against Christian asceticism, including militant heterosexuality. The Greek revival
elevated the status of homoerotic love, practiced by the aristo-
cratic elite in Plato's Athens. The projection of Plato's procreative
metaphor onto homoerotic love, which results in "generation in
beauty," was particularly congenial to the apocalyptic mood of
the times in Russia. In Plato's words, "the partnership between
[those whose progeny is spiritual] will be far closer and the bond

of affection far stronger than between ordinary parents, because the children that they share surpass human children by being immortal as well as more beautiful. Everyone would prefer children such as these to children after the flesh" (*Symposium*, p. 91). The preference for mental progeny, artistic and spiritual, which Plato associated with homosexual love, was imitated in Symbolist culture, in which personal mythmaking and erotic experimentation had homoerotic connotations that went beyond simple sexual preferences. This was true of the Merezhkovsky circle and of some of the inhabitants of Ivanov's Tower, especially Kuzmin. The celebration of homosexuality at the Ivanovs' had a programmatic cultural subtext, whose intention was the reclamation of the original meaning of Platonic eros.

The reappropriation of the homoerotic meaning of Platonic love by Solov'ev and his Symbolist followers took place in stages. The process was characterized by an initial denial of the homosexual nature of Platonic eros, followed by its gradual acceptance. Solov'ev himself rejected homoerotic love, although his theory of eros reflects an unspoken conflict between the heterosexual Sophia, or Beautiful Lady, and the sexually ambiguous androgyne, who can be seen in homoerotic terms. Sophia, whose image informed Blok's and Bely's poetry and life practice, maintained her ties to Christian love symbolized by the Madonna; the androgyne became associated with Plato's Phaedrus and Aphrodite Urania, representing an assault on traditional Christian values. Solov'ev seems to have resolved the contradiction between them by simply fusing the teachings about Sophia with courtly as well as Platonic ideals.

Acknowledging the differences in values between the nineteenth century and Plato's time ("Zhiznennaia," p. 223), Solov'ev exalted heterosexual, not homosexual, eros. His preference was most clearly reflected in his Sophiological treatment of androgyny, which he based on the deification of the feminine principle. The lonely Silver Age prophet of the family, Rozanov, however, accused him of having introduced an antiprocreative homosexual bias into Russian culture. He considered the reinterpretation of Plato by Solov'ev only a mask concealing his subversive intentions. Describing Solov'ev's erotic ideal, Rozanov offered the pejorative syncretic image of "Aphrodite Sodomica," which contaminated Greek and biblical mythology. According to him, she represented a sterile erotic ideal, expressed most powerfully in her words to the earthly Aphrodite: "Oh, if only I could *smash your children against the rock*."[18] It was Rozanov who, at the turn of the twentieth century, first focused on the homosexual nature of Platonic love, which had been consigned to oblivion in Christian culture. "Plato called love of the opposite sex—'earthly' love; 'heavenly' love he calls not philosophical but sensual love and only for the same sex. In making the distinction, he names and quotes the poetess Sappho, . . . this is so indisputable that there is no doubt about it."[19]

While Blok and Bely followed Solov'ev's courtly Sophiological treatment of Platonic love, Gippius adopted the ambiguous ideal of androgyny. Repudiating all forms of physical union because they are founded on power and inequality, she professed androgynous love, which is unconsummated and egalitarian by definition.[20] In this she followed Solov'ev's definition of the "new man" in terms of Aristophanes' erotic myth of the androgyne. In relation to Decadence, she assumed a position of sexual intermediacy. "I do not desire exclusive femininity, just as I do not desire exclusive masculinity," wrote Gippius in an intimate diary. "Each time someone is insulted and dissatisfied within me; with women, my femininity is active, with men—my masculinity. In my thoughts, my desires, in my spirit—I am more a man; in my body—I am more a woman. Yet they are so fused together that I know nothing," wrote Gippius in her diary of unconsummated love affairs.[21]

Gippius's views on homosexuality were ambivalent. She celebrated the highest form of Platonic love—"Love between men *may be* endlessly beautiful and divine"—but rejected its physical consummation. In her private life Gippius was attracted to homosexual androgynous men: "I like the illusion of possibility—as if there were a tinge of bisexuality; he seems to be both woman and man."[22] The biggest love of her life was Filosofov, who was homosexual. A union with him would have come closest to the androgynous ideal as she understood it. Such a love could be described as the fusion of two androgynes, mediated by the mystical presence of Christ.[23] She herself described this love as having elevated her to the status of the utopian new man (*budushchii dalekii chelovek*).[24]

Ivanov treated all love relationships as elaborate reenactments of ancient or contemporary myths. Among them were Dionysian frenzy, which he experienced with his wife, Lidiia Zinov'eva-Annibal; sacred incest, in which he engaged with her daughter Vera; and Platonic love patterned on the myth of Zeus and Ganymede. Although directly connected with homosexual eros, Ivanov's Platonism was much more than a sexual preference; it informed his behavior and worldview as a whole. It defined his path of *de realibus ad realiora*, based on the continuous effort to glimpse higher, absolute reality behind the world of appearances.[25] While experimenting with homosexuality, which in 1906 he identified with the ethos of humanism, Ivanov spoke of its superiority. He described his friend Kuzmin as "a pioneer of the coming age, when with the growth of homosexuality contemporary sexual aesthetics and ethics, understood as 'men for women' and 'women for men,' will no longer deform and destabilize humanity." Yet he rejected exclusive homoeroticism, supporting the ethos of bisexuality.[26]

Viacheslav the Wise (also known as the Magnificent)[27] imitated the Platonic life model that merged the roles of teacher and lover, and saw himself as the divine *pontifex*, mediating between all kinds of people and ideas. Fedor Stepun described him as the most "Symposiesque person" of the prewar period, whose speech was "bewinged."[28] (The image of wings refers, of course, to Plato's *Phaedrus* and the myth of the winged soul.) "His love of discussion was not so much a partiality for polemics, but love of the feastlike [*pirshestvennyi*] play of the spirit," writes Stepun.[29] (*Pirshestvo* is the title of one of the Russian translations of Plato's *Symposium*.) Life at the Tower, especially its Wednesdays, was associated by many with the Platonic symposium.[30] At one of the first Wednesdays, attended by, among others, the Merezhkovskys, Berdiaevs, Bloks, Rozanov, and Bely, the subject of discussion was the meaning of love. "I don't remember who said what," writes Bely, "but from everyone burst the words: 'the erotic soaring [krylen'e] of Plato."[31] In a 1920 drawing of an Olympian gathering at the Tower by Sergei Gorodetsky, he and Ivanov are connected by the image of winged Eros. Blok and Kuzmin are depicted with wings growing out of their shoulders, which may refer to the image of sprouting wings in the Phaedrus and in Kuzmin's Wings (Kryl'ia, 1906).

Ivanov's wife, Lidiia Zinov'eva-Annibal, was known among the cultural elite of Silver Age Petersburg both as Demetra and as Diotima; the former referred to the Dionysian lifestyle of their spiritual commune, the latter to its Platonism. In Nietzschean terms, the two names symbolize the split between the Ivanovs' Dionysian and Apollonian visions, with Diotima, whose image is associated with the elitist ethos of Plato's Athens, representing Apollonian sublimation and aesthetics. In the character of Diotima, the Mantinean priestess who taught Socrates the meaning of divine love, Zinov'eva-Annibal assumed the role of spiritual midwife and Ivanov's counselor.

In Plato's thought, the love of an older, well-educated male for a handsome youth, who combined physical and spiritual beauty, was the starting point of "generation in beauty" and philosophy. Appropriating woman's biological role, Plato's Diotima bestowed procreative power on the male: the procreation of philosophical knowledge was to be engendered in a young man "fertile in soul" by an experienced, refined male friend. Thus childbirth was spiritualized and disembodied.[32] The reclamation of the Platonic ideal became a central point in Ivanov's life strategy: "[He] fell in love with people's souls passionately, in whose depth he heard the call and cry of 'Plato's infant.'"[33]

His most self-conscious attempt to reenact Athenian eros was his relationship in 1906 with the young poet Sergei Gorodetsky, whose soul Ivanov compared to that of Plato's ideal adolescent.[34] Twenty-two years old, tall and supple, Gorodetsky was a clever and talented disciple, to whom Ivanov taught classical Greek, Hellenic religion, and the subtleties of versification. The goal of the relationship was the Platonic contemplation of pure beauty, as well as consummation of passion. In describing the poet's erotic fantasy about Gorodetsky, Olga Deschartes interprets it in terms of the *Phaedrus* and the metaphor of the winged soul: "V.I. hoped that at any moment this young soul would be awakened, would open up and grow."[35] In his diary from this period, Ivanov depicts Gorodetsky naked, looking at himself in the mirror while Ivanov reads to him an aesthetic treatise about the body. Ivanov, cast in the role of the voyeuristic sensualist, watches the young Narcissus indulging in his own reflection.[36] Applying the roles of Platonic teacher and disciple to the Renaissance, he also compared himself to Leonardo, whom he wanted to imitate by teaching Gorodetsky "everything he knew."[37] (Leonardo was a characteristic Platonic image of the Decadence, popularized in European culture by the Pre-Raphaelites and in Russia by Merezhkovsky's novel about the artist; Merezhkovsky's Leonardo also sprouts wings.)

The myth of the winged soul[38] and the erotic relationship between teacher and disciple lay at the core of Kuzmin's famous novel, *Wings*, written in 1905 and published in 1906, at the time when Ivanov was actively searching for a new meaning of love. An intimate of the Tower, which he began to visit regularly in 1906 and moved into in 1907, Kuzmin and his controversial homoerotic novel must have influenced Ivanov and the members of his commune. The novel's mysterious, refined Englishman, Stroop, is steeped in Hellenic culture. In his role of spiritual and aesthetic guide to the young Vania Smurov,[39] Stroop can be compared to Ivanov, who perceived himself as the teacher and initiator of young men like Gorodetsky. One of Gorodetsky's literary prototypes may very well have been Kuzmin's Vania Smurov. The host of a Petersburg salon, Stroop urges Vania to study classical Greek; his relationship with Vania is emblematized by the sprouting of wings: "Just one more little effort and you'll grow wings. I can see them already," says Stroop. "Perhaps—but the growing can be very painful," responds Vania with a grin;[40] it is from Stroop that Vania learns of nonprocreative homoerotic love.

In an explicit polemic with Rozanov, Stroop attacks the Old Testament focus on procreation and its antiaesthetic ethos, contrasting it with love in a higher, Platonic sense: "We are Hellenes: the intolerant monotheism of the Hebrews is alien to us—their rejection of the visual arts, their slavish attachment to the flesh, to the getting of heirs, to seed" (p. 218, p. 32). He also speaks of the interpretation of the biblical Fall by the Jews themselves, who equated it with childbirth: "It is a Jewish legend which tells us that childbirth and toil are a punishment for sin, not the purpose of life. And as human beings put sin behind them, so will they put behind them childbearing and toil" (p. 218, p. 32). Emphasizing the superiority of homosexual love, Stroop relegates the love of men for beautiful women to lust, which takes them away from the true idea of beauty.

Although Kuzmin's posture was aesthetic, not mystical or ideological, it may have utopian connotations in *Wings*, in which homosexual eros is associated with the myth of the new man and the transformation of life and with the myth of the Argonauts.[41] "We are Hellenes, lovers of the beautiful, the bacchants of the coming day. Like the visions of Tannhäuser in Venus' Grotto, like the inspired revelations of Klinger and Thoma,[42] somewhere lies our ancient kingdom, full of sunlight and freedom, of beautiful and courageous people, and thither we sail, my argonauts, over many a sea, through mist and darkness. And in things yet unheard we shall descry ancient roots, in glittering visions yet unseen we shall know our own dear land!" proclaims Stroop in his treatise on love (p. 220, p. 33). This image of the future based on the return to the Hellenic myth of the Argonauts reappears at the end of the novel in the projected opera by the composer Ugo Orsini. Depicting a series of mythological male heroes, including the Argonauts, the opera, according to Orsini, will contain the figures of Prometheus, Oedipus, Icarus, Phaethon, and Ganymede. But only Ganymede will be transformed into a new man, because, contrary to the others, he is motivated by a higher form of love, not rebellion against the gods. His wings are Platonic, unlike those of Icarus and Phaethon, who are doomed to fall from the heavens because their wings have a Promethean, not an erotic, subtext.

Lover of Zeus, the beautiful youth Ganymede alone among

his brothers remained in the heavens: "My poor brothers, of all
who sought to fly up to the heavens only I have remained, for
it was childish curiosity which lured you toward the sun, while I
was lifted up in the beating wings of a love beyond mortal ken"
(p. 320, p. 109). Ganymede, whose homoerotic image was at the
basis of the *Phaedrus*, reflects Kuzmin's conception of the erotic
utopia, as does the figure of the beautiful youth Antinous, who
died for his beloved emperor Adrian. In an inserted tale, Kuzmin's Antinous, like Ganymede, is also transformed by means
of love, becoming a godman at the behest of the emperor. It
is the myth of Ganymede and Antinous that Ivanov invoked in
his desire to transform Gorodetsky into a new man or demigod,
a task that could only be accomplished in the act of love. But,
in contrast to Vania in *Wings* and his mythological prototypes,
Gorodetsky refused to play the role selected for him.[43]

In a typical example of cultural syncretism, Ivanov's Platonic
ideal was intertwined with the Oriental homoerotic image of the
Persian poet Hafiz, chosen as the patron of the playful homosexual coterie that met at the Tower from 1906 to 1907. Besides
Ivanov and his Diotima, its best-known members were Kuzmin,
the artists Konstantin Somov and Leon Bakst, the musician Walter Nuvel', prose writer S. A. Auslender, and Gorodetsky. The
Hafiz Society had its own symposia, or banquets, presided over
by a chorus leader, as in Greek tragedy. In contrast to the public Wednesday symposia, which had a social, even revolutionary
utopian mission, these were intimate, frivolously playful, artistic
gatherings. The members of the Hafiz Society, emphasizing the
importance of "life" over Promethean revolutionary activity, rejected the conceptualization of love in the grand utopian sense.
Associated with "the hashish of fantasy, which led them through
the gardens of pleasure,"[44] they practiced erotic and artistic refinement, effeminacy (except for Lidiia, no women were allowed),
and effete languor, represented by Beardsley's and Swinburne's
androgynes and dandies.[45]

The celebration of intimacy by the Hafiz Society was reflected
in the special focus on its members' diaries, which they read
to each other. Diaries with a fragmentary lyrical structure re-

sembling poetry assumed a central place in Symbolist literary practice in general. Gippius, whose *Contes d'amour*, or diary of "love affairs," reflected her ideology, considered diaries and letters of equal importance with poetry.[46] The diary could be seen as the archetypal Symbolist text, blurring the boundaries between art and life, as well as transforming the life text into art. Ivanov considered Kuzmin's intimate diary, which the poet read to his Hafiz intimates, a "work of art," comparing its form with that of the novel.[47] In doing so, he must have had in mind the fragmented, allusive, open-ended novel that was emerging at the time, not the Russian realist novel of the nineteenth century, with its ideological focus.

And yet, despite Kuzmin's cultivated aestheticism and antiutilitarian stance, his novel celebrating homoerotic love was seen by some contemporaries as a program of action, something like Chernyshevsky's prescriptively ideological *What Is to Be Done? From the Tales About the New People* (*Chto delat'? Iz rasskazov o novykh liudiakh*, 1863). According to Blok, "contemporary criticism has the tendency to perceive Kuzmin as a *preacher*, to consider him the bearer of some kind of dangerous ideas. I heard the opinion that *Wings* for our time corresponds to Chernyshevsky's novel *What Is to Be Done?*"[48]

Celibate Marriage

The Platonic love myth suggests another important cultural model of love—the practice of chastity, including marital celibacy and chaste triple union, which were contrasted to traditional marriage and adultery. Chaste love, of course, goes back to the chivalric ideal of the troubadours, or courtly love, which developed in opposition to the feudal institution of marriage. According to some interpretations of courtly love, it had a triangular structure: the poet-knight's love for the wife of a feudal lord was mediated by the power of the husband. Courtly love, with its mystical and romantic connotations, was celebrated by Solov'ev and his Symbolist followers.[49]

Culturally the most significant chaste marriage among the Symbolists was Alexander Blok's union with Liubov' Dmitrievna Mendeleeva (they were married in 1903), which Bely and Sergei Solov'ev (the philosopher's nephew) saw as a Solov'evian "sacred mystery" heralding the new theocratic era.[50] The realization of this kind of marriage, according to Bely, was a "world-historical task."[51] In his view, Liubov' Dmitrievna, whose name means love in Russian, represented "the image of 'the woman clothed in the sun' or of 'Sophia Divine Wisdom,'" which "received its incarnation in . . . an earthly woman."[52] Bely's later marriage (1910) to Asia Turgeneva, in whom he saw the androgynous Mona Lisa,[53] may have also been conceived as a chaste marriage based on a shared philosophy of life, even though it was not in actuality.

The most consistently celibate and long-lasting chaste union was the marriage (1889) of Dmitry Merezhkovsky and Zinaida Gippius, who lived together for 52 years, without parting for a single day. It is this union that presents the most heterogeneous model of celibate marriage at the turn of the century. The case of the Merezhkovskys is an example of Symbolist syncretism, which combined what may seem to be incompatible cultural sources informing the Symbolist conceptualization of love. The most unexpected ideological aspect of their marriage was the conflation of Solov'evian erotic mysticism with the ideology of love developed in the 1850's and 1860's that was codified in Chernyshevsky's famous novel *What Is to Be Done?*[54]

One of the nineteenth-century prototypes of the celibate marriage between Merezhkovsky and Gippius was Chernyshevsky's concept of fictitious marriage, which influenced marital practice among radical youth in the 1860's and 1870's. Fictitious marriage, originally a legal convenience that allowed a young woman to leave the parental home and thus escape the strictures of traditional family life and marriage, developed into a symbolically significant pattern of human relations. "It was regarded as the ideal marriage, a union that served" not only personal happiness, but also "the realization of the common cause."[55] The young couple, which had married purely *pro forma*, frequently continued to live together on the basis of total equality; refraining from sexual relations, the two worked together for the shared goal of social revolution. Thus chastity, an integral component of courtly love, was grafted onto marriage, whose ideology of love is very different from the courtly ideal. The new radical family of the 1860's and 1870's, based on the precepts of equality, economic cooperation, control over one's emotions and physiology, and ascetic self-denial, was regarded as a prototype of future society. Symbolist marital celibacy can be seen as a continuation of the erotic practice of earlier Russian utopian generations.

If one peels off the turn-of-the-century cultural layers from the Merezhkovsky marital union, their partnership begins to resemble a nineteenth-century radical marriage in some very essential ways. Gippius was hiding a persona of populist persuasion behind the Decadent mask of *femme fatale* and queen of Petersburg social life.[56] Despite the Merezhkovskys' polemic with the preceding literary generation, they appear to have implemented Chernyshevsky's views on love and marriage in their secret private life. It was the concepts of asexual love and marriage, defined by a shared ideology, not by family and procreation, that helped shape the Merezhkovsky marriage. A celibate, spiritual partnership, it was based on what Gippius called a *common cause* associated with the transformation of life in the "Third Testament."

Like those men and women of the 1860's who behaved in accordance with the radical code of celibate love, the Merezhkovskys lived in a fraternal union, which Gippius flaunted during the first ten years of marriage by wearing a single braid, signifying her virginity. In her biography of Merezhkovsky, Gippius depicts their courtship, wedding, and early life in Petersburg in terms remarkably similar to those describing the Lopukhov marriage in *What Is to Be Done?*, the archetypal radical fraternal union in literature.[57] The first uncanny coincidence is Merezhkovsky's name and patronymic, Dmitry Sergeevich, which are the same as Lopukhov's. Both men reenact the radical version of the Pygmalion myth by playing the role of mentor who introduces the bride to a new way of thinking.[58] Merezhkovsky, by marrying the young Zinaida and bringing her to Petersburg, could be seen as delivering her from her provincial environment and exposing her to new ideas.

Like Vera Pavlovna and Lopukhov, Gippius and Merezhkovsky subverted the traditional wedding ceremony and sexual initiation of the bridal night. In contrast to the wedding and marriage of Kitty and Levin, which Gippius invokes in the description of her own, the Merezhkovskys had a conspicuously modest ceremony, lacking in epithalamic symbols. Instead of an extravagant wedding costume (extravagant dress became her trademark only in later years), she wore a grey suit; he was dressed in a greatcoat. The only elements of the wedding ritual that she mentions reflect a feminist concern: the couple stepped on the wedding carpet simultaneously, so as to signify sexual equality. After the ceremony they had dinner as usual, as if nothing had happened; like Vera Pavlovna and Lopukhov, they spent their wedding day in her room, reading a book together: "Our day was the same as yesterday. Dmitry Sergeevich and I continued reading yesterday's book in my room, then we had dinner. . . . D.S. went back to his hotel rather early, and I went to bed and forgot that I was married."[59] The arrangement of the Merezhkovsky apartment in Petersburg is described in almost the same terms as the arrangement of the Lopukhovs'. Like the narrator in *What Is to Be Done?*, Gippius underscores that the couple had separate bedrooms divided by a common dining room. Separate bedrooms were typical of the Russian upper class and intelligentsia in the nineteenth century; the ideologically significant point is the emphasis on the spatial division of Vera Pavlovna's and Gippius's private lives into what they shared and what they did not share with their husbands. In both cases, there was common space for husband and wife and exclusive space designated for the wife's intellectual socializing with her male and female friends. (The husband also had his own room[s], but the narrative focus is on the woman's quarters.) Although this is where the textual similarities with *What Is to Be Done?* end, the later appearance of Filosofov in the Merezhkovskys' personal life may be compared to the role played by Kirsanov in the Lopukhov marriage.[60] Gippius's concerns with sexual equality continue the ideas current in Russia in the 1860's, even though she did not define her theory of love in radical or feminist terms. It may be significant, in this respect, that Filosofov, a major inspiration in her life for many years, was the son of Anna Filosofova, a well-known feminist and populist whose values were formed in the 1860's under the influence of the milieu of Chernyshevsky's followers. (She knew Ivan Sechenov, the third party in a well-known *ménage à trois* of the 1860's, whose role was similar to that of her son in the Merezhkovsky marriage.) Anna Filosofova's ideas are known to have influenced her son and may have contributed as well to Gippius's views, which were tempered by the mystical tendencies at the turn of the century.

Triangular Love

Having rejected the procreative goal of marriage, the Symbolists were seeking more dynamic and open forms of family life, with greater creative potential. Among alternatives to traditional marriage was the expansion of the chaste, as well as sexual, union of two into a more fulfilling erotic union of three. This triangular living arrangement should not be confused with adultery, which is generally illicit and sexual; adultery attacks marriage from within, offering no constructive alternatives. The Symbolist triangular relationship was conceived as a harmonious union, or fusion, of three people into one through the transformative power of love. The triple union represented the triumph of synthesis and was the highest attainment of synthesis in the sphere of private life, fusing together not two elements but three. It was seen as a projection of the Christian trinity or as a reenactment of Greek mythic communalism, as viewed through the prism of Slavophile *sobornost'* (communality). In other words, the new family triad was intended as a prototype of the new community, in which eros was joined to religion and to society.

The experiments with alternative family structures, in which a triangular arrangement was the desired goal, centered around two Symbolist "families": Gippius and Merezhkovsky, and Zinov'eva-Annibal and Ivanov. In the spirit of cultural syncretism, these experiments were informed by a variety of sources. And as in chaste marriage, Platonic, Neoplatonic, and romantic mysticism were combined with the Russian radical utopia of the 1860's.

The belief in the revolutionary function of private life found its expression in the experiments with "collectivity in love" undertaken in radical circles in the 1860's. In their attempts to reorganize established patterns of interpersonal relations underlying the existing social order, the "people of the 1860's" sought to transform the fateful, adulterous love triangle into a form of human relations that would be emotionally fulfilling, as well as socially subversive. Radical versions of the *ménage à trois* and larger love collectives were presented in literary texts and were practiced in some circles.

The harmony of the celibate marriage of the Lopukhovs in the first chapters of *What Is to Be Done?* is destroyed when Vera Pavlovna falls in love with Lopukhov's best friend, Kirsanov. Although the possibility for a harmonious cohabitation of all three is offered, it remains unrealized. Later in the novel, however, collectivity in love triumphs when Vera Pavlovna with Kirsanov and Lopukhov with his new wife settle *à quatre* in a shared household. Their foursome is meant as a prototype of an emotionally, sexually, and economically harmonious society of the future. The real-life examples include two celebrated cases: the triple union involving the radical activists and literati Nikolai and Liudmila Shelgunov and Mikhail Mikhailov and the triple union of the distinguished scientist Ivan Sechenov and Petr and Maria Bokov. In both instances, the establishment of a *ménage à trois* followed what was initially a celibate marriage.[61]

Following Chernyshevsky's linkage of triangular love and political action, Gippius and Merezhkovsky began searching for another person when they decided to build a New Church: "We needed a third person to divide us, while uniting with us," wrote Gippius in 1900.[62] Around 1902, they were actively seeking someone to form with them a triple union that would serve as the secret, conspiratorial nucleus of the Church of the Third Testament. Filosofov became that third person, living with the Merezhkovskys for fifteen difficult years. After their final rupture, in Warsaw in 1920, Vladimir Zlobin, a pale replica of Filosofov, gradually replaced him and remained with them until they died, in Paris, although his life in the Merezhkovsky household was also a cover for his homosexual life style.

Gippius, who was the active force behind the Merezhkovsky *ménage*, modified the populist triangle with Solov'evian ideas, as well as a Decadent ethos. Combining Solov'ev's and Chernyshevsky's views of love, she grafted onto them romantic unrequited love and the *Liebestod*. In a mystical sense, the triangle, which was symbolically associated with the Holy Trinity, represented Solov'ev's idea that the higher form of erotic love must be mediated by God, not the desire to propagate. According to Gippius, divine resurrective love is triangular by definition, with Christ as the third person in the configuration: "The one I love— I love for God," proclaimed Gippius in an early poem ("Truth or Happiness?" ["Pravda ili schast'e," 1904]). "In relation to you and with you," wrote Gippius to Filosofov, "I could do and feel only what I could do before Christ, under His gaze, and even of necessity in His presence."[63] Following Chernyshevsky, however, the notion of mediated desire was also reified in the here and now. Triangular love, according to Gippius, was intended to energize the union, promoting activism in the social sense. Like the role of Vera Pavlovna in *What Is to Be Done?*, Gippius's role was to stimulate the men in the union to action.

The underside of the radical triple union *à la* Merezhkovsky was the romantic ideal of unrequited love and incompatibility, which helped reinforce the principle of chastity. (Since Filosofov was homosexual and Merezhkovsky appeared to be asexual, there was no compatibility among the three partners in purely sexual terms.) Incompatible in their sexual preferences, the members of this triangle were psychologically incapable of physically consummating their love for each other. Instead they sublimated their erotic needs by dedicating themselves to a common cause. Actually, Filosofov was Gippius's ideal "new man"; he combined homosexuality, which she associated with the androgyne's sexual intermediacy, and unattainability. On the surface, the triple union seemed idyllic, and their religious and political cause was well served. Like the Shelgunov *ménage*, they lived together, traveled to Europe in search of collaborators, and even emigrated together. They first went to France in 1906 to "discover in their closeness new things that would be useful later for their cause and for Russia."[64] Like the characters in *What Is to Be Done?*, they equated the triple union with marriage. The religious ceremony they celebrated in 1901 to consummate their relationship reflected this equation: in dedication to each other and to the invisible New Church, they devised a combined wedding ritual and Communion. At the first service, they removed all rings (Gippius had seven) symbolizing past relationships and exchanged crosses to signify the triple marital union.

On the basis of Gippius' triangular model, Anton Kartashev[65] and Gippius's sisters Tat'iana and Natal'ia also formed an ideological *ménage à trois* to promote the Religion of the Third Testament. Imitating the Merezhkovskys and Filsofov, they performed a ritual resembling a wedding ceremony to mark their triple union with the purpose of dedicating themselves to the invisible New Church. Kartashev, who was especially close to Zinaida Gippius at the beginning of the century, claimed that she preached the idea of celibacy and abolition of childbearing among her friends,[66] which included Blok, Bely, and himself. Gradually, however, Kartashev reverted to more traditional notions of love and Christian family, which resulted in the disintegration of his union with the Gippius sisters.[67]

Even more eclectic and more radical than Gippius and Merezhkovsky were Viacheslav Ivanov and Lidiia Zinov'eva-Annibal, whose highly unconventional life practice combined a wide variety of disparate symbols. (The standard example is Ivanov's conflation of Dionysus and Christ, resulting in the powerful Symbolist metaphor of the suffering god who unites pagan

eros and Christian ascetic love.) In spite of his clear preference
for Dionysian (i.e., physically consummated) eroticism, which
set him apart from Solov'ev and the Merezhkovskys, Ivanov expressed a longing for celibacy. "Despite all that has happened
to me . . . , I envy you: virginity like yours,—there is nothing
higher," he said in a conversation with Solov'ev.[68] And although
Ivanov's marital practice was Dionysian, not Apollonian, he was
attracted to celibate marriage and the idea of immaculate, what
he called "seedless," conception.[69] Yet his marriage, unlike the
unions of Merezhkovsky and Gippius, Blok and Liubov' Mendeleeva, and Bely and Asia Turgeneva, was not childless.

It is in a syncretic spirit that the Ivanovs approached the notion
of the triple union in the period around 1905. Their theory
of triangular love was related to the reenactment of the Greek
tragic chorus at the Tower and belief in the transcendence of
individualism and possessive love by Russian communalism: "We
cannot be two, we should not close the circle. . . . Our rings of
love are for the ocean of love!" wrote Lidiia Zinov'eva-Annibal in
her diary from this period.[70] Describing their mythology of love
at the time of the 1905 revolution, Olga Deschartes character-
izes Ivanov's marriage to Lidiia by means of an alchemical image
from his verse: "a melter of souls fused them into one nugget"
(*plavil' shchik dush v edinyi splavil slitok*). But this was only the beginning; according to Deschartes, they were "to 'melt' into their
double union [*dvuedinstvo*] a third being—not only spiritually,
but also physically."[71] Aware of the difficulties posed by physical
intimacy in such an arrangement, Ivanov and his wife perceived
their plans for a sacred spiritual and physical triple union as a
first step on the path to communalism.

Like the Merezhkovskys a few years earlier, they actively
looked for a third person to join them in this radical enterprise.
Margarita Sabashnikova-Voloshina, the Ivanovs' neighbor, who
lived in a celibate marriage with the poet Maximil'ian Voloshin,
became one of the main candidates for such a union. She describes it as the beginning of a new social and religious collective:
"They had a remarkable idea: when two people, like them, had
become one, they could love a third person. . . . Such a love is the
beginning of a new human community, even of a new Church, in

which eros is incarnated into flesh and blood."[72] Discussing the experiment with Margarita Voloshina a few years later, Ivanov referred to it as "marriage"; "my love was in the rhythm of three, not two," he wrote. The marriage, however, did not take place; when Ivanov realized that the inclusion of Voloshina in a triple union was not working, he lost interest in her.[73] As a result of this failure the Ivanovs began to doubt whether their program of triadic love was feasible at all.[74]

Ivanov's active search for the third member of their new collective coincided with his homosexual experiments, which coincidence resulted in the conflation of Platonic love with the triple union. Before the experiment with Voloshina, his choice fell on the young poet Gorodetsky, who was expected to become the third member of the triadic family as well as Ivanov's Platonic lover: "I am seeking from fate happiness in the shape of a threesome," wrote Ivanov to his wife in 1906.[75] And in the poem "Architect" ("Zodchii"), he uses the recurrent image of metallurgical fusion to represent the desired union:

> Dai vedat' vostorgi vershin
>
> . . .
>
> I splav' ognezhalym perunom
> Tri zhertvy v altar' triedin![76]

> Let me know the rapture of the heights
>
> . . .
>
> And melt by means of a perun with a fiery sting
> Three sacrifices into a triple altar!

Like Diotima, Lidiia was expected to play the role of mediator, reifying divine love in the triple union. Her role may be likened to the image of Christ invoked by Gippius in her transformative love for Filosofov, with the exception that in the Ivanov triad the symbol of divine love becomes flesh and blood. It may be argued that Ivanov attempted a kind of transcendence similar to that celebrated by Gippius, and that both failed in their task of breaking down the barrier between homoerotic and heterosexual love.

To conclude, the erotic as well as family life strategies of the Symbolist generation were consummately eclectic and provocatively subversive. In keeping with the Symbolist penchant for life creation, some of the movement's more active representatives attempted to project their favorite ideas and cultural models onto real life. Private life, especially life of the heart and family, became an arena for experimentation with the purpose of creating a "new man" and "new woman." The new man would resemble the divine androgyne; the new woman would be clothed in the sun; new forms of union between men and women would replace traditional marriage. The antiprocreative, androgynous, and triadic life practice among the Symbolists was rooted in Platonic, Neoplatonic, and Christian mysticism, which rested on the substratum of radical utopianism of the 1860's. Combining romantic love with social radicalism, the Symbolist models of love brought together two seemingly irreconcilable cultural myths, romantic and realist, in what appears to be a peculiar amalgam.

Three

Creating the Living Work of Art:
The Symbolist Pygmalion
and His Antecedents

IRENE MASING-DELIC

The notion that the artistic imagination coupled with the energy of sublimated eroticism was a powerful transformational magic, capable of overcoming even death, assumed the form of realized metaphor in the writings of the Russian Symbolists. In keeping with this notion, Pygmalion, who brought to life his own statue, became one of their preferred emblems of the artist. This mythic sculptor as it were anticipated their cherished theurgical aspirations. To them he was the true artist who transcended the confines of mere art, an artist who, knowing the secrets of wondrous transformations, learned how to animate stone in the literal sense of the word "animate." He thus achieved the creation of real life, as opposed to its mere likeness. In their interpretation of the animated-sculpture myth, Pygmalion might even surpass this wondrous transformation by creating, not just real life, but immortality, again in the literal sense of the word. This he would achieve when he transferred the metaphorical immortality of his work of art to the living beloved model. He would transcend the immortality metaphor of pure art, since a work of art sooner or later must disintegrate, whereas the aestheticized beloved would exist forever.

However, the Symbolists were not the first to take an interest in Pygmalion. The motif of a statue coming to life had attracted considerable attention in Russian literature, at least since Pushkin. Culled from Ovid's *Metamorphoses*, the Pygmalion motif captivated Russian writers for the same reason that it did their Western colleagues from Jean Jacques Rousseau to George Bernard Shaw: because it demonstrates "a specific relationship between the artist and his work of art, a specific type of artistry and a specific attitude toward art," one that focuses "on artistic creativity itself."[1]

Within this meta-aesthetic sphere there is room for a great variety of both complementary and contradictory interpretations of the motif: the range of approaches extends to Rousseau's narcissistic self-mirroring;[2] A. F. Boureau-Deslandes's Promethean-Faustian curiosity about the "transmutability of matter within the 'Great All,'" manifested in his *Pigmalion, ou la Statue animée* (1741);[3] Goethe's rejection of Pygmalion in favor of King Midas, since, in his view, the artist must "kill" in order to "turn into gold," that is, make live human beings into statues rather than statues into human beings;[4] Shaw's dismissal of the art-for-art's-sake artist in favor of the one "who aspires, like God, to create life."[5] The motif was not always raised to the symbolic and philosophical heights mentioned above. Often it was treated in purely erotic terms, particularly in eighteenth-century French opera and ballet.

However, the erotic and the philosophical did not necessarily exclude each other in the reception history of this Ovidian metamorphosis. In fact, the two aspects were often interlinked in theories that posited pleasure as a major source of consciousness. Thus the motif of the animated statue attracted the eighteenth-century *philosophes*, who believed in John Locke's theory that the human mind is entirely formed by sensual experiences, as opposed to innate ideas. Diderot, Voltaire, and Condillac speculated on man's ability to penetrate "nature's deepest mystery—the link between matter and mind" and on his potential for endowing matter with sensations in an act rivaling God's creation.[6] A utopian line of thought postulated that not only bodies (organic matter) but also statues (inorganic matter) could be endowed with consciousness by sensual means. Stone could be "caressed to life" (see also note 3).

In Russia, the blend of eroticism and philosophy inherent in the Pygmalion motif fascinated the religious philosophers Vladimir Solov'ev (1853–1900) and Nikolai Fedorov (1828?–1903), as well as those Symbolist "life-creators" who adopted the cause of perfecting a flawed woman into an incarnation of *das Ewig Weibliche* in an act of sublimated eroticism.[7] Almost invariably, the Russian interpreters of the motif took a decidedly anti-Midas and pro-Pygmalion stance, in the sense that they believed, as did Shaw, that the true artist is not the man who is interested "in painting pictures," but the one who wants to "[transform] people."[8] However, Russian life-creators did not need Shaw and his play *Pygmalion* (1913) to formulate their aesthetics; they followed a national tradition of preference for "life over art," already cultivated by the Russian radicals of the 1860's. These, in their turn, clearly were influenced by those *philosophes* who believed in the total malleability of man and all other material forms—organic or inorganic.

In addition, many other native and foreign ideological sources served to inspire the Symbolist life-creators, who placed their hopes in art as a means for transforming life. A survey of some of these antecedents may provide us with some contexts for Russian life-creation aesthetics and its realized-immortality concept. As already briefly stated, Russian life-creators saw the Pygmalion-type artist as powerful enough, literally, to overcome even death: this is their main contribution to the multifaceted and ever evolving Pygmalion myth. They metamorphosed the sculptor Pygmalion into an artist who attempts the immortalization of his living model, following the dictates of a love that is endless and, hence, demands eternity.

What ideological sources and traditions were available to Russian life-creators in their transformation of the myth? Symbolist writers presumably made their first acquaintance with the Pygmalion motif when studying Ovid's *Metamorphoses* in school. Since the turn of the century was a time of particular awareness of myth, classical and national, the Latin text did not sink into post-commencement oblivion. Instead, it was merged with the newer myths of Nietzschean heroic-tragic neoromanticism, preaching the superman, and with Bergsonian vitalism, teaching eternal creativity.[9] Following the precedents set by Friedrich Nietzsche's *The Birth of Tragedy from the Spirit of Music* and Richard Wagner's mythological music dramas, Russian Symbolists, too, sought to revive ancient myths and make them relevant to contemporary life. Many, like Innokenty Annensky, Fedor Sologub, Dmitry Merezhkovsky, Valery Briusov, and Viacheslav Ivanov, celebrated a rebirth of antiquity in their literary works and translations, as well as that Renaissance which resurrected antiquity. The Russian Symbolists showed a particularly great interest in all forms and revivals of Hellenism, including Roman Hellenism, of which the popular *Metamorphoses* forms an integral part.[10]

Earlier, Russian romanticism had taken a great interest in Ovid. The exiled Pushkin repeatedly wrote about the exiled Roman. His own "poetic mythology of miraculous sculptures" may, in its fascination with transition, owe something to Ovid; it explored both directions of metamorphosis, that is, "the triumph of imagined movement over the inertia of matter" and the victory of "eternally immobile matter, overcoming the illusoriness of ephemereal movement."[11] At least, the motif of the statuesque (frigid) woman who is gradually aroused by the poet's caresses offers a Pygmalionesque element in Pushkin's erotic poetry ("No, I do not treasure ["Net, ia Ne dorozhu," 1831]). Continuing this Pushkinian tradition, the realist Ivan Turgenev makes his frigid Odintsova in *Fathers and Sons* (*Ottsy i deti*, 1861) into a statuesque Galatea. She is, however, a Galatea who remains unmoved by Bazarov's efforts to emulate Pygmalion. One reason for his failure is undoubtedly his brutal impetuosity. The Pygmalion motif usually emphasizes the need for creative patience, for caressing life into stone. Thus Madame Odintsova is perhaps rejecting Bazarov not only as a lover but also as a materialistic scientist who believes that unconscious matter may be awakened by crude sensual delights. She refuses to become Bazarov's quasi–test object for his primitive version of Locke's sensationist theories, which entirely dismiss the metaphysical concept of the soul. Turgenev, who studied philosophy at Berlin University, was probably aware of the philosophical implications of the Pygmalion motif, including the notion that pleasurable sense stimuli may awaken cold and lifeless matter.[12]

Russian nineteenth-century poets cultivating anthological poetry devoted much attention to "describing statues and pictures" and often presented people "in statuesque terms" and scenes in pictorial ones.[13] Anthology poets, although influenced by the Ovidian *Metamorphoses*, nevertheless stressed the impossibility of a genuine transformation, viewing life as separate from art; they took a Goethean pro-Midas and anti-Pygmalion stance rare in later Russian literature. Thus Afanasy Fet's persona sometimes toys with the idea of animation, as in the famous "Diana" (1847), where a ripple on moonlit waters makes the poet expect the "milk-white" goddess to step down from her pedestal to look at "sleepy Rome, the city of eternal glory." But he eventually states that the marble "remains immobile, shimmering in its white beauty, forever beyond grasp."[14]

Ovid's *Metamorphoses* fare differently in the poetry of the Tiutchev *pleiade*, where the poet's animating power is emphasized. Thus the *liubomudry* (wisdom lovers) movement paid homage to Ovid's Pygmalion, naming one of its journals *Galatea* (1829–30, 1839–40). And Evgeny Baratynsky, moving toward a "lover of wisdom" stance at the time, wrote the programmatic poem "The Sculptor" ("Skul'ptor," 1841). In this poem, the Pygmalion motif serves the poet's romantic vision of the artist as powerful enough to create *realiora* superior to mere *realia*. This power derives from his sensitivity to form: firstly, he perceives the form of the beautiful nymph hidden in the rough stone, and, secondly, he forms himself, while bringing the envisioned form out of its dark entrapment into the light. The act of artistic creation thus becomes a sublimation of passion and a quest for self-knowledge. Seized by an intense desire for the envisioned nymph, the sculptor does not yield to frenzied passion, but channels his fire into creative energies. Slowly and carefully he "undresses" his nymph hidden in the marble until the last garment falls, revealing her perfect form. At this moment the caresses of his "insidious chisel" yield a corresponding "flush of desire" in his creation. The work of art is perfect when there is no further resistance from the raw material, which now is the ideal incarnation of the artist's vision:

> In sweet, intuitive effort,
> More than an hour, day and year will pass,
> And the last robe will not fall,
> From her, perceived and desired from the beginning,
> Until, *fully grasping* the nature of passion,
> And caressed by the insidious chisel,
> Galatea gives a responsive glance
> And, blushing with desire, entices
> The sage to celebrate with her the triumph of love.[15]

The Galatea of Baratynsky's poem presumably comes to life in a metaphorical sense only. She is liberated from her nonexistence in stone when she acquires a form that entirely corresponds to the artist's ideal of beauty. The created work of art is thus a mirror in which he sees his own evaluations, dreams, and ideals, in short, himself. Galatea revealed is not an imitation of (external) nature but a receptacle of the artist's inner world, a mirror of his personality and, as such, the proof of his creative might, surpassing, in some respects, even that of the First Creator. In nature there is no woman of perfect beauty, but the sculptured Galatea has no blemish.[16] As his externalized anima, Galatea is a work of art superior to any beautiful form found in nature. If one compares Baratynsky's *liubomudry* version of the Pygmalion motif with Western variants, one sees that it approaches the Rousseauan vision of the artist as exulting in his own creative powers and creating a world for himself in which he is able to feel emotionally at home. Intensely erotic as the poem is, it also contains traces of the sensationist philosophy that inspired some *philosophes* to believe that pleasure is the key to the animation of matter.[17]

In spite of its metaphorical-symbolic essence, Baratynsky's poem does cross a magical borderline dividing the inanimate from the animate realm. Within the poem's reality, the statue ac-

quires life, blushing in response to the artist's final advance. Such
animation is impermissible in a realistic text, where a statue cannot acquire life except in dreams and hallucinations. In a realistic
text, however, a beautiful form may be buried in layers of fat
instead of stone and steeped in a spiritual indolence, qualifying
for an inanimate state. This is the case in Ivan Goncharov's *Oblomov* (1859), whose eponymous hero, while representing a distinct
literary type, still may be subsumed under a yet broader heading, namely that of Gogolian "dead souls" in need of animation
and resurrection.[18] *Oblomov* offers a Russian variant of the Western "pedagogical" Pygmalion myth, cultivated by the Enlightenment and its ideological offshoots (such as Sentimentalism, which
stresses both sensation and sentiment).

Goncharov's prose realization of the motif entails several shifts
and reversals. Not only is Oblomov's flesh the "stone prison" in
which his real physical and spiritual form is hidden; it holds a
man who plays the role of passive nymph, whereas his "sculptor"
is a woman.[19] The determined Olga accepts this reversal of roles,
seeing Oblomov as "a kind of Galatea whose Pygmalion she herself had to be." As is well known, Olga's forming of Oblomov
is not crowned by success, perhaps because, like Bazarov and
other radical life-reformers, she is too impatient. For whatever
reason, the beautiful physical-spiritual form she perceives under
the layers of grotesque infantility and baby fat barely emerges
before it is again imbedded in its material prisonhouse, now
to disappear there forever. Olga at times wonders what would
have happened if Oblomov "had come to life," but, unlike Baratynsky's sculptor, she will never find out. What she does learn,
however, is that she herself can be a Galatea in relation to Stolz,
the mentor-husband, who forms her spiritual life, but who also
gains insights and self-knowledge from her.

Stolz and Olga offer a realist intelligentsia version of the
Galatea myth, in which the former is an "artist and thinker" extracting a "new image" of woman out of Olga's current one. Nor
does Stolz lack artistic ambition, since he wants to make his wife
into something "different, exalted, almost unheard of." Although
he succeeds in creating only a "pale reflection" of his ideal, and

although Olga, in her turn, sees that the dreams of her youth are unrealizable, both partners nevertheless do try to live up to their ideal visions of each other, to the extent possible in our flawed world. As realists, Olga and Stolz know that total transformation is beyond reach, but love continues to be an aesthetic force in their life, "as powerful as the life force" itself.[20]

Stolz and Olga mirror and form each other, to the point where they can be seen as merging in a union of spiritual androgyny, that state of human perfection earlier judged desirable by the German romantics and later exalted by Solov'ev in his Platonizing philosophy of love. There is only one fundamental criticism that the "erotic utopian" Solov'ev could have offered of their androgynous union: that their aspirations were not bold enough.[21] Therefore their transformational creativity led to trivial results, namely, a solid and happy marriage, as opposed to a qualitatively new kind of human being, such as the immortal androgyne. The couple certainly does not aim for immortality, as Solov'ev would have demanded. Solov'ev saw the meaning of love in the immortalization of the beloved, the earthly representative of *das Ewig Weibliche*. Although Olga sees her ideal of "masculine perfection" embodied in her husband, and the latter, in his turn, lives in a state of being that is "unfading spring," neither attempts to transcend the empirically possible. Both remain anchored in a solid bourgeois existence, where miracles cannot happen and where spring, however vibrant, eventually must pass.[22] Both Olga and Stolz, who have children, acknowledge the supreme power of death and hence the need to procreate. They accept that either frail Olga or, for that matter, the vigorous Stolz may die at any moment and that eventually both must die and yield their place to a new generation. In other words, their life-creation program does not include immortalization through love, but consists merely in enhancing the "quality of life" while it lasts.[23] Goncharov, unlike his contemporary Solov'ev, wrote not a religious utopia but a realistic educational novel where metamorphosis is reduced to an educational experiment. *Oblomov* is a Russian anticipation of Shaw's educational *Pygmalion*, as is Chernyshevsky's *What Is to Be Done?*, discussed below.

Goncharov wrote a *Bildungsroman* that, although it dealt with metamorphosis, did not include the miraculous but kept within the framework of realism. The religious philosophers Vladimir Solov'ev and Nikolai Fedorov would demand the transcendence of realism in an art that was to model life into an aesthetic text where the laws of current reality would be invalidated. But they were not the only ones to demand miracles in prophetic art serving future life. Some of Goncharov's contemporaries, who claimed to be realists, materialists, and atheists, did so too. Radical realists such as Nikolai Chernyshevsky envisioned and wrote about miraculous transformations of present-day life and flawed human beings. Developing the biblical Mary Magdalene symbolism despite their atheism, they usually took women as the objects of their human-transformation projects. This is certainly the case in Chernyshevsky's famous *What Is to Be Done? From the Tales About the New People* (*Chto delat'? Iz rasskazov o novykh liudiakh*, 1863). It is true that the radicals saw not art but rather the natural and social sciences as the direct agent of metamorphosis. Art was important only as a disseminator of social and scientific ideas. Its purpose was to impart the latest findings to a wider public, as well as to teach the vanguard intelligentsia how to transform current restricted reality into a wondrous future reality where beauty and the imagination reigned.

Nevertheless, both art and science served life, in the nihilist as well as the religious camp, since both camps perceived life as the supreme value. Through their common stance against art for art's sake and for transformational science, in an alchemistic vein, they perceived a basic unity in all material nature. Russian aesthetics of the second half of the nineteenth century offers a materialist-metaphysical blend with a much greater interaction between materialism and metaphysics than is commonly assumed. The materialist Chernyshevsky, as has convincingly been shown, shared many theurgical aspirations with his idealist counterparts, however much he himself may have disputed sharing any common ground with them.[24] The utopian sections of his novel even intimate that a free and creative love between a "new woman" and a "new man" will lead to a "spring without end for all," or, put

in more Symbolist terms, that an androgynous union of two perfect lovers will lead to a radical transformation of life that may
even include immortality.[25] Whatever it is that Chernyshevsky
ultimately envisioned by "eternal spring" for all—an ideal marriage in the style of Goncharov's Olga and Stolz, a Rousseauan
competition among lovers in pleasing one's partner and causing
endless (moral) delight,[26] or yet something else—his notion of
art as serving the supreme value, life, deeply influenced Solov'ev,
himself an ardent radical in his early youth.

The two main versions of the Pygmalion motif—the
materialist-realist version, which stressed education and scientific cognition in the transformation of reality, and the classicist-
aesthetic variant dear to the romantic *liubomudry*—gave the religious philosophers Fedorov and Solov'ev all the ideological raw
material they needed to create their philosophical myths of immortality. It was their synthesized scientific-aesthetic myths that
would inspire Symbolist writers of the "life-creation" persuasion. Thus with the dissemination of the theurgical philosophies of Vladimir Solov'ev and his mentor Nikolai Fedorov, the
uniquely Russian "immortality version" of the Pygmalion motif
first entered literature.[27]

Both philosophers believed that life and reality should be "the
true goal of art," and also that art should become the activity
of "incarnating the absolute ideal . . . in actual reality." [28] The
ideal for each of them was an immortal mankind that had abolished death as a residual phenomenon of biological evolution.
Although Fedorov usually is not seen as being overly concerned
with aesthetics, he did in fact regard art as essential to his immortality doctrines. True, this ascetic moralist emphasized that
aesthetics must transcend itself. Thus he declared that he could
not understand why art critics insisted on the autonomy of art,
divorcing it from life, and why they deemed a stance of de-
tachment necessary for art appreciation.[29] To him it was obvious
that art should be linked to life in an ameliorating function that
served perfection and hence immortality. Illustrating his point
of view, the philosopher asked whether a statue acquiring life
really would become less beautiful in the eyes of the beholder

than it had been in a state of inanimate immobility. If someone, following Pygmalion's example, could fall in love with a statue and imbue it with life, would that really mean that this statue no longer was a genuine work of art? He approvingly quoted the French philosopher Marie Jean Guyau (1854–88), who also had pondered "whether Venus di Milo really was beautiful only because she was made out of marble and immobile." Guyau was inclined to think that, on the contrary, she would improve if her now expressionless eyes would become filled with "an inner light" and she started walking toward her admirer.[30] Similarly, Fedorov found a "living statue" better than an inanimate one. Although Venus certainly was not his ideal of female beauty, severe ascetic that he was, the idea that inert matter could be animated by an artist appealed to him. He seems to have reasoned that if statues could be animated, so could the dead, who had been reduced to inanimate matter.

Solov'ev, Fedorov's disciple in regard to immortalization theories and the Symbolists' favorite philosopher, emphasized aesthetic factors in that perfecting of mankind which would make feasible both the resurrection of the dead and the immortality of the living. He made the well-known Dostoevskian aphorism "Beauty will save the world" the epigraph to one of his essays on aesthetics entitled "Beauty in Nature" ("Krasota v prirode," 1889), but he exchanged the future tense for the present; intensifying the idea's salvatory optimism: "Beauty is already saving the world." In two subsequent essays, "The General Meaning of Art" ("Obshchii smysl iskusstva," 1890) and, above all, the famous "The Meaning of Love" ("Smysl liubvi," 1892–94), Solov'ev specified from what exactly it is that beauty will save the world: death.

In his articles on aesthetics, Solov'ev postulates that what evolution had been in nature, namely, the artistic trial-and-error activity of the "cosmic architect and artist," must be continued in the aesthetic activity of the human artist. The latter should devote himself to the further evolution of nature and mankind. Above all, he should transform woman, the ultimate test object, and through her, himself. Solov'ev's version of the Pygmalion motif may appear irreligious, but, in keeping with his Christian convictions, it is not developed as a defiant challenge to the Creator. Rather it is seen as a further development of His divine plan, sanctioned by God Himself. Realization of His divine plan in artistic creativity was a task given to true lovers.

This creativity involves psychological, spiritual, and aesthetic refinement, rather than any drastic morphological changes. The morphology of nature was basically established during natural evolution, which, however, was not devoid of a progressive spiritualization of material forms. Thus natural evolution, although palpably biological, demonstrates a slow but steady aesthetic progression toward full realization of the principle of "positive all-unity," or freedom in harmony, in its three aspects of the good, the true and the beautiful.[31] Beauty attracted the philosopher's main interest, since progressively beautiful forms not only as it were concretely demonstrate that evolution produced ever fitter species but also mark an ethical and ontological progress. The fact that the human form is aesthetically more appealing than that of the worm, pig, or ape, according to Solov'ev, "proves" man's ethical and spiritual superiority over these species. But, as is well known, there are many extremely ugly human beings. This fact does not invalidate man's claim to superiority over all other species, but merely points to the need for further aesthetic, and hence also ethical-ontological, amelioration of the human species. Mankind, of course, also has remarkably beautiful representatives, capable of outshining any beauty in the animal realm or, for that matter, the vegetable and mineral realms, so rich in beauty. The task lying before mankind, then, is to realize further the human potential for beauty; it is in the aestheticization of mankind that salvation lies. This is the realm where beauty can and already does "save the world."

Instead of mirroring nature on canvas, in marble, or in verbal or musical sound, art should begin to change it from inside, spiritualizing its living forms. Art, in fact, should become a kind of white magic, making man and reality better and truer (to the ideal), by imposing ever more beautiful forms on them. The assumption was that the beautiful cannot possibly harbor evil or deception, at least not for long.[32] The ideal, by definition, is immortal. Perfect beauty gives indestructibility to objects and immortality to living forms. Pygmalion's task, when fully realized, is sublime, since it does not consist in a momentary animation performed for the sake of fleeting pleasures, but puts forward the goal of creating eternal perfection, of immortalizing the beloved.

Solov'ev does not point to the Pygmalion motif in his philosophical articles, but he does mention it in a poem that expresses his aesthetics of immortalization in a nutshell. His "Three Exploits" ("Tri podviga," 1882) places Pygmalion's accomplishments first in a three-phase program culminating in the immortalization of the beloved, who has been made perfect. Thus Pygmalion's deed is not completed when "the divine body" has been fully revealed and seems ready to live and love:

> On the forbidding borderline
> Do not think the deed has been completed.
> And do not expect love
> From the divine body, Pygmalion.

His sculptural achievement is further developed by Perseus, who makes a first attack on the dragon of death by showing him his own frightful visage in the mirror of his shield:

> And reflected in the mirror shield,
> The dragon disappeared into the abyss,
> Having perceived himself.

This painterly attack on the dragon ensures but a short triumph, however, in that the monster does not remain repelled by his own ugly visage for long. He seizes Galatea in her third hypostasis of Eurydice. The musician Orpheus, who challenges "death to a lethal battle" and forces Hades, the "lord of pale death," to relinquish Eurydice, fulfills the ultimate task of the true artist, which is to overcome death, not metaphorically but in reality:

> The sounds of the victorious song
> Shook the vaults of Hades,
> And the Ruler of pale death
> Returns Eurydice.[33]

Solov'ev does not pursue the sad epilogue to the rescue mission, but, as is well known, Orpheus's triumph lasted for only a brief moment. The singer "shook the vaults of Hades" but did not eliminate them altogether; to lead out "the throng of dancing shadows dwelling there" is a task that has yet to be accomplished.[34] This task requires an artist who not only masters the arts of sculpture (Pygmalion), portraiture (Perseus), and "enchanting song" (Orpheus) but also fully possesses that theurgical spiritual discipline that can transform momentary victory into eternal triumph. Art must become no less than the task of divinizing man and woman, of making human beings into perfect works of art, which, being perfect, neither procreate by giving birth to new mortals nor die, but live forever as the immortal gods.

Russian Symbolist life-creators wanted to show how to complete the "task" begun by Pygmalion and continued by Perseus and Orpheus. Striving to transcend mere art for art's sake, as well as mere improvement of the human mortal wrought by lifelong, loving education, they aspired to create the perfect and hence immortal beloved, who is an animated statue, a living picture, and eternally resounding music. The "ultimate exploit" facing their Orphic Pygmalion, on the threshold of a new era and thoroughly initiated into theurgical philosophy, consists in a series of challenges. He is to (a) transform the empirical beloved into an immortal work of art; (b) channel the energies of erotic desire into a sublime creative power capable of working this metamorphosis, which then becomes also a transformation of the self; (c) "marry" the aesthetically formed beloved, who is a mirror image of the artist (he, too, should be a mirror to his beloved), in a nonsexual yet highly erotic union. Thus he can create the immortal androgyne in a nonprocreative act of mutual creative-corrective mirroring that culminates in an "impregnation with Spirit." This is what Solov'ev, following Plato, calls "conception in beauty," as opposed to a mere physical-biological union.[35] The creations that result from the physiological acts of sexual intercourse and birth are human beings as mortal as their parents. Conception in beauty, where the biological seed *metamorphoses* into animating spirit, yields immortal human beings.[36]

Clearly, this version of the Pygmalion motif has metamorphosed far beyond original conceptions. The Symbolists created a new variant that retained the components of the artist who transgresses the laws imposed by reality and a love that thirsts for perfection. But they added their notion of nonsexual conception in beauty that is to result in immortality. Their variants of the motif do not retain the names of Pygmalion and Galatea, but replace them by names taken from congenial myths and motifs, such as Don Quixote and Dulcinea, or from self-created myths, such as Sologub's Trirodov and Elisaveta, or from cultural history turned myth, such as Merezhkovsky's Leonardo da Vinci and Mona Lisa. Regardless of names, the concept of the beloved's metamorphosis wrought in a sublime aesthetic-erotic act unites the myth's variants in a basic structure that may be termed the "Pygmalion structure." This structure is open to further metamorphoses, as well as to art forms other than sculpture.[37]

This three-phase task is presented in at least two major Symbolist texts of the first decades of the twentieth century: Dmitry Merezhkovsky's *Leonardo da Vinci* (1901), where it fails, and Fedor Sologub's trilogy *A Legend in the Making* (*Tvorimaia legenda*, 1907–13), where it is crowned with success. In Merezhkovsky's novel, da Vinci fails to immortalize Mona Lisa in the theurgical sense and even "kills" the empirical woman, in the sense that Goethe's King Midas kills whatever he turns into the gold of art. He immortalizes only her image in a painting that, to be sure, is a superb work of art, but fails nevertheless, inasmuch as it does not merge with its model, Mona Lisa, giving her and its creator the immortality of the androgyne conceived in beauty. Instead of eternal life, its model is given everlasting death. She is sentenced to be buried in canvas and entombed in the picture frame. Instead of becoming an immortal woman, she is made a ghost, exuding her "spectral charm" in a museum, a space entirely devoted to the dead. Her creator too is immortal in the traditional sense; that is, it is known to many that he is dead.

In Sologub's trilogy, Trirodov, a quixotic Pygmalion, succeeds in bringing about a metamorphosis in his *Lisa*, his beloved Elisaveta. He transforms her from a pleasant but trite girl into the

mystical Rose and the immaculate Dulcinea, while himself changing from eccentric "loner" and ivory-tower artist into a king
bearing the name of Georgy. This name indicates that Trirodov
will succeed where Perseus and Orpheus failed, becoming the
one who slays the dragon of death for good. Pygmalion, Perseus, and Orpheus are synthesized in the artist Trirodov, whose
name alludes to a Trinity different from the Church's, and who
becomes a Saint George piercing the dragon with the spear of
theurgical artistry and alchemy for the sake of creating life eternal in a world made legendary.[38]

Why does da Vinci fail where Trirodov succeeds? One answer
is that the former appears before the time is ripe for this metamorphosis, both ideal and real, of the human race. Ever eager to
merge *realia* with *realiora*, the Symbolists by no means despised
the sciences as sources of metamorphosis. They were particularly
attracted to the sciences of transformation, such as chemistry
and agriculture, favored also by materialists such as the French
philosophes, with their notion of transmutability, and the Russian
radicals (see note 24). On the contrary, they attributed important
functions to these in the various processes of creating the immortal androgyne. Sublimation of the base libido into the lofty
Eros is, after all, a chemical (or alchemical) process also. In da
Vinci's times these and other sciences had not developed suffi-
ciently for life-creation, not yet having recovered from the dev-
astation wrought by the obscurantist Middle Ages. Therefore the
painter who takes such a keen interest in the sciences often fails
in his varied and numerous experiments. For example, da Vinci
struggles in vain with a variety of mechanical problems, such as
the construction of wings that would liberate man from the mortal grip of gravity. He dabbles in horticulture and genetics.[39] But
he cannot achieve radically novel results; he belongs to a category of people that may be labeled "the premature forerunners
of too tardy a spring."[40]

The twentieth-century chemist Trirodov, on the other hand,
knows of the energies that are released in radioactive disintegration, and he also knows how to utilize them in resurrective
efforts. To construct a spaceship is no problem for him, the sci-

ences having advanced far beyond the stage at which they were in da Vinci's time. All the knowledge that has accumulated over the centuries gives Trirodov a distinct scientific advantage over da Vinci, the man of the Renaissance. In that time science was being reborn but had not had time to achieve great results. This, however, is not the full explanation. Merezhkovsky's da Vinci is also marked by certain subjective spiritual limitations that hinder him from developing Pygmalion's efforts further. The full truth is that he has the genius, but not the courage, to become a Pygmalion.

One of da Vinci's spiritual limitations is to be found in his fascination with knowledge for its own sake, as opposed to knowledge in the service of immortality. His pupil, the hostile yet fascinated Cesare, states with some justification that the artist relies on "geometry instead of inspiration," wherefore there is a limit that, "with all his learning, he never can surmount."[41] A parallel deficiency in his spiritual makeup is his fascination with art for art's sake, as opposed to art for life's sake. Da Vinci is not a vital Renaissance man "to whom nothing human is alien," but rather an artist who, anticipating the Decadents, is "beyond good and evil" and also overemphasizes the intellectual approach to existence. He believes that an artist's soul should be like a "mirror, which reflects all objects . . . , remaining itself unmoved and clear" (p. 46). This Briusovian aesthetic (expressed in poems such as Briusov's "I" and "To the Poet" ["Ia," 1899; "Poetu," 1907]), together with his scientism, explains da Vinci's inability to fuse knowledge and art into an act of sublime love and faith leading to immortality.

As a great artist, da Vinci is certainly able to restore wholeness of form to an object that he, as scientist, previously had "dissected, like a lifeless body" (p. 358). But the ensuing synthesis, the fusion of art with life, escapes him. His perspicacious pupil Giovanni Beltraffio rightly states, "But now I perceive that he doth but strive yet doth not attain, that he seeketh but findeth not, that he knoweth but doth not realize" (p. 508). Da Vinci himself increasingly realizes that he does not possess the ultimate glue that would fuse his many separate works of art into a single total picture or vision of life. Comparing himself to Columbo (Columbus), he understands that the latter found a "New Heaven and a New Earth" (p. 263) because he had faith in Isaiah's prophecy. However, he himself has no faith in the miraculous potential for metamorphosis inherent in reality, nor in the possibility of unheard-of discoveries, or in the natural magic of life. He believes that reality must remain what it always has been, and by studying its laws carefully he achieves a superb artistic mastery but does not evolve into a life-creator. The "New World" of a new heaven and a new earth where, as the Book of Revelations promises, "death shall be no more" remains undiscovered by him.

In other words, da Vinci rejects the divine promise that a new world and a new heaven are bound to replace the old ones, and that this new celestial-earthly world will hold "no tears and no death." Ultimately, he is the typical modern *intelligent*, who lacks a philosophical or religious vision that would give meaning and purpose to his activities. In fact, in addition to Briusov's Decadently detached poet, he greatly resembles Anton Chekhov's old professor of medicine in "A Boring Story" ("Skuchnaia istoriia," 1889). This uncommitted scientist of the positivist type lacks the cohesive vision of faith and therefore has allowed investigative curiosity to quell the irrational font of being found in love for life and woman. Curiosity is a powerful stimulant to investigation, but only love can give it meaning by establishing a goal that makes investigation a creative act. The immortalization of the perfectly beautiful beloved thus remains an experiment not undertaken by da Vinci, although it certainly would offer him a worthy challenge, one in which his vast knowledge and superb skills could merge with inspiring faith.

In Merezhkovsky's novel we first meet da Vinci as a "resurrector of statues," a kind of Pygmalion. Assisting in the secret excavations of the treasures of antiquity still resisted by clerical bigotry, he resurrects the sculptured gods of the past. On one occasion, a statue of Venus, in Galatea-like fashion, assumes the hue of life: "[The statue] lay like a coffined dead body, yet had not the appearance of death, but seemed rosy, alive and warm in the flickering reflection of the torches" (p. 39). The artist is captivated by the beauty of the sculpture he is "resurrecting": "With the same serene smile as of yore, when she had risen from the foam of the sea waves, she was emerging from the murk of the earth, out of her grave of a thousand years" (ibid.). Determined to find the key to the secret of her perfect form and enticing beauty, he carefully measures the proportions of the statue and subjects these measurements to a thorough mathematical analysis.

In acting thus, he is only partly right. Indisputably it is his knowledge of proportion and perspective that makes him the superb artist he is, as well as his study of the color spectrum and the chemical makeup of various types of paint. This mastery of techniques and excellent craftsmanship, based on exact analyses of empirical data, is not enough, however, to make him a life-creator. Typically, only the surface properties of the statue captivate him, whereas the illusion of life created by the rosy glow of the flickering fire kindles no theurgical ambitions. Archeology fails to become a genuine resurrective act, as Fedorov would say. The artist seemingly is overawed by the laws of nature so recently discovered. He deifies them, attributing to them an eternal validity. This passive stance in regard to natural law bars him from envisioning creative metamorphoses, which could revolutionize nature in a direction initiated by man. He cannot fathom a transition from stone to flesh or from death to resurrection; he therefore does not heed the promise of the rosy glow on the statue's body.[42] Although a creator of beauty, he does not believe that beauty can radically change the world, let alone "save" it. The salvatory potential of beauty's white magic is lost on this overly rational artist.

Though failing to become a life-creator, da Vinci is not a soulless mechanist. He is fully aware of a spiritual reality beneath surface phenomena. But, once again, he seeks to grasp this reality intellectually and analytically, rather than to understand it with both mind and heart. Fascinated with the mysteries of the human psyche, he seeks to penetrate the ultimate secrets of man's emotional world, to grasp the elusive essence of the human soul, this "artist of its body" (p. 171), but he does so mainly by accumulating data and engaging in minute observation. For this reason he watches, with pencil in hand, the faces of men about to be executed. He selects a wide psychological range of pupils, keeping even the one who hates him (Cesare), presumably in order to partake of insights that oppose his own. He attends witch trials, witnesses book burnings and the destruction of art works (including his own "Leda") performed by Inquisitors, "aiming his gaze at everything" (Briusov) with curiosity and perhaps even emotion, but without passion and without faith in change. Emasculated by his intellectual skepticism, da Vinci leads a monastic existence. Yet his pupil Beltraffio is certain that he must have had sexual intercourse at least once, "out of curiosity" (p. 176).

Studying the human psyche with an intense thirst for knowledge, perceiving all its complexities of motivation and wide range of sensations and emotions, da Vinci creates portraits full of accurately observed truth, even inner truth. He fails, however, to transcend experimental psychology. Therefore he also fails to transcend art, since detached analysis and aesthetic amelioration of the human model, however penetrating and beautifully executed, are not enough for the ultimate artistic act of life-creation. This act of genuine creation needs the powerful energy of passion and faith, whereas mere art, in the view of life-creators, remains imitation of existing nature. Life-creation, on the other hand, needs the burning love that discerns the wondrous Dulcinea in the disfigured Aldonsa and passionately desires that Dulcinea exist forever, although eternal life contradicts the laws of nature. Skepticism offers no fertile ground for miracles. Knowledge and faith together overcome all obstacles, changing the very laws of nature. Faith enables man to see that nature is more flexible than positivists assume, and knowledge enables him to discover how the laws of nature are changed.

The dispassionate da Vinci, who persists in but one passion, which is to satisfy his curiosity, cannot generate that powerful spiritual vision that gives reality to the ideal beloved by transforming her empirically. He cannot intensify his willing to the degree that he can will the existing imperfect woman Mona Lisa to become that perfectly beautiful incarnation of the *eternal* feminine who can live forever in a state of perfection. Passionate love engenders, first, pity for the frail beloved, and then the determination to free her from the grip of death. Passion, however, is exactly what Merezhkovsky's da Vinci lacks. Unlike Baratynsky's sculptor, da Vinci does not need to struggle against tempestuous desire, having no elemental passions with which to contend in the first place. Love without desire is impotent. Only desire channeled into creativity, elemental passion concentrated into "will to (creative) power," powerful instinct refined and aimed at a noble goal: only these yield the love that creates perfect life or immortality. The roses of beauty can grow only out of the dark soil of desire, as Solov'ev puts it in his poem "We met not by chance" ("My soshlis' s toboi nedarom," 1892). Addressing his beloved, the poet declares:

> Light emerges from darkness,
> Your roses could not raise themselves
> Above the black soil
> Unless their dark roots
> Were submerged
> In the adumbral earth.[43]

Love cannot subsist on curiosity, however insatiable. It feeds on the energy of desire.

Studying his model, the intelligent and beautiful but naturally imperfect woman Mona Lisa, the artist da Vinci transfers her ameliorated image to canvas with painstaking labor, using the finest techniques. Feeling sympathy for her, even attracted to the mystery she exudes, he yet fails to perceive her potential for living perfection, as a loving life-creator would. Like all art-for-art's-sake artists, he divides his model into a person of limited interest and an endlessly cherished artistic image made by him. The latter he detaches from the original human being in order to immortalize it in art, thus "killing" the person. The fact that the painting usurps the place of the living woman is made quite clear in the novel. Thus one da Vinci disciple observes how the "living beauty of Monna Lisa" is usurped by the "image he had evoked" (p. 480). And there is also the moment when the artist stands before his picture of Mona Lisa, long after she has died.

Letting the drapery covering the portrait fall, he realizes that he had taken the "life from the living woman to bestow it upon the unliving" (p. 496).

There can be no doubt that da Vinci's artistic creativity is "killing," since the painting usurps the place of the living woman, making the latter into a kind of discarded shell.[44] Mona Lisa dies, of a throat disease, to be sure,[45] but also because she realizes that she has no absolute value for da Vinci, either as the imperfect woman she is or as the perfect woman she could become if he loved her enough to desire her forever. She understands that he sees her only as the motif for a beautiful picture, as the raw material to be aesthetically transformed into an eternally dead work of art that will be called "immortal" by connoisseurs. She dies understanding that she is real to him only as the dead woman he created on canvas, as a marvelous illusion of life, a construct of harmonious proportions and color blends, a motif refracted through his genius.

Remaining a perfect artist, da Vinci does not become the perfect lover in the Solov'evian sense of the term. Though he masters the art of painting and mathematics, he does not master the *ars artium*, which is the art of loving the real woman so intensely that this sublime force creates a living work of art out of her, a work of art that, ceaselessly perfected in life-creation, eventually becomes perfectly beautiful and hence immortal, as well as immortalizing. A Pygmalion in reverse, Midas-like da Vinci drains his beloved of life instead of imbuing her with it. This vampiric attitude, characteristic of all traditional aesthetes (like Poe, who regarded a beautiful dead woman the ideal subject of art), can be explained by a failure of communication in the case of Merezhkovsky's da Vinci.

Life-creation posits a mutual "corrective mirroring," culminating in a "conception in beauty" that leads to the birth of the immortal human being. It is this mirroring that does not take place in da Vinci's detached and one-sided act of creativity. The artist faithfully reflects the sense impressions conveyed to him, but himself remains unchanged, being too self-contained to empathize, let alone identify, with the real woman before him. Thus

Mona Lisa remains a model, a challenging artistic task and an intriguing motif, but she does not become the earthly representative of the *eternal feminine* and messenger from the world of the ideal. Accurately observed in the portrait, her mystery is conveyed, but not understood. Da Vinci remains too isolated in his egocentric, ivory-tower world of artistic self-projection to absorb the signals sent out to him; he lacks the empathy with the Other needed to decipher her riddle. Thus he also fails to decipher the riddle of his own self, of his anima and soul.

Whereas Mona Lisa fulfills, and even over-fulfills, her part in the "reciprocal mirroring" by becoming spiritually ever more like the artist, cooperating with him to the extent that she turns into his "feminine double" (p. 166), he remains detached. Though at times hovering on the brink of illumination, da Vinci lacks the daring for the final communication or the reciprocal mirroring that is "conception in beauty." No "impregnation" takes place, and the silent plea of Mona Lisa's smile to immortalize her as a living woman together with his living self fails to reach the artist.

In this novel, then, the mystery of the spiritual androgyne is not celebrated.[46] Even the endlessly obedient Lisa, "a stranger to everything save the will of the master" (p. 468), at one stage smiles mockingly at da Vinci as she poses the question whether "curiosity alone" (p. 484) is sufficient to deal with the mysteries of life and death. Da Vinci understands neither the mockery nor the plea. Shrinking from theurgical activity, he remains a mere artist.

Merezhkovsky's da Vinci, like Walter Pater's, is a Decadent who makes a young woman "older than the rocks among which she sits," since she has been made to absorb all the accumulated experience of past culture and to display a "soul with all its maladies." She is indeed "like the vampire [who] has been dead many times," always returning to "the secrets of the grave," but only because her creator projected his own tired vampire's soul into her, not allowing himself to absorb her vitalizing and immortalizing essence.[47] If da Vinci is seen as a Faust figure, he is one who failed to understand *das Ewig Weibliche*, even on the brink of the "abyss."

But is the creation of immortal art not a supreme act of love? After all, da Vinci paints such an intriguing portrait of Mona Lisa because he does love her, at least in the sense that he sees her potential for artistic re-creation and is willing to devote much time and mental effort to creating her double. Is not the painting, preserving the mortal model for ages to come, the most sublime token of love he could possibly offer her? Can art aspire to more than this, and is not this the "conception in beauty" that Solov'ev himself so warmly advocated? As da Vinci asks himself in the novel: "could he have desired a more perfect union with his beloved than in these profound and mystic caresses,—in the bringing forth of an immortal image, of a new being, which was being conceived, being born of them both, even as a child is born of its father and mother,—and was both Leonardo and Lisa?" (p. 480). The answer to his question is "yes." Merezhkovsky's Leonardo da Vinci should have desired a more sublime union than one of pure artistry. He should have sought one where contemplation and image transfer would have become deed, mutual aesthetic-corrective mirroring and spiritual interpenetration, without becoming carnal knowledge. The perfect union of which Merezhkovsky's painter proves incapable is the merger with the living beloved in that spiritual-aesthetic sphere of transfiguration where a genuine erotic union can take place.

To summarize: da Vinci could have performed an act of life-creation, not by transferring the aestheticized image of the beloved to canvas, but rather by sending it back to her empirical self, having let it pass through the prism of his own psyche; by searching for his own ideal self reflected in her and, having found it there and absorbed it into himself in a process of self-transformation, letting it blend with her divine image in a "conception in beauty." Such a transfigured couple, both ideal and real, forms the *androgyne* of completeness, perfection, and immortality, in whom there is no room for such dualities as the "model and her portrait" or the "artist and his work of art." Da Vinci either does not understand this or shrinks from what he knows. Therefore he repeats the mistake that, according to Solov'ev, the first theoretician of life-creation, Plato himself, had committed. This mistake was to separate earthly and heavenly love, earthly and heavenly beauty, life and art, without building any bridges between them. Platonic love, lofty as it may be, must therefore of necessity remain impotent, while earthly love just as inevitably must remain a crude servant of death, the wages of earthly passion being mortality.

Like Solov'ev's Plato, da Vinci fails to become a *pontifex*, a builder of bridges, halting before the chasm separating art from life, sexuality from Eros, eternal death from immortal life. He fails to acquire those spiritual wings with which man can fly across the deepest chasms, concentrating too much on engineering his clever, intricate, but nonfunctional mechanical contraptions. Creating flying machines is not wrong in itself; it is meaningless only when these replace the wings of faith and love. The artistic engineer da Vinci constructs his flying machines since he is afraid of taking flight on the wings of sublime love. He fears the miracles of novelty (metamorphoses) wrought by love and the breathtaking changes that may occur when the very laws of nature are invalidated, since he does not possess that "love which casteth out fear." Here is the ultimate reason why he hesitates "at the edge of the abyss," where a "leap of faith" is imperative. Fear is also the reason why the artist grapples in vain with painting a truly convincing picture of Christ. The latter was and is a builder of bridges, a synthesizer and redeemer possessing perfect love. It is thus not for da Vinci, the supreme analyst and formalist, to create that image where the idea of positive all-unity is embodied forever, radiating that beauty that is the seamless and total incarnation of the idea.

Sologub's Trirodov in *A Legend in the Making* succeeds where da Vinci fails. He constructs "wings" that can carry not only a man but a whole crew. Trirodov's spaceship bridges any chasms, including the abysses of cosmos. The poet and alchemist penetrates deeper into the mysteries of knowledge and goes beyond mere analysis of abstract structures into actual application. He even resurrects the dead—at least those in certain categories, such as immaculate children. Above all, he succeeds in creating the immortal beloved, for he does not "use" his Elisaveta as raw material for a work of art but makes her his cocreator in the transformation of life. Thus, for example, she is not metamorphosed into Trirodov's chosen art form of poetry. In fact, Trirodov abandons this and all other traditional art forms in order to create the living poetry that is Elisaveta. Not embalmed in a poetic verbal structure (a beautiful grave), she is saved for eternal life. She ceases to be a "bough" (Elisa*veta—vetka*) like other women, becoming instead the "mysterious rose"[48] of immortal perfection that can dispense with reproduction and reduplication in all forms biological and artistic. Trirodov's and Elisaveta's love serves no purpose except "beauty in the making," or immortality.

Like da Vinci, Trirodov abstains from sexual union with his beloved. However, he does this not because he despises the flesh or shuns all physical contact with women except for the sake of experiment, as da Vinci does. He does so because he, like Baratynsky's wise sculptor, is able to control desire. Trirodov even marries his Elisaveta. Thus he not only proves that he regards her as his equal, his partner in a joint venture, but also demonstrates that the flesh is not to be rejected with revulsion, nor lusted for with greed, but rather transformed, illuminated, transfigured. He teaches Elisaveta to sublimate her desires, while also transforming his own into creative energies. There is, for example, one occasion when the "enchantress of the night" whispers to Elisaveta that she should go and offer herself to Trirodov as a "slave and plaything" (pt. 1, p. 244). She obeys this impure voice of lust, but her lover meets her dispassionately, albeit tenderly, and their union remains pure. Before the "chaste moon" (pt. 1, p. 245), the two lovers exchange vows of love, vows that, it may be assumed, express their intent to free their love from convention and greed. Basing their love on an intense admiration for the unclothed body, an admiration that is devoid of even the slightest desire for its physical possession, they achieve a highly erotic yet chaste union of love. This union is formed not for the sake of lust but for the sake of immortality, as Fedorov and Solov'ev demanded.

Elisaveta herself understands that the "art of loving" must exclude all utilitarian procreative sexuality. Even before meeting Trirodov she rejects her suitor Peter Matov because he sees the "meaning of love" in traditional procreation. But Elisaveta knows that in marrying an "old Adam," she cannot have the "great and free union" that liberates mankind from lust and leads to the creation of a "new heaven and a new earth" (pt. 1, p. 40), where, according to Revelation, there can be no death.

On these premises, Trirodov's and Elisaveta's love increasingly assumes the form of a sublime chemical experiment, realizing the mystery of Transubstantiation celebrated by the Church. Unfortunately, the Church's celebration is enacted without any conviction. Purportedly, the mysterious liturgical metamorphosis transforms "cold matter" into "true Flesh and true Blood" (pt. 3, p. 89). But the Church makes no effort to relate this metamorphosis to reality, to apply it to life. Since the Church fails to do so, it is now the task of the artist-lover to realize this sacred mystery in an act of truly holy matrimony. Trirodov therefore does not shy away from woman and love but accepts the actual imperfections of the real woman before him, his own Elisaveta-Aldonsa, while creating with her consent and cooperation her ideal hypostasis, Elisaveta-Dulcinea. In this process he himself is transformed into a perfectly sane Don Quixote who is his lady's true knight.

Upon uncovering the hidden Dulcinea in his empirical Elisaveta, he does not transfer the beauteous image to verbal textures, extracting Elisaveta's essence, as it were, then discarding her as an empty shell and proceeding to "enjoy" the poem. Instead, he reflects her own ideal image back to her, acting as a creative mirror and thus helping her to fuse her ideal essence with her empirical self. In this process of creation Trirodov is himself transformed, receiving and heeding her mirror images of him. The two transfigured lovers can eventually meet in a spiritual-erotic union, which is conception in pure beauty. This refusal to transfer the ideal to art may lead to the disappearance of art (as art for art's sake), but when life itself has become art, or beauty manifest and immortal, there clearly no longer is any need for art in the ordinary sense of the word. Art has then

fulfilled its function of "saving the world," and the world saved
is beauty manifest, the visible manifestation of the true and the
good. A *real legend* is thus created. In King Georgy's realm, dusty
museums are not likely to be found, since his kingdom is to be
a living *Gesamtkunstwerk*, not to be contained by walled-in space.
The hallmark of realized legends is that beauty there is not isolated in certain compartments called "poetry, sculpture, music,"
and so on but is to be found everywhere, not least in those eternally living Galateas and Pygmalions who will inhabit the happy
isles where Trirodov will rule as King Georgy the First, or Saint
George.

In the context of life-creation, a post-Symbolist text that has
many affinities with the Symbolist ethos may also briefly be considered: Pasternak's *Doctor Zhivago* (*Doktor Zhivago*, 1957). Its
warrior-saint cum doctor-poet, Yuri Zhivago, depicts himself in
his poem "Fairy Tale" as Saint George, killing the dragon of
death. This novel, which in its very title intimates its closeness
to notions of life-creation, presents its protagonist as a Christian
Pygmalion, who advances at least as far as Solov'ev's Perseus in
the triple-phased task of overcoming death. Doctor Zhivago is a
Fedorovian-Solov'evian soldier who has declared war on death,
an Orpheus whose poetry immortalizes the beloved, but also a
"doctor" whose healing powers do not (quite) succeed in awakening his Galatea from her lethal sleep for good. In the poem
"Fairy Tale" she does not remain vigilant but succumbs to sleep
periodically. Lara, in Pasternak's novel, remains a "daughter of
earth," who, like Persephone, returns to Hades at regular inter-
vals. Zhivago does accomplish something toward her final liberation from Hades, however, as the progression outlined below
demonstrates.

The first time Zhivago sets eyes on Lara, she is almost lifeless, or at least soulless—a puppet in the hands of Komarovsky, a
rich paradigm of seducer, sorceror, fat Roman, and "ruler of the
underworld," or Hades. It is after her carnal engagement with
Komarovsky that Lara dreams she is dissolving in the earth.[49]
During their first encounter, the youth Zhivago does not attempt
to break the magic spell that has reduced Lara to a doll; he is

merely filled with endless, searing love for her. He is, in fact, charged with the "electricity" of sexual passion. This passion will intensify with the years, but will also grow ever more sublime, providing the energy for his heroic salvatory deed: he will rescue Lara—if not from death, then from oblivion. "Eternal memory" is the foundation of immortality.

Before Zhivago's salvation of "Princess Earth" occurs, the would-be liberator Antipov appears. Pure and brave, he is also pitiless and egocentric, a warrior who believes he is struggling for a new world but who remains a prisoner of the old. During their wedding, Lara is transformed into a Sleeping Beauty, as the whole wedding party falls into a trancelike sleep (caused by fatigue and liberal liquor consumption). Naturally, everyone wakes the next morning, including Lara, but her spirit remains weary—until she meets her Saint George and true liberator, Zhivago.

A saintly Christ figure, Zhivago undertakes a journey to the Underworld and, returning from it, opens the path of resurrection to his Beloved.[50] During their famous stay at Varykino, Zhivago, like Leonardo da Vinci, attempts to immortalize his beloved through art. Unlike da Vinci, he succeeds, at least in the sense that he does not "kill" his beloved by subordinating her to his art. His art is not art for art's sake, but rather serves the purpose of immortalizing the beloved as well as himself. True, Lara and Zhivago both die after their Varykino stay. They remain eminently mortal, and their immortality certainly remains the traditional immortality in art. But there is the difference that Zhivago's art—simple and accessible to all, as opposed to the exclusive kind destined for the museum or library—really serves life. It celebrates the eternal memory of immortal love in the living memory of an entire people, until the last and final awakening will occur. Zhivago commits himself to that Fedorovian and Solov'evian "heroic deed" (*podvig*) that consists in holding up the mirror of art to the dragon of death in images that this monster understands. Therefore, Zhivago's "faithful steed is trampling the Dragon / With its hoof" (p. 547), just as Perseus's did earlier in Solov'ev's poem. Very likely, this time the dragon is even more sorely tried.

Zhivago's art, like Perseus's shield, is held up to death's many ugly faces, reflecting its disintegration, corruption, and evil, wherever these may manifest themselves. Zhivago's is a constant effort to "maintain fidelity to the ideal of immortality" (p. 9). In a sense, he even performs the third deed, that of retrieving his Euridyce from the underworld. Although in a corporeal sense he loses Lara to Komarovsky, he does "save her soul," not allowing her to "fall asleep" again under the influence of Komarovsky's magic sleep-inducing spells. At Zhivago's funeral, Lara, like the women who found Christ's grave empty, is able to assert the illusoriness of death and the triumph of sublime love over death. The flowers filling Zhivago's grave are living proof that life and beauty will triumph over death. Galatea-Persephone-Eurydice-Mary-Magdalene-Lara has thus escaped Hades (Komarovsky and his prehistoric Mongolia), and Lara's liberation from Komarovsky's clutches is not to be taken in too metaphorical a sense. Lara dies, but her concrete immortality lies before her in a future when the dragon of death will be crushed for good. Solov'ev's three tasks are taken seriously in Pasternak's world, which is very much a Christianized Hellas, as Solov'ev hoped Russia would become. Zhivago may well be seen as an Orpheus who, metamorphosing into Christ, will accomplish the task of annihilating death in the creation of a new heaven and new earth. In this he will join with other artists engaged in life-creation. The task of saving mankind from death is a "common task," as Fedorov and Solov'ev postulated.

Pasternak's novel is not the first of his texts to explore these notions. Much earlier, the protagonist of his *A Tale* (*Povest'*, 1929), young Seryozha, is also engaged in "resurrecting." In a central episode of this prose fragment, Seryozha, seeking out his beloved Mrs. Arild, finds her lying on her bed "as if dead" (*kak pokoinitsa*). She is extremely pale, and for a long time the hero looks at the "blinding paleness of her closed, heavy eyelids."[51] He too is near fainting, but at this moment she returns to consciousness, as if resurrected by his despair, which is vented in his heavy breathing. Seized by endless pity for her, he senses how his heartbeats resemble galloping hooves. In short, he is a Saint

George on his steed and a Prince Charming breathing life into
his beloved, just as in the later poem "A Fairy Tale," discussed
above. He is a prince resurrecting his raven-haired, deathly pale
Snow White. She, without a drop of blood left in her face (*ni
krovinki*—in other words, usually pink-cheeked), clearly evokes
the image of the fairy-tale princess Snow White, who, "white as
snow, red as blood and black as ebony," is resurrected by love.
Nothing supernatural takes place in this episode, to be sure. Yet
it is intimated that the artist's task lies in overcoming death as
urged by Solov'ev and Fedorov. He is to be the theurgist who subordinates his art to the task of slaying the dragon of death and
freeing Princess Life from her subterranean imprisonment or,
alternatively, from the wicked stepmother whose name is Death
(of feminine gender in Russian).[52]

Ultimately, then, the Pygmalion motif is part of the myth, all-
pervasive among the Russian intelligentsia, of reality's ultimate
metamorphosis into earthly paradise. It was a myth pursued by
realists and Symbolists with equal fervor but in different philo-
sophic and stylistic registers. The Symbolists of the Solov'evian
persuasion envisioned this last transformation as the era of
Merezhkovsky's "Third Testament," or Christ's "Second Coming," or the "Triumph of the Woman Clothed with the Sun."
They saw themselves as theurgists bringing about this change
of the real into the ideal. They were thus fulfilling a legacy be-
queathed by those who had raised the Platonic question of the
relationship between the true, the good and the beautiful, and
who had emphasized the salvatory function of beauty. For beauty
possessed the magic force capable of enchanting even beasts.
In their opinion, Gogol clearly belonged to such Platonists. The
creator of *Dead Souls* (*Mertvye dushi*, 1842) had shown that even
the hopeless vulgarian Chichikov could be enchanted by a fleeting vision of beauty. Rooted in the mire in which he was wont
to wallow, this "pig" was captivated by the radiance of beauty
when glimpsing the Governor's daughter. Another forerunner,
naturally, was Dostoevsky, whose Prince Myshkin formulated the
theurgical program in his aphoristic statement on beauty as the
force that could and would save the world.

However, both Gogol and Dostoevsky also demonstrated the impotence of beauty, invariably letting it perish in a world where beauty and love of beauty are either the most ephemeral of all phenomena or, where they are entombed in works of art, the most exclusive of all phenomena. How can beauty save the world when it either leaves no lasting traces or is locked away in museums, books, and concert halls? The Symbolists have an answer to this question. Beauty shall save the world permanently when it no longer is removed from the world into the realm of pure art. On the contrary, it must be carried forth from art's ivory towers into the world, with the help of that divine love that demands to see beauty realized and eternalized. Then the feeble manifestations of beauty found in the world even now will become a "joy forever." Then life-creators, as opposed to mere artists, will make the sublime Eros the potent agent of aesthetic metamorphoses that transform all mortals into their ideal proto-types (the likenesses in which God created them). When this happens, the world will be at last saved, for it will have become a place of positive all-unity, where only two principles cannot coexist: the ugliness of death and the beauty of immortal life.

Four

Andrei Bely and the Argonauts' Mythmaking

ALEXANDER LAVROV

The "Argonaut" circle, formed in Moscow in the first years of this century, was destined to play a notable role in the establishment of Russian Symbolist culture. Perhaps more persuasively than other realizations of the Symbolist worldview, this circle underlined by its very existence that artistic system's striving to become a life-creating method. The Argonauts declared "life-creation" to be their basic, primary task. This effort then generated a collective striving to mythicize daily life, human relations, and artistic activity.

The Argonaut circle was least of all a literary association. Among the creators and enactors of the Argonaut myth, only three were writers whose creative work entered Russian literary history: Andrei Bely, Ellis (pen name of L. L. Kobylinsky), and Sergei M. Solov'ev. Indeed some members were remote from artistic practice and from any creative activity in the usual sense. But this fact did not keep them from being full-fledged Argonauts, for "talent for writing" and "talent for living" were regarded as of equal worth.[1] The basic unifying themes of Argonautism were a sense of the "end of the century" and the rejection of all the ideals, tastes, illusions and beliefs the century had generated. Along with this came the feeling of "the frontier," beyond which must lie the "all new." The Argonaut circle came into being—without any deliberate organizing—as a union of people who found one another to be like-thinkers, sympathizers, and fellow-seekers. "At a time when every individual thought that he alone was wandering in darkness, without hope, with a sense of disaster, it turned out that others also were traveling that road," wrote Bely to Alexander Blok, after discovering with joy that he and Blok had feelings and hopes in common.[2]

The embryo of the future Argonaut circle is discernible in the school friendship of Bely and Sergei Solov'ev, dating from the autumn of 1895. Acquaintance with the ten-year-old Solov'ev's parents, Mikhail Sergeevich Solov'ev, brother of the philosopher Vladimir Solov'ev, and his wife, Olga Mikhailovna, helped the young Bely become aware of his creative possibilities. At the end of 1896 a common interest in art drew Bely to his classmate Vasily Vladimirov. Their friendship grew closer in 1898 and took on a more conscious character. In fall 1899 Bely entered Moscow University, where he met Alexei Sergeevich Petrovsky. These two promptly found a common language in debates about Friedrich Nietzsche and Vasily Rozanov.

Bely's relations with these three friends, intensified by shared youthful interests and enthusiasms, already by the end of the 1890's anticipated to a significant degree the thematics and style of future Argonaut meetings.[3] In 1901 Bely wrote, "S. M. Solov'ev is telling me about his new acquaintance L. L. Kobylinsky, a raving Marxist and at the same time a Nietzschean, active in workers' organizations and simultaneously going out of his mind reading Nietzsche. I am becoming very interested in him."[4] In that same year Bely found himself participating in several congenial groups: "I, Batiushkov and Ertel at one time made up a sort of trio; another group was: the Solov'evs, Petrovsky and I; finally, at the university I grew steadily closer to my school friend V. V. Vladimirov. And around him gathered Pechkovsky and S. L. Ivanov."[5]

By 1903 all these friendly clusters formed one loosely organized circle, the moving force of which was Andrei Bely. The regular meeting place was the Vladimirovs' apartment. Bely also began to arrange "Sundays" at his home. Even more important, Argonautism took the shape of "conversations with friends" that "occurred in the university corridor, in the open air: in the Kremlin, on the Arbat, at Novodevichy Monastery or in a shop on Prechistensky Boulevard."[6]

This circle was in no sense formally structured, and it promoted no concrete program—ideological, creative, or publicational. It therefore remained, as it were, outside the literary process or on its distant, barely discernible periphery. In any case, no news of its existence appeared in print. Even to establish exactly the number of members is difficult. The nucleus was Bely and his friends—young people (chiefly fellow students at the university) who promoted the "Argonaut" myth. The initial membership included Ellis (then a student of economics), A. S. Petrovsky (a chemist), V. V. Vladimirov (an artist who became, as did Bely, a student of the natural sciences), S. M. Solov'ev, still in the last classes of the gymnasium, who enrolled in the university's philological division in 1904.

There were others: the student of organic chemistry Alexander Petrovich Pechkovsky; the student Sergei Leonidovich Ivanov, later to become a prominent botanist; Alexander Sergeevich Chelishchev, "mathematician and student at the conservatory, a composer";[7] medical student N. M. Malafeev; philosophy student Sergei Kobylinsky, Ellis's brother; the student D. I. Ianchin; the historian and theosophist P. N. Batiushkov; and the historian M. A. Ertel. At that time, Bely noted,

some came to be regarded as Argonauts simply because we felt they were close to us, often without their suspecting that they were Argonauts. Rachinsky, who rarely visited me and was never at Ellis's, had no suspicion of his "Argonautism"; neither did E. K. Metner, who in the spring of 1902 did not live in Moscow, suspect that he was an initiate.[8]

Considered one of their own by the Argonauts was Blok, whose poetry, along with Bely's work, was a primary source of their mythmaking conceptions.[9]

In addition, each of the Argonauts created around himself a sort of field of influence, which made the establishment of boundaries between the "initiates" and the "noninitiated" in the final analysis impossible. Thus, primarily through Bely, Argonautic moods penetrated both centers of Moscow Symbolism: Valery Briusov's sphere at the publishing house Scorpio and the publishing house Gryphon, headed by S. A. Sokolov (Krechetov). And through other Argonauts these moods were diffused into the broad milieu of the Moscow intelligentsia ("the Argonaut center developed a *parterre* made up of those who came to watch the performances of Ellis, Chelishchev, Ertel").[10]

The Argonaut circle, so varied and ill-defined in its membership, turned out to be equally so in its participants' modes of thought. The circle's meetings produced odd encounters: the translator of *The Light on the Ways* and the *Bhagavadghita*, a theosophist who offered "a vinaigrette of Buddhism and Brahminism" (P. N. Batiushkov), met an admirer of the populists Gleb Uspensky and N. N. Zlatovratsky, a man of peasant origins (N. M. Malafeev) who "fantasized his own sort of new peasant commune."[11] A Baudelairean and Nietzschean who was attracted to economic theories (Ellis) met a seeker for truth in Russian Orthodoxy who venerated Seraphim of Sarov (A. S. Petrovsky). "Only the slogan that promised some kind of future united us all at that time," wrote Bely.[12] Presentiments and omens of that approaching future, veiled in a fanciful system of images, constituted the essence of Argonautism.

"Our youthful strivings toward the dawn in whatever guise it appeared—in ideology, in life, in personal relations—served as a kind of plan for our common life in new spaces and new times."[13] Bely thereby stressed the projective principle of Argonautism: the "plan" of the anticipated common life must involve world-transforming goals. The ordinary "artist" sets himself the goal of creating a perfect work and only that. But an Argonaut's goal holds eschatological meaning: it is the re-creation of the world following an ideal model that arises in his consciousness.

Later Bely often recalled how Argonautism united people for reasons least of all literary in nature. He was profoundly right,

nonetheless, in calling that association Symbolist in spirit. Argonautism embodied with great consistency the primary and most
characteristic feature of the Symbolist attitude toward reality: to
perceive the world as a quasi-artistic phenomenon, to attribute
to reality the qualities of a literary text.[14] In this the Argonauts
took the extreme position: either they abstracted totally from
their own artistic creation or they looked on the artistic texts they
created primarily as emanations of the universal "life text." This
hierarchy of values appeared in the complex of myth-creating
conceptions. At the same time all separate, concrete, individual
myths were isomorphic with the basic myth that gave the association its name.

The Argonauts became conscious of themselves as a group
relatively late. It was 1903 when the collective's membership and
its conceptual contours took definite shape. They then needed
only a designation to serve at once as symbol and as manifesto.
The plot line of the ancient Greek myth of the heroes' journey in
the ship *Argo* seeking the Golden Fleece was brought into service
by Ellis, whom Bely with reason called "the soul of the circle—
the gadfly-agitator, the propagandist."[15] In autumn 1903 Ellis
wrote to Bely:

A symbol is a roadmark of experience, it is a conventional sign saying,
"Remember what was revealed to you at such a time, about which it is a
sin to rationalize and *comic* to argue . . ." Sometimes a symbol says, "I will
help you remember and once again experience this." . . . This is the way
I look on my own symbol—the Golden Fleece. It is a conventional sign,
it is a hand pointing out the entrance to the house, it is a phonograph
shouting: "Arise and walk" . . . But the content of that symbol is given
to me by my intellect and moral instinct, which were developed before
I invented the symbol of the fleece.[16]

On March 26, 1903, Bely wrote a letter to Emil Karlovich
Metner, his chief partner in discussions of worldview. This letter
offers possibly the first interpretation of the "Argonaut" myth
used as both a "conventional sign" and a "pointing hand"—a
myth ideally suited to expressing mystical life-creating desires
that were at once bold and extremely unconcrete and undefined:

By the way, I and another young man (L. L. Kobylinsky) are planning to establish a sort of secret society or association in the name of Nietzsche—a union of *Argonauts*: the exoteric goal is the study of literature devoted to Schopenhauer and Nietzsche and of those authors themselves; the esoteric goal is a journey by way of Nietzsche in hope of finding the *Golden Fleece*. . . . Emil Karlovich, do you hear what rings in that combination of words pronounced in the twentieth century by Russian *students—Argonauts traveling by way of Nietzsche* in pursuit of *the Golden Fleece*!! . . . For others this journey beyond the horizon that I want to undertake will seem like disaster, but let them know also that at the moment when the sail sinks beyond the horizon in the view of *shore* dwellers, it continues to fight the waves, sailing... to the unknown God.[17]

This letter already outlined the created myth's basic contours, though not all the intentions Bely expressed were fulfilled by the Argonauts. Thus the "exoteric goal"—organized study of Schopenhauer and Nietzsche—probably was discarded or forgotten: such study would have contradicted the style and sense of the Argonaut meetings. The stress on Nietzsche as the single inspirer of the quest for "the Golden Fleece" stemmed chiefly from Bely's mood at the time of writing the letter. (His second surge of interest in Nietzsche began in the summer of 1902: "For the first time am reading *Zarathustra* in the original—am intoxicated by its rhythms.")[18] It can also be explained by his close communication at that time with the "Nietzschean" Ellis and his dialogue with Metner, who considered the philosophy of Nietzsche the most brilliant and significant event of modern culture.[19] Notable in this connection is the fact that the Argonauts did not take from Nietzsche the real content of his philosophical-aesthetic views. Rather, their ideals resonated chiefly with his stance of bold opposition to traditional attitudes and commonly accepted value systems, his conflict with the age, and his attempt to move beyond the limits of the permissible and the possible. For the Argonauts Nietzsche was a sign that the positivist bases of the life they rejected were undergoing a crisis and that the world was standing on the brink of renewal and transformation. In that same letter to Metner, Bely wrote: "It seemed that Nietzsche was a madman, whereas he merely *sailed away*." The

Argonauts understood Nietzsche's insanity as the just madness of the prophet rejected by his age; it gave yet greater meaning to his philosophical discoveries. Thus in Ellis's sonnet sequence "To F. Nietzsche" ("K F. Nitsshe," unpublished) the philosopher is presented as a "demigod" and "shattered titan":

> He rose, like a waterfall boiling in white foam,
> Nodding like a phantom in nocturnal darkness,
> Like a gloomy mountain ridge in frozen armor
> That holds aloft the heavenly vault, endlessly blue.[20]

To the myth of Nietzsche—"prophet" and "madman," who had penetrated the "abysses" and embodied the Argonaut ideal —was conjoined another myth, also to become a foundation stone of Argonautism: that of Vladimir Solov'ev. Having announced "the end of world history" and the coming catastrophe that would crush the world of evil, disunity, and egoism, Solov'ev forced the Argonauts to believe in the genuineness of their "mystical summons." "He became for me the teacher of the way," wrote Bely.[21] Solov'ev's testaments and revelations, his prophecies of the early coming of eschatological time and of the struggle with the "Antichrist," to be followed by the mystery of the final harmonious union of earthly and heavenly principles, generated the thematics of Argonaut meditations. Also important for them was the fact that Solov'ev was a Russian philosopher: they saw in him their immediate forerunner, and they proposed to see his prophecies of Russia's messianic fate fulfilled concretely. Wrote the philosopher's nephew, the Argonaut Sergei Solov'ev:

> Entering into battle with the power of darkness,
> Amid the murk you fearlessly lit your fire
> And the holy fate of Russia
> You foretold, prophet aflame with God's spirit.[22]

However, Argonautism did not fit entirely into the system of Vladimir Solov'ev's later views. Comparing the Argonauts with Russian Hegelians of the 1840's, Bely later concluded: "The position of the Bakunin circle was simpler: he had Hegel behind him. Our awaited Hegel was ahead, we had to create him, because

Vladimir Solov'ev was for us only the call to push off from the shores of the old world."[23] These strivings to abandon the stagnant present and move into the future, unknown and awaited with trembling and inspiration, found a complete symbolic embodiment in the image of the *Argo*.

Insofar as Argonautism "was only the impulse to reject the old life, the launching out on a sea of searchings, the goal of which glimmered in the fog of the future,"[24] its mythmaking (unsupported by "real" prognostic constructions) tended solely toward self-development. Argonautism soon assumed all the characteristic features of the Symbolist sphere. Saturated with details and organized in accordance with the Symbolist conception of life, the Greek myth of the *Argo* turned into a kind of eschatological myth. The search for the "Golden Fleece" was likened to the striving for the sun, which in turn revealed itself as the pursuit of a final harmonious reconciliation of "earthly" and "heavenly" principles. Thus the antique world is interpreted in Bely's poem "The Golden Fleece" ("Zolotoe runo," 1903), which became the Argonauts' distinctive password and their oath of initiation:

> The arch of heaven is embraced with flame...
> And there, the Argonauts sound to us
> The horn of departure...
> Listen, listen...
> Enough of suffering!
> Don your armor
> Of sun-fabric!
>
> An ancient Argonaut
> Summons us,
> He calls
> With golden
> Trumpet:
> "To the sun, to the sun! Loving freedom,
> We race forward into
> The blue ether!.."
> The ancient Argonaut summons to the sun's banquet,
> Blowing his trumpet
> In a world turning gold.

> The sky is all in rubies.
> The sun's globe has gone to rest.
> The sky is all in rubies
> Above us.
> On the mountain heights
> Our Argo,
> Our Argo,
> Preparing to fly away,
> Is replete with golden wings.[25]

The fullness, energy and force of the mythmaking experience stimulated the construction of detailed symbolic pictures with a carefully elaborated plot. This created the effect of a phased progression in Argonaut strivings. At the same time as the programmatic poem "The Golden Fleece," Bely wrote a letter to Metner (April 19, 1903) in which he acknowledged his Argonautic hopes: "My desire for the sun constantly grows. I want to hurl myself through black emptiness, to swim through an ocean of timelessness; but how to conquer emptiness?" Further on he describes the path by which he intends to reach "the sun":

Stenka Razin constantly drew a *boat* on the walls of his prison, he constantly laughed at the executioners, saying he would board it and sail away. *I know what this is.* I will behave in much the same way: I will build myself a sun-vessel—the Argo. I wish to become an Argonaut. And I am not alone. Many want this. They do not know it, but it is so.

Now a flotilla of sunclad vessels stands in the bay of expectations. The Argonauts will hurl themselves toward the sun. It required some kind of despair to smash their little idols, but in return that despair turned them toward the Sun. They demanded to go to him. They thought the unthinkable. They lay in wait for the sun's rays, woven of gold, reaching out to them through the vast chaos of emptiness—constant summonses; they cut leaves of gold fabric, using them for sheaths for their winged desires. The result was sun-vessels radiating streams of lightning. A flotilla of such vessels now stands in our quiet bay, ready with the first favorable wind to set off through terror for the Golden Fleece. They themselves forged their black contours in golden mail. Shining cuirassiers now walk among people, evoking now laughter, now fear, now veneration. These are the Knights of the Order of the Golden Fleece. Their shield is the sun. Their dazzling visor is lowered. When they lift it, a gentle, sad face full of courage smiles at the *seeing ones*; those who cannot see are frightened by a *round black spot* that, like a hole, yawns at them in place of a face.

These are all Argonauts. They will fly to the sun. But there, they have boarded their vessels. A burst of sunlight has set the lake afire. Golden tongues spreading about lick the stones that protrude above the water. In the Argo's prow stands a shining warrior, and he trumpets departure on the horn of return [*rog vozvrata*].

Someone's vessel has taken off. That vessel's spreading wings have marked a shining zigzag and then disappeared upward beyond the curious gaze. There another. And another. And all have flown away. Like lightning they sundered the air. Now a dull peal of thunder is heard. Someone is firing from a cannon at the surviving Argonauts. They have far to go... Let us pray for them: and indeed we intend to follow them.

Let us gather *sunness* [*solnechnost'*] so as to build our own vessels! Emil Karlovich, the spreading golden tongues lick the stones protruding above the water; streams of sun break through the glass of our dwellings; there, they have struck against the ceiling and the walls . . . There, everything around is alight . . .

Gather, gather that sun! Scoop up with buckets that flowing radiance! Every drop of it is capable of producing a sea of light. Let the Argonauts pray for us![26]

Each picture drawn here by Bely expresses the general sense of the myth. Replacement of one picture by another, of details by general plans, merely imitates the movement of developing thought. It represents in a multitude of images the many-faceted, many-leveled embodiment of a single, integral spiritual condition. A kaleidoscope of images is created, each of which proclaims its identity with the whole. Here the "sun" ("the Golden Fleece") is the goal of the Argonauts' striving and also their shield, and they themselves are "shining cuirassiers" enclosed in "golden mail" swept by a "burst of sunlight" and moving toward the sun in "sunclad vessels." The very striving toward the sun is presented as pure movement outside of space; a vessel's sailing from the "bay of expectation" with a "favorable wind" becomes a flight on wings "upward beyond the curious gaze."

Yet more fantastic pictures issued from Bely's consciousness in the prose fragment "The Argonauts" ("Argonavty," February

1904). Here the myth is elaborated with such care that there emerges a fantastic-utopian project of transferring mankind to the Sun, a project to be carried out by the "Order of Argonauts" "at the dawn of the twenty-third century." A journal called *The Golden Fleece* (*Zolotoe runo*) is published; the ship *Argo* is constructed at a plant called The Interplanetary Society of Communications, and so on. "Sunness" absorbs into itself all plot and image structures: "clouds of autumn leaves" ("all resounded . . . and rang with gold")—and "the golden leaves of lamps that were arrayed about," "the windows of houses taking fire" and "flotillas of sunclad vessels." The sun itself is here "a golden walnut pouring forth 'sunness.' "[27] Bely was capable of multiplying these mythemes to infinity, but they were all swallowed up in the global myth that ruled his consciousness.

The general idea inspiring the Argonauts also colored their daily attitudes and behavior. The everyday became the favorite material for mythmaking: for "the Argonauts felt themselves to be not only symbolists but symbolists-in-practice, theurgists."[28] Life appeared as a text full of signs, hints, and allegories demanding to be decoded; the most ordinary happening threatened to be a "Sphinx with an ancient riddle." The Argonauts' behavior was akin to the actions of fairy-tale heroes in magical space. Everywhere there lay in wait for them "abysses" and "horrors" that might give place to blessed revelations. "Not long ago there were horrors—an apparition of a menace in lightning that demanded from me, under threat of immediate destruction, an affirmation of my readiness for battle. I gave the affirmation. And for a time *they* let me go": Sergei Solov'ev confided this experience in a letter to Bely.[29] In February 1901, according to Bely, Solov'ev underwent another shattering spiritual trial: "[A]ccording to the newspapers, a new star burst forth in the sky (it soon disappeared). Sensational news was printed, saying that this star was the very same that accompanied the birth of the infant Jesus. [He] ran to me, much agitated, with the words: 'It has already begun.' "[30] "Almost *every member of our circle possessing the Argonaut spirit has experienced horrors—at first mystical, then psychic and, finally, in reality*," stated Bely, preliminary to describing his own experiences, which he perceived as a test of his fitness to fulfill the destined theurgical plan.[31] A. S. Petrovsky wrote from Moscow to Bely in Serebriany Kolodets on August 27, 1903, about his observation of the moon:

> I have never seen a more revolting animal than that which I saw in the sky at seven o'clock in the evening on August 23. . . . Huge, turbid, like a greasy sheet of paper, yellow-green (I avoid the more precise epithets that run through my head, so as . . . "not to provoke the geese"), to the horror of the earth-born the moon rose, foretelling at the very least one of the punishments of Egypt, the plague or some such. . . . The atmosphere, sticky, oppressive, was saturated with an evil fog and the filthy fumes of Tsvetnoi Boulevard. A saffron-yellow sunset completed the picture. I had to go to Sretenka, and I felt clearly that something would happen to me. And in fact I was ill with insomnia and so on; but in spirit I am strong and calm.[32]

Thus a walk from one end of Moscow to the other, quite ordinary from a commonsense point of view, took on sacral meaning, foretelling mystical "threats" and trials. Encoding one's torments and premonitions in descriptions of nature was a general motif among the Argonauts. Their communication was constantly fed by their common observations, filled with esoteric meaning, of sunsets, dawns, and, generally, the normal transitional states in nature, in which they recognized signs of global changes in the world's destinies. A half-joking note from Sergei Solov'ev to Bely speaks eloquently of this sort of "Argonautic" contact: "O Astra, it has begun .... A small cloud turned into the devil knows what. Many things are much closer than might be expected. Please come here for a minute. I have something to tell you. Inspector Lunakov [from *luna*, moon]."[33]

The Argonauts saw the outlines of their myth not only in natural phenomena and everyday scenes but in the basic episodes and prophecies of the New Testament as well. The mystery of Christ's coming was reflected as in a mirror in the anticipated new "coming." In Sergei Solov'ev's poem "The Virgin of Nazareth" ("Deva Nazareta"), Old Testament Judea and pagan Rome are shown awaiting divine revelation. But beyond the historical pictures can be glimpsed the contemporary life situation as the

Argonauts understood it. The good news to Joseph resonates
with the Argonauts' "secret" signs, and Nazareth, the place where
the mystery was accomplished, evokes Moscow of the "epoch of
sunsets":

> Joseph strode swiftly along steep streets,
>   Between steep houses and deserted squares;
> His soul burned in him with holy premonition,
>   Open to its depths for marvelous revelations.[34]

Christ's birth is symbolized in Solov'ev's poem by the spiritual
awakening and brightening of all nature, and here once more
the Argonaut "sun" motifs emerge:

> The time has arrived
>   To become blissfully happy...
> The blue mountain
>   Is blossoming with olives...
> An angel with white wings
>   Shines from the corner,
> With radiant arrows
>   The darkness is pierced... [35]

The Argonauts appropriated more than evangelical figures
and the Christian thematic generally. In their perception, any
text, of whatever provenance, could in principle become an emanation of the Argonaut text. For example, in 1902 the publishing
house Scorpio printed Knut Hamsun's play *The Drama of Life* in
Sergei Poliakov's translation. The play produced a very strong
impression on Bely. "It is possibly the best thing that has appeared in recent years here in Russia," he wrote to Metner.[36] Bely
authored a special review of this edition, in which he included a
large number of quotations from the play and also his own ideas
and impressions:

Over the speeches of Kareno and Teresita in Hamsun there hovers an
inextinguishable northern light... An inextinguishable northern light...
A tender snow is falling. One stops. One closes one's eyes. Let the whole
world rush by, speed away—gently, gently. And that mood accompanies
one through the horrors into a tender silence. And of horrors there
are many. The orgiastic waves of life splash... . . . And a gentle sadness

settles on the soul—the eternal glimmering of clumps of snow, eternal
rest after a long storm, the gleam of gold, the intoxicating champagne
of the horizon, a whitish quiet... Hamsun's heroes are people who, once
they have heard their inner music and learned something, can no longer
be stirred.[37]

The problematics of Hamsun's play, which concerned chiefly
the themes of fate and retribution, were, as a whole, rather far
from Argonaut ideals. Nonetheless, they generated in Bely's consciousness moods and pictures that were inserted *in toto* into the
conceptual and stylistic system of his "symphonies" written in the
early 1900's. Bely was not interested in the direct, intrinsic content of the "speeches of Kareno and Teresita." He cared about
what lay behind them and how they might serve as hints.

The Argonauts needed another's text as a point of departure;
they hoped to glimpse in it possibilities for creating their own
text. And having fallen into a system of mythological relations,
that other text in the process lost its authorship. Thus they constantly turned to the texts of others. (Along with his chief "rulers
of thoughts," Vladimir Solov'ev and Nietzsche, the works of, for
example, Fet, Lermontov, Poe, Dostoevsky, and Ibsen had great
meaning for Bely in those days.) But inevitably they saw in these
other texts either a text of their own or some kind of stepping
stone, a transitional stage to their own text. For Bely each poet's
individual features were only "veils" behind which could be discovered the ideas that consumed him or an analogy with them.
He valued Mikhail Lermontov insofar as Lermontov's poetry anticipated the possibilities of Solov'ev's creation. But the "search
in the beloved for the reflection of Eternity" found in Lermontov's love lyrics forced Bely to take "one more step—whereby
the beloved being becomes only an inexhaustible symbol, a window through which gazes an Eternal, Radiant Companion."[38]
Valery Briusov's work spurred him to meditate on conquering
the "chaos" reigning in the world: "The hope glimmers that Russian poetry will move toward the great task of organizing chaos
in preparation for its final conquest."[39]

Bely regarded the history of Russian poetry generally as
incarnating the potential for revealing the "countenance" of

"the Woman clothed in the Sun." Solov'ev and Nietzsche, while sharply contrasting thinkers, in Argonaut mythmaking fulfilled essentially the same function: each of them was "no longer a philosopher in the previous sense, but a sage." They met at the Argonauts' point of departure, and Nietzsche was graced with that same theurgical aureole that Solov'ev wore by right: "The theurgists' task is complex. They must go on where Nietzsche stopped—they must walk on air."[40] Both Solov'ev and Nietzsche were allotted the two-in-one mask of "Argonaut-forerunner." The enthusiasm of Argonaut striving toward a final harmonious world structure erased the cardinal differences between their world outlooks, giving these only secondary significance.

The Argonaut circle did not long retain the outlines it had assumed in 1903–4. One reason for this is the amorphousness of its intellectual credo and the unstable formal nature of the circle, which was actually halfway between friendly meetings that obligated no one to anything and a goal-directed organization. It was due also to the inevitable changes in the Argonauts' attitudes and convictions. Gradually their youthful character faded, and the link between idealistic strivings and real-life practice came to count for more. Generally, their horizons widened. The stormy events in Russian social life and above all the 1905 revolution brought new accents into their attitudes. Their eschatological moods predetermined their consistent radicalism: the Argonauts "sympathized with the revolutionary parties and laughed at the Octobrist and Cadet postures."[41]

From outside it seemed that the circle grew steadily stronger: new active participants were added (M. I. Sizov, V. O. Nilender, N. P. Kiselev, K. F. Krakht, and others), connections were widened, and so on. However, Bely admitted with good reason: "Argonauts are multiplying, but Argonautism is degenerating."[42] Many years later he wrote: "The tragedy of *Argonautism* was this: we did not actually board the *Argo* all together, we merely lingered in the port from which embarkation was possible. Each one discovered his own vessel, which he subjectively called *Argo*."[43]

To the degree that the initial keenness was lost or the spiritual force that once united a few Moscow students into a circle receded, the link became increasingly formal. It appeared less in common spiritual moods and intimate experience than in participation in meetings and delivering lectures and papers. The center shifted from Bely's "Sundays" to Pavel Ivanovich Astrov's "Wednesdays." These later gatherings were organized by Ellis, who found a common language with Astrov. A member of the Moscow circuit court and a lecturer on civil process, Astrov was interested in religious questions, most of all in the Christian-Democratic views of Grigory Petrov.[44] He offered his apartment for regular meetings and lectures, in which, along with the Argonauts, Astrov's friends and his two brothers, as well as members of their families, participated. "Astrov's 'Wednesdays' continued for several years," Bely recalled.

A wide variety of people appeared there: Professor I. Ozerov (who talked with us on the theme "Social Spirit and Art"), Professor Gromoglasov (from the Academy), Privat-Docent Pokrovsky, Berdiaev and Viacheslav Ivanov; P. D. Boborykin once read a paper there. The most varied topics followed each other. In the 1904–1905 season I remember: my papers ("On Pessimism," "Psychology and Theory of Knowledge," "On Scientific Dogmatism," "Apocalypse in Russian Poetry"), Ellis's (two papers on Dante), M. Ertel's ("On Julian"), Sizov's ("The Moonlight Dance of Philosophy"), Shklarevsky's ("On Khomiakov"), P. Astrov's ("On Fr. Petrov"). V. P. Polivanov read his tale and the long poem "Saul"; Sergei Solov'ev read his poem "The Virgin of Nazareth," etc.[45]

At the Astrov "Wednesdays" Bely saw evidence of the degeneration of Argonaut hopes and the dissipation of the circle's primary tasks: "[O]ut of pure duty I appeared at the Astrov circle to wallow in Argonaut verbiage."[46] The fruits of the Argonauts' union with the Astrov circle were the literary-philosophical anthologies *Free Conscience* (*Svobodnaia sovest'*, the first of which came out in the fall of 1905, the second in 1906), in which, along with the writings of Bely, Ellis, Sergei Solov'ev, and other Argonauts, were included various dilettante writings. Bely told Blok that *Free Conscience* was "an unbearable institution."[47] After the second collection appeared, the relations of Bely and Ellis with Astrov broke down, and the last locus of the Argonauts' meetings and cooperative activity ceased to exist.[48]

Possibly, for some of the circle's participants, Argonautism remained an example of immature youthful "good aspirations,"
a student game. Still, relations formed in the Argonaut period
resurfaced in common theosophical and, later, anthroposophi-
cal interests, as well as in such new associations as the Society
for Free Aesthetics (*Obshchestvo svobodnoi estetiki*), the House of
Song (*Dom pesni*) of the d'Algeims, and the circle of the sculptor
K. F. Krakht. Finally, the former Argonaut collective (E. K. Metner, Andrei Bely, Ellis, A. S. Petrovsky, M. I. Sizov, and others)
became the kernel of the publishing house Musaget, founded
in 1909.

Argonautism's basic ideas and principles found their most consistent embodiment in Andrei Bely's writings between 1900 and
1904. The corpus of Bely's "Argonaut" texts (broadly understood
as his creative searchings in the years mentioned) consists first of
all in the three "symphonies"—*The Northern Symphony (1st, Heroic)*
(*Severnaia simfoniia, 1-ia, geroicheskaia,* 1900), *Symphony (2nd, Dramatic)* (*Simfoniia, 2-ia, dramaticheskaia,* 1901), and *The Return.
III Symphony (Vozvrat. III simfoniia,* 1901–2)[49]—and fragments
of the first versions of *The 4th Symphony* (Chetvertaia simfoniia,
1902). The corpus included as well poems and prose fragments
making up the book *Gold in Azure* (*Zoloto v lazuri,* the largest part
written in 1903); articles and prose studies from 1902 to 1904
(the most significant being "Forms of Art" ["Formy iskusstva"],
"A Lightsome Fairy Tale" ["Svetovaia skazka"], "On Theurgy"
["O teurgii"], "The Poetry of Valery Briusov" ["Poeziia Valeriia
Briusova"], "The Singer" ["Pevitsa"], "Some Words of a Decadent Addressed to Liberals and Conservatives" ["Neskol'ko slov
dekadenta, obrashchennykh k liberalam i konservatoram"], and
"Symbolism as World Understanding" ["Simvolizm kak miroponimanie"]); "Apocalypse in Russian Poetry" ("Apokalipsis v
russkoi poezii," 1905); and the unfinished, unpreserved long
poem "Child-Sun" ("Ditia-Solntse," 1905).[50] Bely's letters of these
years, in which he expressed his ideals even more declaratively
and directly, must be considered of equal importance with these
works.

Bely's "Argonautic" world-perception shows a certain evolution divisible into several stages. "From 1901 to 1905—from thesis to antithesis," Bely himself summed it up, surveying his life's course.[51] The first, actually pre-Argonaut, stage, which preceded construction of the collective myth, takes in 1901–2. At that time those notions of the world and those creative challenges that were to be fundamental to the Argonaut brotherhood were taking shape in Bely's consciousness:

The eternal appears in the line of time as the dawn of the ascending century. The fogs of grief are suddenly split asunder by the red dawns of completely new days. . . . The rupture of old ways is experienced like the End of the World, the tidings of a new epoch like the Second Coming. We felt the apocalyptic rhythm of time. We reached toward the Beginning through the End.[52]

Thus Bely described his sense of the world at the turn of the century. That temporal boundary, as he saw it, was the frontier between the accustomed and the new, historically unknown life; it separated not centuries but eras.

These moods defined the tonality of Bely's life at the time of his creative formation. Vladimir Solov'ev's "A Short Story of the Antichrist" ("Kratkaia povest' ob Antikhriste," 1899–1900), Bely's acquaintance with the philosopher, and Solov'ev's death shortly thereafter strengthened the mystical longings of the young Bely into life convictions. The year of "quiet sunsets," 1901, became the most important phase of his life: that was "*the only year of its kind: it was lived with maximal intensity.*" In February 1901 "our expectations of some kind of transformation of the world were at their peak"; "during the entire summer of 1901 there visited me blessed revelations and ecstasies; in that year I became fully conscious of the intimations of the Unseen Bride [*Nevidimoi Podrugi*], Sophia the Most Wise [*Sofii Premudrosti*]."[53]

His acquaintance in September 1901 with the poems of Blok, who was experiencing a similar rebirth, was a remarkable event for Bely: "recognition was clear: this was a tremendous artist—ours, completely ours, he voices the most intimate trend of our Moscow strivings."[54] The premonition of a coming new era and encounters with the "Unseen Bride" were symbolized for Bely in the person of Margarita Kirillovna Morozova, whom he first glimpsed in February 1901 "at a symphonic concert during the performance of a Beethoven symphony."[55] This chance "meeting of eyes" was taken in the Solov'evian key as a meeting with the "Eternal Bride" (s Podrugoi Vechnoi), and in the wife of a Moscow manufacturer was perceived the "Woman clothed in the Sun" (Zhena, oblechennaia v Solntse): thus was born one of the first and most significant myths in Bely's creative consciousness. The confessional letters that Bely sent to Morozova, signed "Your Knight," in the medieval courtly spirit, represent the quintessence of his pre-Argonautic perception of the world. In the first of these, composed immediately after the "prophetic meeting," Bely wrote:

We are all living through the dawn [zori]... Is it sunrise or sunset? Can you possibly know nothing of the great sadness at dawn? Illuminated sadness turns everything upside down; it places people outside the world, as it were. The dawn-glow sadness—only that called forth this letter...

The near is becoming the far away, the far away, the near; not believing the incomprehensible, one is repelled by the comprehensible. One is immersed in a dreamy symphony...

Can you possibly know nothing of the great sadness at dawn?.. . . .

But all has changed... I have found a living symbol, an individual banner, all that I have sought but for which the time had [not yet?] come. You are my dawn of the future. In You is the coming event. You are the philosophy of the new era. For you I have denied myself love. You are the fated one! Do you know that?[56]

The year 1901 cannot be compared with any other phase in Bely's biography—for its purity, strength, and clarity of world perception and for the vitality of its experiences. What he then implanted in himself bore fruit for many years. In 1901 his self-definition as a writer took place: the Second Symphony, with which he made his literary debut, was written then in its entirety. The year 1902 marked a transition from experiences in seclusion to their proclamation to a broad audience: through entrance into literature and publication of the Second Symphony, through acquaintance with writers (Merezhkovsky, Zinaida Gippius, Briusov, and others), and through attempts to enter into esoteric contact with them.

In 1902 Argonaut Symbolism already had begun to grow: "for me there first began the cult of *the sun's gold* and the moods linked with it; the note of the feminine dawn was superseded by the note of masculinity; . . . the tone of the dawns [and sunsets] of 1901 was rosy; the tone of those of 1902 was a brilliant gold."[57] The tonality of Bely's worldview was changing—from the "feminine," "rosy" "dawns" of 1901 to the "sun" of the Argonautic 1903. To the contemplativeness and intimacy of experiences (which still reflected his youthful attraction to Schopenhauer and Buddhism—"reminiscences of Nirvana," in Bely's words),[58] to the effort to sense the sacral meaning of events and submit joyfully to cataclysms that daily threatened were now added the enthusiasm of optimistic daring, the summons to actively re-create the world. Quiet ecstasy retired before the gospel of action, of real life-creation. Solov'ev retreated somewhat to the secondary plane, but the figure of Nietzsche loomed large. The bold prophecies of Zarathustra began to prevail over the fatalistic oracular sayings of "A Short Story of the Antichrist." Bely's inner searchings now led to a self-definition of the myth, which was losing its initial purity as it was sublimated into a conscious symbolic structure:

[E]verything *apocalyptic*, which is a historical concept, begins to be for me only a symbolic prayerful ascent to Christ; *Apocalypse* is an *Apocalypse* of the soul: the path to initiation into the mystery of Christ's Name; "She" is becoming only the gate to the inner Christ in me: Sophia is becoming Christosophy: Christ's raiment.[59]

The year 1903 brought the final maturation of the Argonaut myth: Bely became the acknowledged leader of an esoteric union. He was filled with faith in his creative powers and full of radiant hopes for the world's rebirth:

> Let us fly to the horizon: there through the crimson curtain
> shines the never-dimming light of eternal day.
> Hurry to the horizon! There the crimson curtain
> is all woven through with dreams and fire.[60]

Now came the time for that which had been found and experienced earlier to multiply and propagate. Most of the poems in *Gold in Azure* were written in the summer of 1903. However, consolidation of Argonautic convictions, now finally found, named, and explored, did not make for a calm existence in an established mythological continuum. In fact, quite the opposite occurred: from all sides came palpable blows. Ever more keenly he felt the gap between theurgic expectations and everyday, trivial conditions, the ineradicable sluggishness of life. He later wrote: "In all those poems of that period can be heard clearly the note of the 'fracture' of hopes . . . , the leitmotif of that summer was 'not this,' 'not these'; I no longer felt in myself the vital current of spirituality that had lent me wings during those two years."[61] "The year 1903 was the year that saw the start of the inner extinguishing of the *dawns*."[62] "The dawns' unusual nuances gave way to ordinary ones."[63] And that sense of the loss of life-values warned of a painful crisis of Bely's entire worldview.

For Bely the "external" spread of Argonautism was accompanied by a serious review of the world perception that had generated this current of ideas. At the beginning of 1904 he experienced a crushing blow to his theurgical ideals. A "definitive break was acknowledged; a period was put to the past."[64] The events proceeding from Bely's relations with Nina Petrovskaia cast the ultimate light on what had been inexorably approaching. In his relationship with Petrovskaia he had wanted to see the prototype of "mysterial" love, but it had turned into a trivial "romance."[65] Bely gradually suffered disillusionment with his "prophetic" mission. So too with his aim to achieve a direct "brotherly" closeness and unity of ideas with other Symbolist writers. And he became disillusioned with the Argonaut brotherhood itself. His participation in Argonaut enterprises became more and more perfunctory, and his creative work underwent such a profound evolution that many poems from 1904 and 1905, later included in the volumes *Ashes* (*Pepel*, 1909) and *The Urn* (*Urna*, 1909), in form and mood resemble a full antithesis to works from the Argonaut period. "The commune, desired since

1901, for me turned into a madhouse": such was Bely's verdict on his Argonautism.[66]

The primary reliance on autobiographical and epistolary materials in tracing the basic phases of Andrei Bely's Argonautism is not accidental. More than anything else these provide direct evidence of that particular epoch's experiences. The evolution of Bely's worldview was so headlong that frequently the artistic works that were supposed to manifest a particular phase lagged behind in time. They were written when he had fallen under the sway of other ideas and beliefs, and they appeared in print yet more tardily.

This general rule in Bely's creative career was very apparent in his Argonaut period. Indeed, only the *Second Symphony*, written in the course of several months in 1901, synchronized with the moods that generated it. And Argonautism became a unifying principle only when the exhaustion of the mine he had opened was already quite apparent. Nonetheless, for some time writings maintaining the tonality of that world perception dominated his work. The article "Apocalypse in Russian Poetry," the swan song of Bely's Argonautism, was written at the beginning of 1905. Still later he worked on the poem "Child-Sun." By his own admission that poem, "written in June 1905, was satured with *gold*, with *azure*: in approach, in colors."[67] Many of Bely's articles from 1904–5 were written in the Argonaut vein and filled with faith in the imminent realization of hopes that to the author himself, on the plane of personal destiny, now hardly seemed achievable.

In all of these works, of course, new tendencies are observable. The original purity of world perception is absent; "phantoms of chaos" constantly intrude. Yet creative inertia is evident in them. For a long while Argonaut thematics and style remained in Bely's intimate correspondence also. Only late in 1905 and early in 1906 was he able openly to announce a major revision of his creative work's defining themes.

The lagging of "art texts" behind "life texts" observed in Bely's case serves to confirm the subordinate position of the first in relation to the second. The "life text" for Bely the Argonaut was primary, valuable, and perfect; the "art text" was flawed from the start, like an imperfect emanation of a myth actually experienced, like a matrix of something single and unrepeatable. Bely's remarks about *The Second Symphony*, written in 1901, are significant: it was "a chance excerpt, an almost stenographic record of that genuine, huge symphony that I lived through for many months of that year."[68] One of the many "supertasks" that occupied him was to overcome the narrowness, confinement, and "literariness" of artistic creation and to elevate it to a genuinely functioning force. It was necessary to unseal art's world-transforming nature, to rise to the level of "life-creation." Here was a principle of genuine value.

Bely chafed at hearing words only *"about* bliss," *"about* duty," *"about* universal happiness." *"I want heroic exploit, duty, happiness,* and not the word *'about,'* " he averred to Margarita Morozova.[69] He prized Symbolism not as artistic creation but as a way of understanding the world. Art was valuable not intrinsically but only as a step to something larger and more meaningful: "When that future becomes the present, art, having prepared mankind for what will come after it, will disappear. The new art is less art. It is a banner, a forerunner."[70] Only the orientation of an artistic text along the coordinates of a "life text" gives the former meaning and justification. An artistic text receives the right to exist from the reality of the moods and experiences that evoke it; its specifically artistic parameters play only the most subordinate role. The dominating principle here is strict autobiographism. The more a text follows its "life" source, the more accurately it presents the variations of the life myth, the more it is justified.

"I wrote the third part of the *Symphony* in the country, at my mother's, in Serebriany Kolodets, between the first and fifth of June, galloping for whole days in the fields on my fast horse and jotting it down in the saddle, scene after scene," Bely recalled about that summer of 1901 and his work on the *Second Symphony*.[71] Such deliberately uncontrolled recording of experience appears also in numerous "lyrical prose fragments" of those years, a large part of them unpublished. In general Bely's creative path was remote from established notions of authorial activity. The rhythm of his work on the *Second Symphony* is indicative: "[D]uring Holy

Week I hastily, in 2–3 days, sketched out the 1st part of the *Symphony*."[72] During one night in May almost the whole of the second part was written, and that summer, also in a very short period, the third and fourth parts were created. This is paradoxical. Yet if one approaches Bely's early work, which was outstandingly innovative and unusual to the point of eccentricity from the point of view of the author's creative psychology, one can apply to it S. Ia. Nadson's famous lines: "If only somehow might be poured forth / That of which the richly sounding heart is full!" Bely's closest friend, E. K. Metner, wrote of *Gold in Azure*:

[I]n its own way [it] is like *The Robbers* of Schiller, who considered genius (whose? of course of *his own* type) almost incompatible with taste. . . . In that genius there is something Schillerian, easily broken, extremely impetuous; the result is a lack of taste or, more correctly, insufficient subordination of one's outbursts to one's taste.[73]

Even such an admirer as Briusov pointed out the carelessness and formal imperfections of Bely's poems, amazing as they were in their vividness and originality of world perception:

Bely's language is a vivid but random amalgam; the most "trivial" words collide there with the most refined expressions, fiery epithets, and metaphors with feeble prosaicisms; it is a royal cloth-of-gold mantle with unsightly patches. . . . Bely awaits the reader who will pardon his lapses, who will yield along with him to the mad cataract of his golden and fiery dreams, who will throw himself into the abyss foaming with pearls.[74]

The dialogue between the critic N. F. Nikolaev and D. V. Filosofov concerning the "symphonies" is also highly typical. Nikolaev, evaluating Bely's works from the strictly "aesthetic" point of view, concluded: "If Flaubert were alive and acquainted with him, he would perhaps advise Mr. Andrei Bely to consign to the flames *almost* all that he has written, just as, following his advice, Maupassant did with his youthful experiments."[75] Filosofov, who with incomparably greater sensitivity grasped the phenomenon of Andrei Bely, argued reasonably that such criticism

cannot possibly plumb the creative personality of the author of the "Symphonies." In fact it is impossible to force Bely into a strictly literary frame. . . . He constantly splashes over artificial barriers, constantly

destroys the integrity of forms and gives himself to prophecies of a decidedly unliterary nature. This is a sign of the time. It is not the fault of
Bely only.[76]

Bely emerged as an adept of the spontaneous creative process
not only as an artist but also—and primarily—as a "life-creator."
Later, halfway through the decade after 1900, the task of transforming the world having retreated to a secondary plane in
his consciousness, he was able to understand the meaning of
those artistic demands that had seemed to him despicable and
"formal." And from that point of view he criticized his early
works for inexperience, stylistic imperfection, the naïveté of
youth, and so forth.

If the artistic texts of Bely the Argonaut tended toward the
directness of a document about a myth in the making, those texts
usually thought of as "nonartistic" (for example, letters, articles,
reviews) in their turn took on marks of artistic organization.
Intended as the concrete expression of a life myth, they could
not take form otherwise than through those "secondary" means.
More than that, a contemporary consciousness might perceive
the life myth embodied in words as a recognized and unavoidably
artistic system. Such is the case, for example, with one of Bely's
first confessional letters to Margarita Morozova, which opened,
like a long poem or a philosophical article, with epigraphs from
Vladimir Solov'ev, Blok, and Lermontov:

Radiant is the philosophy of the dawns. Veil after veil falls on the horizon, and there, while the sky is dark overhead, on the horizon it is pearly.
It is pearly. Yes.

If You embody the World's Soul, Sophia the Divine Wisdom, if You
are the Symbol of the Radiant Bride—the Bride of the lightsome ways,
if finally the dawn is radiant, it will illumine also the horizon of my
expectations.

My fairytale, my happiness. And not mine only. My revelation incar-
nate, my blessed tidings, my secret banner.

The banner will unfurl. That will be on the day of the Ascension.[77]

Ultimately, texts that are normally disposed in a strict generic
and stylistic hierarchy merge to the point where demarcations
are impossible.

For two years Morozova had no notion who the man was who wrote letters to her signed "Your Knight." She recalled:

In the spring of 1903 in a bookstore I bought a small book by the poet Andrei Bely, *The Second (Dramatic) Symphony*, since I had heard about it from many people. Coming home I opened the book and was stunned to find in it literally the same expressions as in the letters of the "Knight." And I understood that under the name of "Fairy Tale" in that symphony he spoke of me.[78]

The first letters to Morozova were written simultaneously with the *Second Symphony* during 1901, Bely's year of transformation. In this way the "life text" generated secondary texts, "artistic" and "nonartistic," all built on the same model. They differed only in the degree of intentional poetic organization and the degree of distance from their creator. The "intimate," "nonartistic" text most often embodied ideas and images only just generated, not yet established in consciousness, as was the case with Bely's programmatic letter to Metner, singing the praises of "sunness." The pathos of the Argonautic striving toward the sun penetrated also the 1903 story "Lightsome Fairy Tale." In it is traceable a certain likeness of plot, the first sketch of the theme of childhood, which was later to receive fruitful development in Bely's work. Individual episodes are written with some pretensions to "everyday" verisimilitude, but the story's central idea and pervasive images are the same as those about which Bely wrote to Metner:

The Sun's Children desire to hurl themselves through fathomless darkness to the Sun. Like velvety bees who gather honeyed gold, they treasure in their hearts reserves of sunny gleams. Their heart will hold the noonday ecstasy: it will widen like a chalice, because their soul must become the huge mirror reflecting the lightning of suns, etc.[79]

The burden of tasks greater than those usually borne by any specific type of text (artistic, philosophical, epistolary, etc.) equalized these texts in some way, establishing their similarity and permitting "interchangeability." A letter might figure at the same time both as an intimate confession addressed to a specific person and as a philosophical study aimed at the widest audience, insofar as it contained theurgical ideas and anticipations of the apocalyptic transformation of the world. Merezhkovsky understood this very well when he published in the journal *New Way* (*Novyi put'*) excerpts from a letter of Bely's to him under the title "Concerning D. S. Merezhkovsky's book *Tolstoy and Dostoevsky*." And Blok, in February 1903, asked Bely's permission to publish one of his letters. Bely did not consent, but the very fact that the question was put in a correspondence only a month and a half old, between two people who had not yet met in person, is striking.

The "life text" also generated a special mythological space—a proscenium for Argonaut rituals. Bely felt deeply the importance of the place where the realization of the "world mystery" was expected. "The time has drawn near. The center has been designated in Moscow," he wrote to Metner.[80] Moscow (more specifically its "professorial" region—the Arbat, Prechistenka, Prechistensky Boulevard and the nearby Deviche Pole [Field]) was awarded the precious distinction of being both the witness to the mysteries being consummated and the living backdrop of the life-creating "act." Moscow's streets, lanes, boulevards, and churches inspired the specific image structure of Argonaut expectations and was itself encircled by an eschatological aureole. Bely confided:

Moscow is the center simply because [in Moscow] one feels most acutely what will come to pass. It is revealed with stunning clarity, is easily grasped. Not long ago I was at Devichy Monastery. The ecstasy of the snows was above all measure. The snows marked the border between life and death. A transparent pine cried out about what has secretly crept to the soul.[81]

The individual and unrepeatable features of the city known since childhood occurred in one synonymic series with the global phenomena on which the gaze of Andrei Bely and the Argonauts was trained. Bely stressed that for him Moscow then symbolized the entire life universe: "the place of our strolls was not the Arbat, not Prechistenka, but—Eternity."[82] He felt himself to be, as it were, not in the real topographical space of the city but in the cosmos, in inner proximity to the forces directing the world. "In Symbolism," he stated, "there is added to the five senses a sixth one—the sense of Eternity. This is the coefficient that marvelously refracts all."[83] That "sixth sense" dictated the original portrait of Moscow in "the epoch of dawns" that Bely sketched in the *Second Symphony* and re-created twenty years later in the narrative poem *The First Encounter (Pervoe svidanie)*:

> And I recall: beyond Deviche Pole
> A whitish swarm of clinics would go by;
> We will the luscious mystery,
> And sigh in joyful play:
> In waves of radiant ether,
> We read the chronicles of the world.[84]

The cosmic features of these experiences expressed themselves most vividly in the "symphonies" of sunsets and "music of dawns," in their mythologized "philosophy" and "aesthetic." The act of watching the sunsets and dawns took on a liturgical meaning and was for Bely the most cherished of collective "acts." Remembering his outings with Sergei Solov'ev, Bely wrote, "the hour of our strolls was sunset; we yielded ourselves especially to the evening glow." With A. S. Petrovsky he "climbed out onto the balcony, surveyed the sleepy Arbat and watched how the rosy light began in the east."[85] In letters to Metner, Bely "narrated" and interpreted the sunsets:

[T]wice there occurred in the sky something unexplainable—joyful, expressed in its "externals" as the synthesis of incompatible (and, rarely, of compatible) sunsets: a synthesis of a rosy, religious, mystical, feminine sunset, symbolizing the holy Church, the World Soul, Sophia, the Light of Heaven, the Holy Rose (Merezhkovsky) with a golden, Nietzschean, mangodlike, self-affirming sunset.[86]

The most portentous place in mythological Moscow was Novodevichy Monastery, where, even as early as the end of 1900, Andrei Bely and Sergei Solov'ev visited the graves of Vladimir Solov'ev and L. I. Polivanov, their beloved gymnasium teacher. "We mythicized their graves," Bely subsequently noted.[87] In 1903 Sergei Solov'ev's parents and N. V. Bugaev, Bely's father, were buried there. "Novodevichy Monastery was the goal of our walks," Bely later recalled of his meetings with the Petersburg Symbolist L. D. Semenov.

We would come there, visit the graves of my father, Polivanov, Vladimir Solov'ev, M. S. and O. M. Solov'ev, all still completely fresh, . . . and often in the midst of the most elevated conversations about the tomb and Eternity we would fall silent, observing the very still turquoise-colored sky; it would grow rosy toward sunset. . . . After a silence sometimes we would summon words from the silence: words about the last things, the quiet, our own concerns, and generally what was precious to us.[88]

The Argonauts' behavior at the graves of those dearest to them turned into a ritual act. "I run to give myself to these delights," Bely wrote in *The First Encounter* about these visits to Novodevichy Monastery.[89] Death presented itself to their consciousness less as a frightening event bringing the sharp pain of loss than as a portentous phenomenon in the providential destiny of the world. In anticipation of apocalyptic changes it lost its concrete tragic meaning and was equated with other, "mysterious" reflections. On January 16, 1903, M. S. Solov'ev died, and O. M. Solov'ev, unable to bear her husband's death, shot herself. These were Sergei Solov'ev's parents and Bely's spiritual teachers. Briusov, who was present at the funeral, left a diary entry of interest as a bystander's view: "Bugaev [Bely] bore himself majestically; Serezha behaved very strangely."[90] In this deeply affecting event Bely felt above all the breath of eternity and the approach of the eschatological epoch. Death was experienced not as an end but as assurance of the inevitability of resurrection, as the sailing away beyond the horizon to the "Argonaut" sun. "Heaven has drawn near. I rejoiced at the grave of the Solov'evs," he wrote to Metner, adding about Sergei Solov'ev:

He accepted his misfortune heroically—it could not be otherwise. Even on the day of his parents' death he said to me that he was ready for anything (it seems he already knew that his mother too would not survive—he knew it *all*). He prepared himself for terrible things, reading "Readings on Godmanhood." He said: "There has risen in me a wave of messianic feelings, and it will sustain me."[91]

Moscow was the scene not only of majestic rituals but also of all possible games and "harlequinades." These pranks served the function of humorous intermedia in a mystery play, setting off the sacral meaning of the events:

We ourselves threw a veil of jokes over our cherished dawn . . . and we began at times to play the fool and joke about how we seemed to the "uninitiated," and about what sophisms and paradoxes would result if we exaggerated in overblown forms what was not put into words; i.e., we envisioned a "harlequinade" of ourselves.[92]

Thus Bely commented on one of their "Argonautic" jokes, in which he and Sergei Solov'ev invented two researcher-philologists of the twenty-second century, the Frenchmen Lapan and Pampan, who disputed about the correct understanding of the "Blokian sect," that is, the Argonauts. Insofar as Bely and the Argonauts constituted a kind of "order of initiates," "devotees of the mystery," their behavior had to be at all times extraordinary, breaking with accepted conventions. Thus Bely, V. Vladimirov, and S. Ivanov organized "in the fields" a "gallop of the centaurs." They devised a peculiar ritual—the "kozlovak." And in the appearance of Moscow acquaintances they surmised fauns and other mythical creatures. Typical was an entry in Briusov's diary:

Bugaev dropped in on me several times. We talked a great deal. Of course of Christ, of the Christ-feeling . . . Later about centaurs and silenuses, of their way of life. He told how he went to look for centaurs beyond Novodevichy Monastery, on the other side of the Moscow River. How a unicorn walked around his room . . . My ladies, hearing how one man seriously said these things and the other seriously listened, thought that we had gone off the rails.[93]

"Harlequinades" were one means of interpreting Argonautic moods in everyday life ("a 'centaur,' a 'faun' were for us in those years not some kind of 'elemental spirits' but means of perception"),[94] and at the same time they were a profanation of the "everyday." The existing world had outlived, exhausted itself; it was not righteous and therefore deserved mockery and provocation. It was necessary to reveal its senselessness and to oppose to it other values and another type of behavior. Argonautic follies and escapades, related to medieval "holy foolishness," were understood as a kind of "holy madness." "If what is *to us* so splendid is madness, then long live madness," Bely exclaimed. "We will knock the spectacles of sobriety from myopic noses!"[95]

With Petrovsky, Bely undertook a demonstrative action ("an

incautious joke in which Alexei Sergeevich played a not unimportant role in that he ordered the cards").[96] To a whole series of acquaintances and to the editorial offices of *New Way* and *World of Art* (*Mir iskusstva*) he distributed printed visiting cards from mythical beings: "Vindalai Levulovich Belorog [Whitehorn]. Edinorog [Unicorn]. Bellendrikovy Fields, 24th Izlom [Fracture], No. 31"; "Ogyga Pellevich Kokhtik-Rrogikov. Edinorot [Singlemouth]. Vechnye boiazni [Eternal Fears]. Sernichikhinskii Tupik [Deadend], Omov House"; "Paul Ledoukovich Thathyvva [written in Greek script]. Mius. Kozni [Intrigues]. Rogovataia [Horn-like] Street. Sharzhanov House."[97] This prank created quite an uproar. "Not long ago Bugaev raised a commotion with his Ogygs, Edinorogs, etc.," Sergei Solov'ev wrote to Blok. "They almost called a psychiatrist for him, and there was a good deal of unpleasantness, for him and for us as well."[98] Bely's "Unicorns" with their "addresses," which parodied Moscow topography, were not merely prizes drawn by acquaintances. They were also hints wrapped in jokes pointing to phenomena concealed from quotidian vision and open to his own inner gaze, emphasizing their vital daily presence to him. Briusov (the only one who accepted the "rules of the game")[99] perceptively noted that for Bely this was "not . . . a joke, but a desire to create an 'atmosphere'—to do everything as if these unicorns existed."[100]

Moscow, the arena for life-creating acts, changed its image with the disintegration of Argonautism. It was no coincidence that the crisis of the Argonaut world perception expressed itself in part in the fact that Bely "fled" Moscow, on the physical level, in April 1904 ("I am fleeing from Moscow to Nizhny Novgorod," where "I will recover somewhat from the series of [cruel] blows dealt to my utopian dreams regarding the mystery").[101] On the creative level his flight consisted in the writing of poems that sang of flight "into the open" and the free life of wandering. Moscow seemed a "roaring city," and his dominant feeling was now the "yearning for freedom." The latter became the title of a poetic cycle announcing new currents in his creative work.[102] The myth of a Moscow that opened on eternity ("There for a year I talked about the Eternal"), all compact with "secret" signs, collapsed and was transformed into its opposite—the image of the urban torture-house with "stuffy chambers" and rusty window grills, poisoned with dust, where the dawns and sunsets dear to Bely were disfigured by the smoke of factory chimneys:

> Through dusty, yellow clouds
> I run, opening my umbrella.
> And like smoke the factory chimneys
> Spit at the fiery horizon.[103]

Inwardly Bely abandoned that place of unfulfilled "mystery." Motifs of exile and bitter freedom in "the empty field" became predominant.

The "mystery" of human relations took a central place in Argonaut mythmaking. Here the prototype of the universal "mystery" could be glimpsed. For the Argonauts human relations came in many ways to resemble artistic texts: they had their plot, their pragmatics, their system of stylistic definitions. "Essences began to emerge. The mask was torn away—and everywhere there were amazed, amazing, unmasked faces," wrote Bely in his article "On Theurgy."[104] Facts of human interaction seemed to signal phenomena and events hidden from the ordinary gaze; they were perceived as the direct self-expression of "essences." Everyday relations occupied one of the highest places in the Argonauts' scale of values. Their realization in the desired sense—the dialogue of "essences," and not of "masks"—was an exceptional phenomenon and required a "path of dedication." Esoteric contact took place without regard to everyday links, sometimes in spite of them. As early as in his first letter to Margarita Morozova, wishing to be correctly understood, Bely stressed that his confessions had nothing in common with the usual motives of human behavior: "[F]or fear that You will misinterpret my love, I declare that *I do not love You at all.* . . . I do not have to know You as a person, because I have come to know You better as a symbol and have announced You as the great prototype." In another he repeated: "I do not need to know You personally, nor to know how You feel about me. My bliss lies in the fact that *I* consider You a sister in the spirit."[105]

Typical is the emphasis Bely put here on the first-person pronoun: he did not strive to know and understand this person who meant so much to him. He only gazed rapturously on the mythic aureole with which he himself had endowed the object of his veneration. He was even ready to admit the artificiality, the randomness, of his choice, but he believed in his experience because he was prepared to see in the least human being a gleam of greatness. As in medieval courtly ritual, veneration might bear a conventional character, for all the object's precious qualities were generated by the effort to glimpse in a concrete phenomenon the ideal image. All these were brought from without and were not intrinsic to the object of veneration. He explained to Morozova: "I am not from heaven, and I am not with You, I am with *myself*, I speak with myself: I summon myself, I am in love with myself—there beyond the boundaries of time I summon myself, I summon You, I summon all: 'It is time, it is time . . .'"[106] Not surprisingly Bely rejoiced at learning that Sergei Solov'ev had discovered the "World Soul" (*Dusha mira*) in the granddaughter of L. I. Polivanov, and that in Petersburg Alexander Blok had found her in Liubov' Mendeleeva. The important feature for Bely was the likeness of moods, not the direct addressee. The ideal image—the intermediary between the phenomenal and the noumenal worlds—loses its real outlines and, being assimilated to all of nature, speaks with the language of the universal elements. "Sky," "ether," "azure," "blizzard," "rapture of snowstorms," "pearly cloud," "dawn": Bely's letters to Morozova are dotted with these "ethereal" definitions symbolizing nature's essence, perceived as revelation.

In the mythmaker's consciousness, the specific individual and his myth need not even intersect. Morozova as "World Soul" and the "Idea of future philosophy" (*Ideia budushchei filosofii*) in no way coincided with Morozova the arranger of lectures and meetings to whom Bely was introduced in the spring of 1905. She recalled how Bely "would approach me, and we would converse a little and in snatches about the most general themes. I invited him to call on us, and he came two or three times, and never, not by one word or one gesture, let it be known that he had writ-

ten to me." [107] The subsequent confidential relations established
between them, if indeed inspired by Bely's youthful letters, in
no way constituted their continuation. With Bely, relations with
one and the same person generally developed along two lines. In
the sphere of daily life they were regulated by ordinary, everyday circumstances. But myth-creating notions lay totally within
the confines of the myth being created and the strict system of
stylistic means and "artistic" devices it generated. As a rule, the
myth-creating notions involving an individual were primary for
Bely. Only later were these overlaid by "life-related," individual
features, but even so the myth remained the chief criterion for
evaluating the individual's behavior in everyday life. Even many
years later, after the disintegration of Argonautism, Metner reasonably concluded: "I very much doubt (in relation to Bugaev)
whether I was ever genuinely understood and loved. And I wonder whether the 'old friend,' as Andrei Bely calls me, was not
simply one of the characters in the *Symphony*, while I myself, the
living person, was merely a model." [108]

Often it was not easy to reconcile a person's myth with his
actual appearance and behavior. The myth's inevitable "accom-
modation to life," the discovery in the person of previously unknown human traits not allowed for in the system, was a dramatic
process. The first meeting of Bely and Blok was preceded by
acquaintance with each other's creative work and by a year of
intensive correspondence on the most important questions concerning worldview: on art and theurgy, on the paths for seeking the "Radiant Bride" (*Luchezarnaia Podruga*) and dangers and
"threats" arising in the process, and so forth. A striking similarity of life ideals and creative principles emerged. Nonetheless,
the long-awaited first encounter, in January 1904, did not yield
the expected result. Both poets were ill at ease: "It was difficult
to find immediately an authentic tone toward each other. . . .
We didn't know what to do with each other, what to talk about:
it wasn't worth talking about the weather, but to talk about the
Splendid Lady was impossible." [109]

Bely's words here sketch vividly the situation typical in Argonautic mythmaking, where out of the familiar "text" about a

person there stepped an unknown real person, and it was necessary to look for points of contact between them. In the relations of Blok and Bely that desired synthesis of "text" and "real life" was achieved, but again in the specific form of "a special, involuntary esotericism that was incomprehensible to the 'uninitiated.'"[110] Their relations took on the character of a distinctive "soulfeast" and produced a peculiar jargon, beneath which the moods affecting each might be discerned. Appropriately, the most convenient and expressive language in Bely's and Blok's communication turned out to be silence:

I would sit on the divan, resting my arm on the edge of the table. A.A. would sit in an armchair facing the table, and Liubov' Dmitrievna [Blok's wife], joining us, would perch on an armchair by the window. And there would begin our silent, hours-long sitting with essentially no conversation, but only the occasional foaming up of some kind of uninterrupted spiritual gurgling of a stream. And if there was any conversation, it was chiefly I who carried it on, and A.A. and L.D. were the landscape across which my stream of words cut.[111]

On the other hand, the plot constituted by Bely's relations with Nina Petrovskaia demonstrates the disintegration of a myth that did not sustain the test of "life." Petrovskaia, who in 1903 drew close to the Argonauts and especially to Bely, aroused in him hopes for a concrete realization of "mysterial" love. He confided ecstatically to her: "I believe that we are linked for Eternity. I believe there is not 'us,' separate, individual, but only 'us' insofar as we face toward Eternity, toward the One Source that gives us its single law, fulfilling which we draw close with Faith, Hope, and Love to Him—the Source of all love."[112] But Petrovskaia turned out to be a refractory pupil on "the paths of initiation." She wanted to see in her love not only the symbol of higher principles but something of intrinsic value. And she resisted Bely's "mysterial" rigorism, defending her right to a complete earthly feeling. She answered a reproachful letter from him in these words:

There sound in me "false notes from the point of view of religious love"? . . . I know one love, *holy and sinless* always, even in its vivid earthly beauty. . . . I do not think that you and I are "somehow special in Christ."

In Him all are equal. . . . But you split apart, destroy, divide, instead of accepting love's holy fullness.[113]

Bely was not a fanatical opponent of "earthly" union with a woman, yet this seemed natural to him only in the category of "everyday life." When it was a matter of a myth's realization, the emanation of a "lofty," "supersensible" principle into the "low sphere" of "fleshly" sensations seemed sacrilegious and impermissible. Bely perceived the evolution of his relations with Petrovskaia from hopes for "heavenly love" toward "common romance" to be a tragic "fall." "Everyday life" annihilated the "mystery," the exceptional degenerated into the trivial, the symbolic and providential to the one-dimensional and unambiguous. Insofar as Argonautism was characterized by the universal striving "to show in the common act its uncommon meaning," [114] the collapse of his relations with Petrovskaia in its turn held significance beyond that of an individual event. It was a symptom of the discrediting of the global Argonaut myth.

The episode with Nina Petrovskaia marked the downfall not only of Argonautism but also of Bely the prophet. The myth of Bely, *coryphaeus* of the Argonaut choir, created by his contemporaries and by himself, obligated him to such a mission. If Blok's experience in those years was markedly individualistic, Bely, despite the similarity of his moods to Blok's, felt driven to make his revelation available to many. Never mind that the "many" did not extend beyond the limits of an esoteric circle.

> Preaching an imminent end,
> I stood forth like a new Christ,
> Donning a crown of thorns
> Decked with the flame of roses,

wrote Bely in the poem "Eternal Summons" ("Vechnyi zov," 1903).[115] He went on to describe the lot of the newly appearing prophet: the "asylum" and the "madman's cap."

His sense of election and his conviction of his right to proclaim what was "unspoken" were firm in the young Bely, and they were strengthened by the readiness of many to hear his pronouncements. "The beardless student Bely played the messiah, and we *all* applauded": thus was the Argonautic situation later characterized by Ellis, who was by that time disillusioned with Bely.[116] Even those who were not Bely's voluntary pupils spoke of his genius, of the uniqueness of his life-creating credo. This did much to aid the mythicization of his personality. "You possess such insights, such a sense of God, as none of the rest of us has," Merezhkovsky told him.[117] After contact with Bely, A. A. Kublitskaia-Piottukh compared herself to the Samaritan woman enlightened by Jesus: "If you will sometimes write to me, I will be able once more to take an alabaster vessel and sit by the roadside." She signed another letter: "She who sits by the roadside with an alabaster vessel."[118] At one time, the myth of Bely as "the Chosen of God" was zealously propagated by Ellis in tones like those of his highly colored poem "To Andrei Bely" ("Andreiu Belomu," unpublished):

Yes, you did not know love, but, full of loving-kindness,
You thirsted, not for pleasing dreams, but for visions,
And sometimes joyfully on life's way
You thirsted to melt, not into tears, but into sounds,
And you suffered much, aroused from dreams,
And in thought more than once were nailed to the cross;
But training your radiant gaze on the *cupola of eternity*,
You heard the silvery chant of celestial angels,
In the flight of turtledoves and the sound of gray wings
You caught the lineaments of another realm,
In chants you heard, too, with fainting heart
The whisper of heavenly strings and the murmur of heavenly
    streams,
You saw mother-of-pearl in heavenly skies
And the bright face of God rising above the waters.[119]

The germ of the myth was already contained in the very pseudonym "Andrei Bely [White]." For him the color white embodied the absolute fullness of being and at the same time most adequately reflected the noumenal essence of the world. Later Bely reminisced about himself and Sergei Solov'ev in 1900:

Our mystical experiment of that time was the discovery of apocalyptic experiences in connection with the color "white"; laughingly we told each other that we were tracing the "white sources" of life; in them was the intimation of the approaching great era of the coming of Sophia the Most Wise and the Holy Spirit-Consoler.[120]

The mystical semantics of the color white persistently bubbled up in the "symphonies" as well. Thus the choice of pseudonym was first of all an affirmation of Bely's participation in "transfiguration." It was an anointing in preparation for the splendid "life-creating" deed.

The pseudonym fit extremely well with conceptions of the writer-theurgist and more than once served to good effect in various interpretations of the Bely myth. Moreover, it is directly linked to contemporaries' perception of Bely's appearance. To many he seemed a messenger from other worlds. His "angelic likeness" and "light-bearing" quality were constantly noted. "In his presence everything seemed to change instantly, to be displaced or illuminated by his light. And he was indeed radiant," as Vladislav Khodasevich remembered him.[121] "He was as if disembodied, unphysical," noted N. Valentinov.[122] And these opinions belonged to the most "sober" of Bely's acquaintances, individuals who did not share the Argonautic ecstasies.

Around 1905 the Bely myth was alive and developing. Briusov affirmed its active existence when, in his novel *The Fiery Angel* (*Ognennyi angel*, 1908), he endowed his Count Henrich with the likeness of Andrei Bely. In historical guise Briusov reconstituted not only the basic features of the Argonaut myth (a sort of secret mystical society) but the phenomenon of Bely itself, even to the "hypnotic" features of his external appearance.

The disintegration of Argonautism brought about the dispersion of dreams and illusions. And the myth of Bely either collapsed or was modified into very different forms. (Symptomatic of the first was the characterization of Bely given by Konstantin Bal'mont in 1908: "He was a handsome blue-eyed poet of the most delicate type, but he became a shrill journalist 'furiously clamoring on the stage.'")[123] In 1904 Bely saw himself as a "self-proclaimed prophet." But in the years following—despite Briusov's caution: "No, you cannot be a mere man of letters"—

his consistent and conscious participation in the literary process per se was increasingly noticeable. His maximalist strivings to be "more than a writer" were for a time replaced by authorial, and only authorial, work.

From his transports into the uncharted spheres of Argonautism, Bely thus gradually moved away into the tragic element of real life. Yet with all the zigzags of his creative evolution, his personality retained its wholeness. And Argonautism for a long time retained its meaning as a source of all his creative potency. This showed in the years when Bely's myth-creating mood had ebbed, but especially in the years of its resurgence. Again he felt the call to transform the world: in the epoch of "the second dawn" of 1909–11, by way of anthroposophic "discipleship"; and, finally, in the years of revolutionary upheaval.

Five

Valery Briusov and Nina Petrovskaia: Clashing Models of Life in Art

JOAN DELANEY GROSSMAN

In his retrospective essay "The End of Renata" ("Konets Renaty," 1928) Vladislav Khodasevich bitterly condemned the whole Symbolist enterprise of merging life with art for its ruinous effect both on talents and on human lives.[1] The impetus for that essay was the suicide in Paris in 1928 of Nina Ivanovna Petrovskaia, minor writer and critic, long-time mistress of Valery Briusov, and model for the witch Renata in Briusov's historical novel *The Fiery Angel* (*Ognennyi angel*, 1908). The history of the Symbolists, Khodasevich maintained, became the history of broken lives. At the same time he conceded to some of his former associates—and preeminently among them Nina Petrovskaia— a talent for life-creating that left a mark on their epoch independent of their actual literary gifts.[2] Moreover, Petrovskaia's power to draw others into her enterprise amounted almost to an act of living artistic creation. For this achievement Khodasevich rendered her tribute: "More artfully and more resolutely than others she created the 'poem of her life.'"[3]

The daughter of a petty official, Nina Petrovskaia was only eighteen when, in 1902, events took her into the center of emerging Moscow Symbolism.[4] As the wife of Sergei Sokolov (Kre-chetov), a minor poet and literary entrepreneur soon to found the publishing house Gryphon, she took her place as hostess to frequent literary gatherings in their apartment. From obscure, probably provincial origins she thus plunged quickly into the Moscow artistic vortex, where, though only a minor participant, she was soon known to all who moved in its circles.

Nina Petrovskaia may have differed from numerous other "average" members of that culture, chiefly in the intense seri-ousness with which she sought escape from its more flagrant banalities and vulgarities.[5] Andrei Bely contrasted the public Petrovskaia with the small somber woman, curled up on a divan, head on hand, who was capable of dreaming for hours "of some-thing simple, something fine; and was ready at such moments for heroic exploit, for sacrifice."[6] She remembered those early times as tracts of misery and spiritual loneliness where life was mean-ingless, where "days passed as if under a stupid glass bell from which, little by little, the air was being sucked out."[7] Devouring every page by Konstantin Bal'mont, Valery Briusov, Zinaida Gip-pius, Fedor Sologub, and other Symbolist "lights," she assimilated what she could of the new tastes, new ideas, and new strivings. Thus she sought access by any means available to the rarified but undefined spiritual regions they seemed to herald, where life and one's own self might be transformed. Yet, as Khodasevich acidly observed, the formula for merging life and art was not found, and Nina Petrovskaia, like too many others, became "a genuine victim of Decadence."[8]

In the rapidly overheating milieu of early Symbolism and Decadence, intense emotions of all kinds, but especially love, were greatly cultivated for the precious instants—*migi*—of ec-static transfiguration they promised. "It was enough to be in love," wrote Khodasevich ironically, "for then one was supplied with all the subjects of highest necessity for lyricism: Passion, De-spair, Exultation, Madness, Vice, Hatred, etc." Nor were halfway feelings tolerated. "The Symbolists wished to nourish themselves on the strongest essences of emotions."[9] Nina Petrovskaia learned this lesson quickly and from a highly regarded authority. Khodasevich's description of her first teacher in this matter clearly refers to Konstantin Bal'mont.[10]

In 1903, recognized as the leading Russian Symbolist, Bal'mont was a major figure both in Gryphon's publishing designs and in Petrovskaia's initiation into the cultural code of early Decadence.[11] From a distance of some twenty years she described the demands Bal'mont placed on his female admirers: "either to become the companion of his 'mad nights,' throwing into these monstrous bonfires all one's being, including one's health, or to join the ranks of 'incense-bearing women,' humbly following behind his triumphal chariot."[12] Their relationship cooled quickly. Nonetheless, it was probably Bal'mont who introduced her to the Polish writer Stanislaw Przybyszewski's philosophy of love.

Bal'mont's influence on Nina Petrovskaia in all spheres was relatively short-lived.[13] However, Przybyszewski was an influence of another order. Publication of his works began in Germany in the early 1890's. Russian translation apparently began in 1901 and by 1904 was in full flood.[14] His novels, plays, prose poems, and other small genres seemed to his readers to give shape and dignity to inchoate longings through their daring, broad-brushed pronouncements about life, love, death, God: the "accursed questions." Petrovskaia later called *Homo Sapiens* (1895–96) a "new moral testament."[15] In so saying she apparently spoke for many in her generation who tried to fill a painful emptiness with whatever promised relief: poetry, literary activity, spiritualism, alcohol, drugs, love.[16]

Meanwhile, along with Przybyszewski, another guide appeared for Nina, one who for a time took precedence over all others. In the spring of 1903 she became acquainted with Andrei Bely, around whom the circle known as the Argonauts was forming. (See Alexander Lavrov's essay in this volume.) For the next months she frequented Argonaut gatherings, attracted to the "fraternal mystery" of Argonautism and increasingly infatuated with Bely. Despite its kinship to Symbolism, Argonautism was not a literary movement. Its adherents were drawn together by common hopes and apprehensions about the future. A sense of approaching total change in all aspects of life, in which they might hope to play a leading role, was a central unifying theme in their fellowship.[17] Their visions of the new life were extremely vague. Still, the aura of mystery, the promise of a new life, and, above all, the quasi-messianic figure of Bely were irresistible to Petrovskaia. Bely attempted to account for his relationship with her on the grounds, first, of genuine friendship and, more, of spiritual mission:

I felt in myself at that time the potential for creating *a ritual*, a rite; but I needed . . . a helper, more accurately, a *sui generis* female hierophant; she had to be found and properly prepared; I began to feel that such a kindred soul existed: Nina Ivanovna Petrovskaia. She related to me with a certain special sensitivity. I began to visit her often; and—to teach her.[18]

However, he soon found this relationship not only that of priest and assisting priestess but something more complicated and troubling:

My attraction to Petrovskaia is at last defining itself; she is becoming the person closer to me than any other, but I begin to suspect that she is in love with me; I am trying to transform the very feeling of love into mystery. . . . I don't know what to do with Nina Ivanovna; moreover, I feel that she attracts me as a woman; relations between us are becoming difficult.[19]

His published autobiographical account was written later, from a different perspective, and in some respects is less candid than the private one just cited.[20] Like Khodasevich, he looked back on events that had occurred 30 years earlier with the knowledge of Nina Petrovskaia's decline and suicide. From that vantage Bely might blame his naive pride, as well as sexual attraction, for having blinded him to the complexity and perils of trying to save the woman whom he now compared to Dostoevsky's Nastasia Filippovna.[21] In addition, he could now acknowledge his need for the adulation and sympathy Petrovskaia provided. "She was good and sensitive and sincere; but she was too responsive: almost criminally receptive."[22]

Petrovskaia's intense attachment to him, his words, and his presence frightened, flattered, and fascinated Bely. He protested the role of "teacher of life" in which she cast him, at the same time encouraging her obedience to his precepts. This role was not of her sole devising, since in Argonaut circles Bely generally wore a prophetic cloak. Moreover, he wrote later of his youthful delusion that his newly constructed "rules of life" had the power to heal Petrovskaia's deeply troubled soul.[23] Both his published and his unpublished biographical writings show Bely as slow, possibly loath, to grasp the situation in which he found himself. Perhaps only after reading Briusov's novel did he come to understand the nature of this woman who became the "original" of the sixteenth-century witch Renata. But various adventures in the meantime prepared him for that outcome or at least for a Dostoevskian interpretation of the situation.

For a time Bely cast himself and her in the roles of Orpheus and Eurydice. This myth was popular among the Symbolists as a paradigm both for life situations and for creative activity where fantastic images are drawn from the artist's soul into the world of reality.[24] However, its application here held unforeseen perils, as became clear on an occasion in 1904 when Petrovskaia summoned Bely and, "with sobs, with a revolver in hand, with poison in a container and, reducing *symbols* to material reality, demanded that I 'lead her out of hell.'"[25] The fact that she took Symbolism's "life-creation" with deadly seriousness was demonstrated frequently over the next few years in her relations not only with Bely but even more with Briusov. Long afterward Bely summed up more than just his own experience when he wrote: "Around her there was an atmosphere of danger, ruin, fate."[26]

Bely's Solov'evian conception of love as celibate mystery long outlived his Argonautism, as various accounts of his relationship with Asia Turgeneva show. (See Olga Matich's essay in this volume.) However, what he referred to as "my fall with Nina Ivanovna" accompanied the collapse of Argonautism as a means of life-creation for Bely. He elaborated on his disillusion: "instead of dreams of mystery, brotherhood and sisterhood, there was simply a romance," a common, ordinary love affair (unconsummated, to be sure) based on sensuality.[27]

Nonetheless, Bely did not immediately flee the perceived danger but continued an ambiguous and ambivalent relationship for some months.[28] During this time, according to Petrovskaia, his close followers looked to him still in expectation of "the miracle." Even after three decades she resented his abdication of responsibility to those he had hypnotized with prophecies evoking "cold white halls, white garments, white flowers, pure candles with white tears flowing, and we, radiant in the mystery of serving the new Christ," whom she and others considered to be "Bely himself—the 'false prophet.'"[29] For Petrovskaia there was no such conflict as that endured by Bely. If he saw their relationship as an experiment in Solov'evian "mystic love" that precluded the physical, she read the situation otherwise. Wounded and angered by Bely's rejection, she determined to demonstrate, with Przybyszewski's guidance, how life might indeed be transformed by love. Valery Briusov became her willing partner.

Bely's relations with Briusov, already complicated by other circumstances, speedily worsened as he became convinced that Briusov, urged on by Petrovskaia, was persecuting him with hypnosis and black magic. However, what began, at least in part, as an intrigue to avenge thwarted love developed quickly into a passionate love affair, with Decadent overtones, that set a model and standard for Symbolist "life-creation." That both parties were married to others was, if anything, a positive factor.[30] In a milieu that throve on such spectacles the Briusov-Petrovskaia liaison was an invaluable means of elaborating the cultural code.

The chief artistic result was *The Fiery Angel*, obviously based on the real-life triangle of Petrovskaia, Briusov, and Bely. In Briusov's novel the driving force was the obsession of the witch Renata (Petrovskaia) for the fiery angel who visited her dreams and whom she recognized in Prince Henrich (Bely). The soldier of fortune and narrator Ruprecht (Briusov) was her protector, slave, and lover. Bely later wrote with some admiration that Briusov had achieved here an almost clinically exact description of Petrovskaia's nervous malady.[31] Certainly Briusov drew heavily for his novel on the personalities and behavior of both his models, and, at least in Petrovskaia's case, he had her willing cooperation. Khodasevich's picture of Briusov as exploiting Petrovskaia for the purposes of his art and then callously abandoning "Renata" to the inquisitorial flames stood for many years as the life drama's definitive interpretation. Later information, including Petrovskaia's own memoir written long after in emigration, has modified and greatly added to that picture.[32] However, at the time, for the participants and their associates the triangular relationship, with its dramas and turmoil visible to all, exemplified the Przybyszewskian dictum that love was a force of cosmic significance.

Przybyszewski's writings, as well as his biography and character, presented in concentrated form many of the elements embraced by the notion of "Decadence." In the aggregate these features offered a frightening but also flattering interpretation of Decadence to a generation trying to be convinced of the radical newness of its aesthetic vision and its worldview. To demonstrate the point, its spokesmen flaunted their defiance of conventional standards of morality and even sanity, chanting a litany of such names as Poe, Hoffmann, DeQuincey, Nerval, and Baudelaire. Przybyszewski, despite his links to the positivist scientific view, seemed to many a splendid addition to the list.[33]

Przybyszewski's career began in Germany in 1890 with the writing of his study "Chopin and Nietzsche."[34] In Nietzsche's psychology (which Przybyszewski saw epitomized in *Thus Spake Zarathustra*, 1883–92) he found a prime exemplar of "the genius," which he renamed "the individuum."[35] The modern "individuum-decadent" he likened to "the crevices after an earthquake, which point to places where the earth attempted to shape itself anew."[36] Through such crevices human nature's profoundest depth, the "individuum" or unconscious, becomes visible, along with the sexual ferment that sets it all stirring.[37] Because Nietzsche had reached "the highest level of human development and even something higher, because with one half of his being he had already penetrated into the new period of development, because the center of gravity of his organism's development had shifted to his brain," he was able to analyze these secrets within himself. He was destroyed by "the mysterious law of nature by whose force in some fatal manner all such 'bridges' are destroyed. . . . But Nietzsche's destruction was caused by the very thing that at the same time constituted his might."[38]

Nietzsche's life and fate, then, formed for Przybyszewski a paradigm for the most advanced members of society, and he called this early piece a program for all his later work.[39] Its first major application came in his 1893 poetic study, *Totenmesse*, which opened with the notable line: "In the beginning was sex."[40] His protagonist, Certain, narrates his own psychological dissolution, which is due to the dislocation of sex within his nature.[41] The fate that destroys him befalls the most sensitive, advanced individuals, in whom this dislocation, potentially present in all human nature, is experienced more acutely. These advanced types are the decadent-neurasthenics, often artists, who are able to understand, though not cure, their sickness.

In his introduction, Certain sketches the history of human development, powered by that primeval sexual impulse amounting to the will to life. Starting from the lowliest level of human being, this impulse is so exuberant as to result in increasing multiplicity and diversity of types, often achieved by violent struggle. The final goal is reunification at the highest level. But as the soul becomes ever more refined, it loses touch with its original driving force, elemental sex. The outcome for both higher and lower parts of man will be, not ecstatic reunion with its necessary other half, but death and reabsorption into the "primary idea." Certain traces the final terrible stages of this process in himself and ends with the words "The reverse metamorphosis may begin."[42]

The ancient myth of androgyny as the original state of all being and humanity's ultimate transcendent goal was widely disseminated in turn-of-the-century European culture. Przybyszewski, like his Russian contemporaries, had access to it in many forms and many sources, from the Cabala (in which he was interested) to modern Decadent writers like Joséphin Péladan.[43] Przybyszewski's studies in biology and psychology were presumably influential in making his notion of androgyny itself something of a hybrid. For the notion of androgyny the result of this kind of bias was frequently, as Olga Matich put it, "to plunge it from the mystical realms of divine harmony into the murky waters of sexual ambiguity."[44] However, Przybyszewski's version, at least in his work *Androgyne* (to be discussed below), retained a strongly mystical tone. But, like many of his generation, he—through his characters—showed mankind unresigned to merely projecting the return to final androgynous harmony onto another plane beyond time. Their struggle against psychological and physical limits led inevitably to the tragedies and despair experienced by such as Certain.

Though this pessimistic, fatalistic scenario recurs variously in Przybyszewski's work, glimpses of another, ostensibly more optimistic, outcome also occur. The foreword to *Sons of Earth* (1904; Russian translation *Syny zemli*, 1904), which appeared in the Russian Symbolist journal *Libra* (*Vesy*) in 1904, presented another picture with distinctly different terminology and tone, carrying an echo of Edgar Allan Poe: "The axis of our life is Love and Death."[45] The focus here, however, was on love:

In my understanding, love . . . is a cosmic element, the fate weighing on all mankind, the blessed force that preserves it from expiring.

. . . love is the unknown power that regenerates and resurrects life again and again unto eternity.

. . . love is the unrestrainable striving (it may also become the source of unquenchable sufferings) toward the full merging of the two sexes so that the human race may be ennobled and reach Perfection.

In the name of that love and that striving toward Perfection, man suffers, labors, torments himself, struggles, kills, and the result of this is progress and the perfection of the human race.

Despite his talk of progress toward ultimate human perfection, Przybyszewski is not so much presenting a program here as attempting to illuminate a mystery: "I have tried to penetrate into this essence of life. . . . I have studied all the manifestations of love so as to form for myself a complete worldview. But the road is long, very long."[46] His works, he assured his readers, have been devoted to "this holy love and aspiration for the perfect merging of the two sexes, who strive toward perfection."[47]

Here indeed was encouragement for those who, like Nina Petrovskaia, found the Argonaut doctrine, with what Bely later

called its "left Solov'evian" cast, a hard and puzzling and ultimately disillusioning word. Bely had finally retreated in confu-
sion, taking his "mystery" with him. But meanwhile there was
Przybyszewski, who taught that fully consummated sexual love
might be a life-transforming mystery.[48]

The first phase of Nina Petrovskaia's relationship with Briusov
extended from autumn 1904 to the end of June 1905. Briusov
wrote, "For me that was a year of storms, a year of mael-
strom. Never have I experienced such passions, such torments,
such joys."[49] The high point was a month's stay in Finland, on
Lake Saima, already hallowed for their generation by Vladimir
Solov'ev.

While, thanks to Briusov's novel and Khodasevich's memoir,
much attention has been paid to the Briusov-Petrovskaia story,
little effort has been given to examining the element of personal
myth that informed their expectations and actions. The ideological baggage they, and especially Petrovskaia, brought with them
to Saima carried materials for an experiment with profound,
life-shaping meaning for both. The mixture's explosiveness came
from the incompatibility not only of their personal expectations
and demands but also of the very models inspiring their projects
of life-creation and life-discovery. The experiment was doomed
from the beginning, but of this, as often happens, the principals
were at first happily unaware.

Solov'ev's Finland held many mysterious elements that nour-
ished his spirit, and his visions subsequently entered the Symbolist culture.[50] The core of his Finnish landscape poetry was the
"Saima" series, written between October 1894 and July 1896.[51]
In these poems the lake was portrayed variously: as the turbu-
lent captive of granite cliffs who remembered her waters' im-
memorial dominance over the earth; the languorous beauty of
changing enchantment; the luminous vessel of revelation, "Dark
chaos's radiant daughter."[52] Solov'ev's Saima was a place where
heaven and earth came together in visionary union. The image
of the eternal feminine hovered over it. Andrei Bely wrote: "For

Vladimir Solov'ev the Finnish lake Saima served as the source
of inspirations about Her: in the watery elements he saw Her
countenance."[53]

It is no exaggeration to say that Saima and southern Finland generally became a place of pilgrimage for Symbolism. That
Petrovskaia and Briusov likewise went there with high expectations is evident in the writings of each over the next several years.
His 1906 volume of poetry, *Stephanos*, and her more modest 1908
collection of short stories, *Sanctus Amor*, as well as *The Fiery Angel*,
all in various ways interpreted the "revelations" that had come.
Of these the cycle "On Saima" in *Stephanos* gave the most immediate response.[54] No love poetry in the usual sense is found there.
Instead, the poems express the mood wafted to the poet by Saima
itself in midsummer, in the season of fair days and white nights.
There is little indication of any other theme. But the experience
is clearly a shared one: Saima casts a spell of silence, peace, and
clear beauty that penetrates the spirit. The first poem shows the
poet, so recently inspired by the city's hum and roar, now su-
premely peaceful and receptive to the wordless messages that
flow as "her" image rises over him.[55] Saima, Petrovskaia, "she" (in
Briusov's case always his muse) blend into one. The next three
poems are purely descriptive, though the personal point of view
is expressed in syntax and punctuation.[56] In the fifth poem bliss
becomes too much to contain: "I am ravished—I need nothing
more! / If only this bright dream could last."[57] Here is the first
hint that "she"—now Petrovskaia unmistakably—does not totally
share his lightsome mood, but longs instead for darkness.[58] The
sixth poem finds them in a boat, at one, sharing interior peace.
In this and in the final, seventh poem the poet's imagination is
carried away to thoughts of Finnish legend and history.[59] This
closing poem's "thou"—Saima—comes nearest to Solov'ev's eternal feminine, but the vision is Briusov's: "all languor, all love!" as
she weaves endless tales of Finland's legendary past.

An undated unpublished letter to Petrovskaia filled with Briusov's ecstatic reminiscences of the month on Saima evokes the
metaphor of the lake. It is also suggestive of his highest hope in

going there: "You showed me the profoundest depths, the final secrets of my soul."[60] For Briusov the artist's soul was the source of all art, and if that source was muddied or dried up, the artist was dead. In effect, by revealing to him his soul's depths—stirring the waters, as it were—she acted as his muse. A year later he wrote to Petrovskaia, recalling his depleted spiritual condition shortly before their first encounter. He had just finished his book *Urbi et Orbi* (1903): "I remember . . . exhaustion, weakness, inability to create, the wish to run away, hide, disappear, so that no one might force me to think, act, and most of all *feel*." Then came the miracle:

And suddenly—you came, like something new, unexpected, unrealizable, that was long ago dreamed of and suddenly came true. A love came of which I had only written in poems but had never known; a woman came about whom I had only read in books (in your Przybyszewski) but had never seen. You have often told me that that year was a resurrection for you; but it was a resurrection for me as well. My eyes suddenly opened and became a hundred times keener; in my hands I felt new strength. Suddenly I saw around me treasures that my earlier vision had not discerned.[61]

The stay on myth-laden Saima brought this resurrection to its fullness for Briusov. Moreover, as he indicated in his letter, another magnetic field was in play, for Petrovskaia carried with her an aura from another literary source. Thoroughly steeped in Przybyszewski by the summer of 1904, she now had a mission: to impart to Briusov a true understanding of the Przybyszewskian mystery of love and to try with him to achieve its promise of life-creation. Przybyszewski's foreword so recently published in *Libra* (under Briusov's editorship) concluded with a passage that promised much for both of them:

Love and aspiration toward something better, higher . . . alone are the source of inspiration for the true artist.

   And the man and woman linked by the bonds of such love instinctively strive ever forward, forward—into the radiant future, . . . trusting in the great strength of Love, eternally regenerating toward ever more perfect life.[62]

Such a statement, with its vision of regenerative love leading mankind toward future perfection, could almost have been extracted from Solov'ev's "The Meaning of Love" ("Smysl liubvi," 1892–94). However, as any reader of his novels and poems knew, Przybyszewskian "love" was of an entirely different character. Nina Petrovskaia herself formulated this difference, with apparent oblique reference to Solov'ev, in a 1906 review of a new Russian translation of *Totenmesse*:

There are two paths of ascent for the human spirit. One is the calm self-affirmation, the blessed olympian clarity, the even and majestic advance of powerful inspiration. This is the image of the "wise man and poet" on a lofty mountain peak, in rosy dawn rays. The other is the *via dolorosa* of the human soul passing through chaos, through tragic self-division, the terrible path of deep darkness accompanied by flashes of blue lightning against the black sky of despair.[63]

If Solov'ev's theory of love was Platonic, premised on unconsummated Eros, Przybyszewski's required not only passionate consummation but physical as well as spiritual suffering. Petrovskaia summarized it in Przybyszewskian language and imagery: "Love . . . comes drenched in sacrificial blood. . . . It is the intoxicating eucharist, the sacrificial giving of body and blood, the divine dionysian ecstasy."[64]

The discussion and reconsideration of love from new viewpoints was as central to Briusov's work as to Przybyszewski's. From the appearance of his first book of poems, *Chefs d'oeuvres* (1895), Briusov had been noted—and often abused—for his treatment of love and passion. He strongly believed that experience of intense passion was the *sine qua non* for an artist who would penetrate the soul's depths. Yet in a December 1902 letter to Liudmila Vilkina he confessed to what he considered his greatest failure: "No, I really do not know passion—blinding, frenzied. I cannot enter its domain. I only stand at its heavy gates. . . . Fate has refused me her best gift—the bliss of suffering!"[65]

But Briusov continued to ponder the subject. In the August 1904 (no. 8) number of *Libra* he published an essay entitled "Passion" ("Strast'"), which might be seen as a companion piece and answer to Przybyszewski's recently published foreword to *Sons of Earth*. "Passion" opens by defending the new art's alleged "immorality." Its free treatment of sexuality and the physical generally was, Briusov maintained, a celebration of the equal rights of body and spirit. Pointing to the Hellenistic roots of this new attitude, Briusov noted that the modern cult of physical passion is merely the full recognition of rights suppressed during twenty centuries of European civilization. For this he credited Nietzsche and, independently, the new French Symbolists (and in Russia Merezhkovsky). But there is, he asserted, another cult yet more effective in elevating passion to its preeminence: the cult of mystery. Moderns have learned again to see beneath the surfaces of immediate realities: "Our art is again becoming a key to the mysteries." Here Briusov refined Przybyszewski's notions by drawing a distinction between love and passion:

Passion is first of all a mystery. Love is a feeling on the level of other feelings, elevated or low. . . . Passion does not know its genealogy, it has no likes. . . . Passion in its very essence is a riddle; its roots are outside the world of people, the earthly, our sphere. When passion rules us we are close to those eternal bounds that encompass our "blue prison," our spherical universe swimming in time. Passion is that point where the earthly world touches other spheres of being—always closed, but there is a door.[66]

Besides refining Przybyszewski's concepts, Briusov obviously intended a shift of emphasis in two respects. One concerned the place of art in their respective schemes. For Przybyszewski "Love and the striving toward something better, higher" is an artist's best inspiration and the subject of all his own work.[67] In Briusov's analysis art seems to play a more active exploratory role. Passion is a phenomenon of another order than what surrounds us and cannot be fully embodied in earthly forms. It is a mystery that, moreover, pierces the boundary of our world. Yet art, Symbolist art, can catch a glimpse of passion's real visage and thus open a door out of the "blue prison." By entering into the earthly, physical sphere of passion, it would seem, art is able briefly to lift the veil from the mystery.

Briusov's second difference with Przybyszewski was a fundamental one: he rejected the utopian feature of the latter's vision.
Przybyszewski wrote constantly about the state of perfection that
humanity strives for. The total reunion of the two sexes in androgynous unity is a problematic outcome, as he showed in *Totenmesse*. However, it is presented in radiant terms as a goal worth
striving and suffering for. On the other hand, Briusov's negative
view toward any utopianism is derivable from his writings, early
and late.[68]

This attitude was already articulated in his diary, in essays,
and in poetry, particularly beginning with the collection *Tertia
Vigilia* (1901).[69] In a poem dedicated to Zinaida Gippius, only
partly intended to provoke the recipient, he wrote:

> For a long time I have not believed
> In unshakable truth,
> And all seas, all harbors
> I love equally.[70]

His art gave him the freedom to explore the endless secrets of
a universe without limits. To his friend Mikhail Samygin he had
written as early as 1899: "I have been amused by our striving for
a unity of forces or principles or truth. My dream has always been
the pantheon, the temple of all gods."[71] In the essay "Truths"
("Istiny," 1901) he wrote: "Thought is the eternal Wandering
Jew. It cannot be stopped, its path can have no goal because the
path is itself the goal."[72] Belief in any final state of perfection was
fundamentally contrary to his worldview, which was premised on
an endless array of paths open to the adventurous spirit. Art is
"the way out," and outside the "blue prison" the possibilities are
infinite.

Before 1904 Briusov showed no obvious interest in Przybyszewski.[73] Yet the latter's burgeoning popularity in Russia and
Scorpio's own project of publishing his works made certain of
Briusov's acquaintance with those works. Moreover, in many
ways their concerns intersected. In "Passion" Briusov may well
have been asserting his own position before a competitor. Indeed, retrospectively this essay should be regarded as the first

hint of Briusov's polemic with Przybyszewski—a polemic that developed in the course of his relationship with Nina Petrovskaia and reached a climax in *The Fiery Angel*.[74] For the time, however, he may have suspended his skepticism in the face of her persuasion and his own desire to explore a path hitherto closed to him.

The reminiscences of both Briusov and Petrovskaia after their Saima sojourn hint at attempts then and over the previous months at a rather literal enactment of the Przybyszewskian mysteries. It will be remembered that Petrovskaia later called *Homo Sapiens* a "new moral testament." This trilogy presented the history of the Decadent Falk, a tragically superior being, driven by sexual fatality to destroy one woman, abandon others, cause the suicide of a friend, and stalk onward alone, carrying his torment with him. That torment resulted, as one critic put it, from the inability "to dissolve totally in the loved being, to unite oneself with it so as to re-create this being in its primitive unity, the Androgyne."[75]

In Decadent literature, death looms large. This is especially so when the subject is man's quest for the androgyne. European Decadence's obsession with suicide and death was partly derived from romanticism, but developed its own peculiar character. Sometimes death was seen as a total rejection of existence, sometimes as the ultimate ecstasy, sometimes as the prelude to some species of transformation. Przybyszewski's work suggested the second and third possibilities. At the peak of her love affair with Briusov, Nina Petrovskaia seems to have considered all three:

In January of that year [1905] such an unbearable sadness came over my heart that I decided to die. . . .
    He . . . asked:
    —Will you find a second revolver? I don't have one. . . .
    —And why a second one?
    —Have you forgotten about me? . . .
    —You want to die? You... you? Why?
    He said:
    —Because I love you.[76]

In the language of Decadence Petrovskaia recalled how in those days "he thirsted to be intoxicated with the instant of ecstatic death."[77]

In a letter to her later that summer of 1905 Briusov relived the extreme happiness, the "madness" (*bezumie*) of that time "when death came so near."[78] What was there in the stern *maître*, the efficient manager of publishing enterprises, that permitted such sentiments? Petrovskaia answered from the vantage point of later years:

The striving toward something unheard of, impossible on this earth, the sadness of a soul that longed to tear itself not only from all the established norms of life, but also from the arithmetically exact perceptions of the five senses—from all that constituted his "severe mask" for three-quarters of his life: this he carried within himself always.[79]

That inner striving was usually well hidden, except in his poetry. But she offered him one of the "keys to the mysteries." To be sure, her formula differed from his own. Embedded in her recollections is a quite specific reference to the androgynous "mystery" that Przybyszewski offered as the ultimate, if uncertain, fulfillment. Many years later, Petrovskaia could still think of their relationship as that of two lovers sharing one soul. "What did Valery Briusov find in me. . . ?" she asked. "In me he sensed the organic kinship of my soul with one half of his own, with that—'mystery' that those around him did not know, with that part of himself that he loved and, more often, fiercely hated."[80]

The work that seems to have crystallized Przybyszewski's message for Petrovskaia was *Androgyne* (1900), which appeared in Russian in 1905 as *In the Hour of the Miracle* (*V chas chuda*), with its concluding section called "The City of Death" ("Gorod smerti").[81] The plot is slight. A concert pianist is presented with a huge bouquet at the end of a performance. He has only a fleeting impression of the young woman who presented it, but, seemingly under the influence of the flowers' intoxicating scents, he is haunted by her face and becomes obsessed with finding her. Varied visions feature in his obsession. Thoughts of the fresh fields of his home are replaced by much less innocent sensations:

the erotic, snakelike flowers twine before him; he is a king who commands the beauties of his kingdom; he is a magician who summons up Astarte, mother of love, daughter of Satan. Dreams, drugs, fever, hallucination take over his existence. He glimpses her on the street, only to lose her again after their eyes have met. In a terrible dream he finds himself in a hall where the sought-for face appears many times multiplied, wearing all the visages of love from innocent tenderness through sadness and pain to devilish laughter and debauch. He sees her crucified to the wall in all her hellish beauty, but this vision is followed by angelic consolation. Awakening in fever, in a sudden access of hatred he orders her crucified and dreams of watching her tortures. Finding her again in the street, he tells of his love—and his hatred. At last she comes to him: the "hour of miracle" is accomplished. But in the morning she is gone.

During his mad search for her, he comes to realize that she is within him. He then understands that they must await their reunion in the "city of death," where an even greater "miracle" will occur. At last, in the "city of death"—a ghostly Moorish city bereft of human life—she comes to lead him to a realm of unimaginable wonder. Is it death? Is she a ghost? a vampire? a part of himself? "He and she must unite in one bosom so as to merge into one flame, into one holy sun. There the miracle will be accomplished—the great unearthly miracle. . . . He is She. Androgyne!"[82] She summons; he responds: "I am coming!" (*Idu!*)

Przybyszewski's hero (be it noted, a famous artist) undergoes months of ecstasy and torture before the "miracle" is revealed to him. The sometimes wraithlike female figure is the instrument of revelation. She comes to him at first mysteriously, unexpectedly, a young admirer paying homage to his art. She then leads him through tortuous nights and days of passion, joy, and suffering. Finally in the wondrous "city of death" he understands the "miracle": total, inseparable union of two lovers in one soul. This marvelous life-transformation was to be the reward for those who believed and persevered.

For Petrovskaia this Przybyszewskian path was almost certainly the goal of the experiment at Saima. But, however exhilarating, it was an experiment that Briusov could not sustain. Later that summer he warned her of the ephemerality of that stage of their love. But he promised a new, more permanent stage now to begin. If only she would believe "that love is not always madness, and madness is not always love!"[83] Nina argued energetically against this view. On July 3 she wrote: "You speak of 'descent,' the summit is past, . . . I do not feel this. . . . No, believe it, dearest, this is no descent, *this is the beginning*." Of what? Her letter the following day gives the answer in unmistakable Przybyszewskian terms: "Believe in the miracle!"[84]

But Briusov rejected the improbable program she offered, as he rejected any final translation to a perfect state: for him there was always "more." Over the next months and years it grew painfully clear that whatever revelation came at Saima reached them with deeply divergent meanings and consequently different implications for their future separately and together. For him, sexual passion was *one* of the keys to the mysteries, but there were others that he pursued with new energy, and he invited her to share them. If she could only see the clarity of his horizons, feel his thirst to breathe, work, be alive, he wrote on August 29. If only she would consent to go forward with him. "In my soul there are no more answers to what you again are seeking." Instead he offers "what I am now: without madness, with a stubborn, unquenchable thirst to work, but with undying love for you."[85]

However, a few months later, Briusov fell into the depression that regularly followed his completion of a book of poems. (*Stephanos* came out at the end of 1905.) He found himself searching with increasing desperation for a new stimulus, a new direction.[86] However much Przybyszewski may have seemed to offer at one time, Briusov's own model of constant quest required him to move on now, despite Petrovskaia's relentless insistence on continued adherence. In June 1906 he wrote to her: "I cannot go on living by outworn religions, those ideals that I have moved beyond. I can no longer live by 'Decadence' and 'Nietzschean-ism,' in which I believe, believe."[87] This last paradoxical assertion suggests that indeed Briusov was torn. But his own deep fear of stopping on the road, of having nothing new to say that would justify continuing to write poetry, pushed him forward. "There are truths of some kind—beyond Nietzsche, beyond Przybyszewski, beyond Verhaeren, ahead for mankind. Whoever will show me the road to them, I will be with him."[88]

In the meantime *Stephanos* was acclaimed by Symbolists and others, with the notable exception of Nina Petrovskaia, who, according to Briusov's reproach, never bothered to read it. He wrote bitterly to her of this lapse: "That was a cruel blow for me. You don't know how many threads between your soul and mine you broke then."[89] The reasons for this pointed neglect are extremely significant for understanding the clash of perceptions and models operating in that highly charged relationship.

In spurning *Stephanos*, Petrovskaia seemed to spurn the very poems that embodied Briusov's experience at Saima. Upon close examination, some of these reveal his subversive interpretation of what happened there. But probably even more important in understanding this is the structure of the book itself. Briusov was the first of the Symbolists to employ the full structure of a book of poems to convey meaning. He made the method explicit in the foreword to *Urbi et Orbi* (1903): "A book of poems must be, not a random *collection* of poems of various sorts, but exactly a *book*, an enclosed whole united by a single idea."[90] With this in mind Petrovskaia presumably would have scanned *Stephanos* for some testimonial to the doctrine she had so tried to inculcate in Briusov at Saima. In this she would have been gravely disappointed.

The first edition of *Stephanos* contained five lyric sections and four longer poems.[91] The first three sections, "Evening Songs" ("Vecherovye pesni"), "The Idols' Eternal Truth" ("Pravda vechnaia kumirov"), and "From Hell Delivered" ("Iz ada izvedennye"), followed the history and progress of the romance. Following lyrical recollections of Saima and Finland, the next two sections have clearly biographical elements. In the second of these, several poems that refer to the Briusov-Petrovskaia-Bely triangle employ a favorite Briusov device: embodying contemporary emotions in antique images. The most memorable of these poems—and one of Briusov's finest—is perhaps "Orpheus and

Eurydice" ("Orfei i Evridika"). Here Bely, the "Orpheus" of the Argonauts, might see reflected his efforts to save Nina from "Hades."[92] But the section's closing poem, "Orpheus and the Argonauts" ("Orfei i argonavty"), shows the hero-poet in another relation: now free of encumbrances, he is called to take up his lyre again among his fellow heroes. This might refer equally to Bely and Briusov.

However, the centerpiece of the book, the section in which Petrovskaia is featured, is "From Hell Delivered." Here are seventeen numbered pieces. The epigraph, "from an Assyrian epic," describes the descent into hell of the goddess Istar (Astarte) to lead forth souls "so that they may again eat and live."[93] Some poems included were written earlier and some after the return from Saima, but the section, while clearly assembled to focus on Petrovskaia herself and their relationship, was obviously also designed to place these in a larger context. The opening poem, "At Noon" ("V polden'"), already signals as much.

"At Noon" was first written in 1903 as a farewell to youth and a resignation of higher hopes. Briusov revised it to suit his new mood, celebrating the "miracle" of "flaming noon," when the soul's hidden dreams come to light, the vault of heaven is expanded by love, and it is granted to him to "tremble over measureless expanses on the wings of passion."[94] Yet he will inevitably fall into the abyss below, from where, unable to rise again, with his whole being he will drink in the heights. It is, in short, a poetic statement of his warning to Petrovskaia that the peak was past, the "miracle" short-lived.

She could not have quarreled with the three portraits of her that followed. "Portrait" ("Portret"), describing a spiritual waif, corresponds very much to her own recollections. The two pieces entitled "To the Moon Priestess" ("Zhritse luny") cast her in an unearthly light, in league with Astarte and Hecate. Then comes a series of lyrics about passion, several of which greatly augmented Briusov's reputation for mingling soft pornography and sacrilegious imagery.[95] "In the Torture Chamber" ("V zastenke") most strongly evokes Przybyszewski's *Androgyne*, with sadism, masochism, and a hint of incest that is not quite androgyny.[96] Briusov's

previous poetry was not innocent of these themes, but the con-
catenation here is new. At the center of the section is a diptych:
two of Briusov's best known poems, "Antony" and "Cleopatra,"
raise the twin themes of passion and suicide to the universal
plane of "The Idols' Eternal Truth."

Yet nowhere is the Przybyszewskian formula proposed. Love,
passion, torture, suffering, even death are in no way presented
as the path to the higher synthesis, the androgyne. Briusov has
retained his own vision. Passion has allowed a glimpse beyond
the earthly, but it has not translated its votaries to another state
of being. Throughout these poems are hints of unearthly visions:
there is startling Christian religious imagery, as well as Astarte
and Hecate. But the treasured vision thus attained is not transformed life, but art.

In the section's final poem, "Marguerite" ("Margerit"), all that
has preceded is suddenly and pointedly transfigured into "art."
The medieval conceit by which this is done involves several transformations: "You are like the pearl. . . . I am like the coal" that
burns out, leaving a diamond. The "pearl" becomes *The Pearl*,
St. John Chrysostom's work of wisdom, a precious book of "mysteries," on the binding of which, in a gold setting, gleams the
diamond.

> I am the coal, you the pearl.
> But my transformed visage
> Glows before your soul![97]

The proximate source for the "coal-into-diamond" image of aesthetic transformation is of course Vladimir Solov'ev's "Beauty in
Nature" ("Krasota v prirode," 1889), but Viacheslav Ivanov's en-
thusiastic use of the same imagery may have influenced Briusov.
(See Irina Paperno's essay in this volume.)

The book's two remaining sections, "The Everyday" ("Povsed-
nevnost'") and "The Present" ("Sovremennost'"), emphasized
Briusov's energetic return to outward life, in particular to public
events of 1905. Given this fact, the concluding poem (in the first
edition) is unexpected: it is an adaptation from Tennyson entitled "From the Songs of Maeldune" ("Iz pesen Mal'duna"). But

its theme reminds one of Tennyson's "Ulysses" (1833), in which the hero urges his men never to rest but always to seek, always to dare. Briusov's Maeldune exhorts:

> Enough! Happiness has been tasted!
> The empty goblet is overturned.
> Sweeter than the trembling of passion,
> The free waves rush upon us.[98]

It is, then, not surprising that Petrovskaia rejected *Stephanos*—the book whose foreword was concerned only with the fate of its private songs in a time of public turmoil, the book that was dedicated "To Viacheslav Ivanov, poet, thinker, friend."

The next few years saw constant and increasing tension between Briusov and Nina Petrovskaia. Still locked in a close relationship that neither wished to break, each tried to win the other to a life strategy based on one of the conflicting life-and-art models put into play at Saima. For a time Petrovskaia spread her gospel in the journals *The Golden Fleece* (*Zolotoe Runo*) and *The Crossing* (*Pereval*), where, in reviews of new Scorpio volumes, she told her readers: "All of Przybyszewski's creative work is the presentiment of future revolutions in the sphere of the human spirit."[99]

Writing for the section "Moscow Theatrical Life" in *The Golden Fleece*, Petrovskaia also had occasion to review productions of Przybyszewski's plays, then popular in Moscow and Petersburg. She used her review of *For Happiness* (*Dlia schast'ia*, trans. 1904) both to reassert some central tenets of her faith and to present Briusov publicly with a life-model in art. Happiness, she wrote, cannot be achieved until "the soul in its entirety, in the orgiastic joy of suffering, throws itself onto the bonfire," from which it will arise like the phoenix. However, "they are not to know this mystery, this miracle, they who are perishing in the contradiction of feeling and duty: they who are poisoned by pity, which is worse than death for those to whom they give it as a precious gift."[100]

The drama's plot is simple. Four characters are fatally intertwined in a circle of love and torture. One of the women, Olga, is "the eternal image of the love that the world has not accepted."

All is possible, she tells her lover, Mlicki, if only one loves. Elena, the woman Mlicki has deserted for Olga, is a mediocrity who, according to Petrovskaia, cannot know "the bliss of crucifixion, of passionate-submissive torture in the name of Love."[101] Mlicki and Olga might have lived in each other, but he, poisoned by the past, is unable to sustain their happiness. In Petrovskaia's plot summary, she herself is clearly identified with Olga, and Elena stands for Briusov's wife, Ioanna Matveevna. The strictures against those who let a false sense of duty stand in the way of happiness were a rebuke to Briusov that many readers would understand.

In 1908 Nina Petrovskaia published some creative work of her own: a collection of stories entitled *Sanctus Amor*.[102] These stories, like her reviews, were conceived to blazon forth Przybyszewski's teachings on love and were addressed to Briusov. Three are cautionary tales about a pusillanimous man who deserts the great mysterious love of his life and returns to a commonplace wife.[103] His fate is bitter despair and personal diminution. Other stories, less specifically referential, nonetheless all feature the mysterious love that comes but rarely and is even more rarely recognized for the treasure it is. The style and diction are reminiscent of Przybyszewski's poems in prose. Characters have no names, and settings are impressionistic, though sometimes suggesting a northern landscape. The first-person narrator is always masculine, but the bearer of the mystery is feminine. The story "Vagabond" ("Brodiaga") serves as keystone.[104] "He" has often seen "her" with her husband in society. On one occasion her sadness prompts him to ask: "What are you thinking of?" The answer of course is "Love." When she comes to him, he feels something new and alarming entering his room: "the mystery of a strange, unknown soul." To his questions she responds: "I am a vagabond—I roam from soul to soul, always seeking a meeting with the love that I see only in dream." And what is this love?

My love is what they call "madness." It is unfathomable joy and eternal suffering. When it comes, like a fiery whirlwind it sweeps away all that is called "life." In it are drowned all the small, calculating, cowardly things with which we destroy our days. Then the most insignificant person becomes a god and will understand forever the great unknown word "boundlessness."

This tale, unlike most of the other stories, has two characters who seem well matched. He responds: "That love of which you speak is a miracle, and I feel that it has already touched my soul."[105] However, he makes a misstep: he proposes marriage. In many well-chosen words she pictures a comfortable relationship declining into habit and tedium. They part apparently forever, but this Love remains their shared possession: not yet the ideal, but still potentially so.

The Fiery Angel, or at least the character of Renata, was as greatly to Petrovskaia's taste as *Stephanos* was alien. She gloried in her role and watched intently as the character of Renata took shape.[106] Living and traveling abroad in the summer of 1908, she wrote to Briusov from Italy: "I wish to die . . . so that you will copy Renata's death from me, so as to be the model of the splendid last chapter."[107] A few months later she described to him her visit to Cologne, where she lay on the cathedral floor "like that Renata whom you created and later forgot and ceased to love" and where she "relived all our life minute by minute."[108] Briusov's Renata had become her true identity. Sometime during or just after the First World War, years she spent in Rome, Petrovskaia became a Catholic. She wrote to Khodasevich: "My new and secret name, written somewhere in the unerasable scrolls of St. Peter's is— Renata."[109]

Much as she admired and delighted in *The Fiery Angel*, Petrovskaia could hardly have overlooked its covert polemic with the Przybyszewskian vision. Yet if she chose to see the unhappy, bewitched, and bewitching Renata as a tribute, the novel gave ample grounds. From the moment when the stalwart but somewhat stolid and pedantic soldier of fortune Ruprekht finds Renata in a state of diabolic possession, he is lifted to another plane. This is a woman such as he had "read about only in books," if that. The Latin dedication to his history (translated by Briusov) pays tribute to this fact, as well as to the heroine: "Not to any of the famous people lauded in the arts and sciences, but to you, radiant, mad, unhappy woman, who loved much and per-ished from love, the author, as humble servant and true lover, dedicates this true narrative."[110] Renata's ecstatic but ambiguous death, which obviated her sentence to burning, takes place in his arms. But thereafter, much as he has suffered with and from her, Ruprekht is able to gather his wits and make his escape. In his closing paragraph, while swearing his unconquerable love for Renata, Ruprekht wonders whether, given the choice, he would relive the experience. Perhaps he would. "But with strict certainty I can here swear, before my conscience, never again to give myself so blasphemously . . . into the power of one of God's creatures, no matter in how tempting a form that creature appears."[111] Ruprekht now has other business, in the New World, where further discoveries await.

The correspondence of Petrovskaia and Briusov in the years between Saima and her final departure from Russia, in 1911, is filled with complaints and misunderstandings on both sides. In her letters she now rebuked, now challenged Briusov in language very like that in her published writings. As S. S. Grechishkin and A. V. Lavrov describe it, the style of her stories is so close to that of her letters that her book without exaggeration can be called a fictionalized diary.[112]

Briusov's letters form a saga in themselves. A thread running through them leads directly from Saima to the final admission that their two different life models could not coexist. In his letter of June 10, 1906, he laid out some bones of contention between them, several of which seem derived from her cult of Przybyszewski: her uninterest in his current artistic concerns, her disdain for literary artistry and her overemphasis on the artist's idea, her maneuvers to bring all conversations back to the subject of their love.[113] Some two years later he made his position abundantly clear: the experiment is over, finally and definitively. He cannot offer her the kind of love she requires. Instead he offers something higher: "the divine closeness of two souls, similar and separate, united and distinct, blended in one and *forever unfused*" (emphasis mine).[114] No clearer rejection of the Przybyszewskian androgyne could be imagined. A short time later he dismissed another of her earlier Przybyszewskian inspirations. Trying earnestly to persuade Petrovskaia to rethink her future, he wrote: death, murder—all that is in the past. The browning revolver from "our famous days" is now only a symbol. The question now is "how to live." [115]

Petrovskaia came reluctantly to admit that she had two enemies within Briusov: his need to retain his domestic ties (no matter how he abused them) and his single-hearted devotion to his art. The former she treated with scorn, the latter with grudging admiration. In key with the milieu in which they functioned, she conceived of the struggle between herself and him as a clash of worldviews: her Przybyszewskian erotic-androgynous utopia against his life-expanding, nonutopian vision in which art played the central role. Much later, when her Przybyszewskian faith was no longer in evidence, she still protested what she saw as his total sacrifice of all the human elements in his life to art. And to the very end she believed that Briusov had taken the lesser way, refusing to fulfill his spiritual potential. For she remembered him always as a man of "bottomless spiritual depths." [116]

Vladimir Solov'ev's erotic utopia, developed in "The Meaning of Love," with its patently religious base, inspired theory and practice in what may be called high Symbolist culture. The models of love derived from Solov'ev are reviewed in Olga Matich's essay in this volume. Przybyszewski's was yet another manifestation of that ethos, though including other sources. But, though his writings were known, read, even translated in the "higher culture," the aura of Decadence surrounding both the man and his works seemingly disqualified his utopian model from serious consideration there. Moreover, that model was less intellectually coherent and fastidious than Solov'ev's. Both philosophies offered the androgyne as the ultimate goal of mankind, but Przybyszewski stressed the dark side of the road of attainment, which is "love." As he explained in his foreword to *Sons of Earth*, love "is the unrestrainable striving . . . toward the full merging of the two sexes so that the human race may be ennobled and reach Perfection." But the goal and the means, he warned, are in painful contradiction: "In the name of that love and that striving toward Perfection, man suffers, labors, torments himself, struggles, kills, and the result of this is progress and the perfection of the human race."[117] This dark and tortuous way is the only route, and in fact the ultimate cleansing, transforming step requires a miracle.

Przybyszewski's critics called his writings an invitation to unbridled indulgence and vice. Others, presumably like Nina Petrovskaia, found his words to correspond to their life experience and grasped at the glimmer of hope they found there. Thus in the more broadly based culture where Symbolism and Decadence mingled, and where Nina Petrovskaia, for all her aspirations, had her place, the Przybyszewski variant was not only acceptable but welcome. In many ways Petrovskaia was an "average" member of the culture, of modest talents and undistinguished attainments, but thoroughly *au courant* and fashionably notorious. In other ways—in intensity, in commitment, in honesty, in tenacity—she was clearly exceptional. She went to unbelievable extremes, yet she was "typical." Przybyszewski offered to such individuals both solace and a sense of participation in the higher strivings of their culture. That she played a woman's role in the Symbolist milieu is no doubt significant.

Briusov's position in high Symbolist culture was always marked by ambiguity. His early relations with both Bely and Blok featured a misunderstanding of his artistic and philosophical position and a tendency on Blok's part, at least, to seek parallels between Briusov and Solov'ev that led to unwarranted conclusions.[118] Blok saw both as seers privy to secrets of the contemporary soul and bearers of new visions. He and Bely soon looked to Briusov to assume leadership of Symbolism in the theurgic direction inspired by Solov'ev's ideas. Briusov assiduously corrected what he saw as a misconception. Moreover, he insisted on the freedom of art from ideological commitment. Ultimately these issues converged in the "crisis of Symbolism" debate in 1910.[119]

However, the fundamental disagreement that has always been discernible between Briusov and the other major Symbolists may come down to the question of utopia. The mystical belief in life-creation and life-transformation that was central to the main branch of Symbolist culture was totally alien to Briusov. This was so not because, as is sometimes thought, mysticism itself was alien to him: his veneration for art might indeed be called mystical. Thus he resented and rejected the notion put forward by Bely and Viacheslav Ivanov that art, once its transforming task was completed, will disappear into a life that has become art. As Briusov viewed it, art is no mere instrument but a cosmic reality. It is the eternal and ever expanding universe refracted in the soul of the artist and embodied—incarnated—in his medium. As Irina Paperno notes in her essay, the principle of incarnation that, in its mystical sense, was for Bely the foundation of Symbolist art was for Briusov devoid of theological connotations. The eschatological dimension had no place in his vision. If the universe—spiritual, physical, moral—eternally unfolds, so must art. Neither it nor the artist, whose soul must at every instant be open to its messages, may submit to closure. The notion of utopia is incompatible with such a vision.

But the utopian vision was fundamental to the followers of Solov'ev. It also was fundamental to the beliefs of those who saw in Przybyszewski more than sensationalism. Nina Petrovskaia was clearly one of the latter, though she had earlier tried to join the former. The experiment on Lake Saima may have failed not only because of two unsuited temperaments but finally because of two clashing life-models based in two fundamentally opposed visions of reality.

Six

Viacheslav Ivanov: From Aesthetic
Theory to Biographical Practice

MICHAEL WACHTEL

Viacheslav Ivanov occupies a secure place in Russian literary history as the leading theoretician of the Symbolist movement. This reputation, while undoubtedly justified, has led to a one-sided reception of his work. Ivanov's theoretical essays have continually attracted critical attention while his poetry has been accorded a secondary position. Biographical materials (diaries, letters, etc.) constitute the most neglected area of Ivanov's legacy. Many scholars appear to share a tacit assumption that personal documents contribute little toward understanding such a "cerebral" figure. Yet, in the Symbolist context, all facets of a writer's life have relevance to his work. Ivanov's biographical writings, no exception in this regard, are fundamentally linked to both his theoretical work and his poetry.

The dearth of studies that integrate Ivanov's life and work in a meaningful way can be partially attributed to a paucity of sources.[1] The vast majority of Ivanov's personal writings remain unpublished and inaccessible. The present emphasis, on a single period in Ivanov's life (1907–10), has been dictated in part by the availability of a number of "personal" documents from these years. Yet this pragmatic reason alone neither explains nor jus-

tifies the emphasis. The period under consideration marked the
height of Ivanov's fascination with *zhiznetvorchestvo*, the Symbolist longing to fuse life and literature. These years also coincide
with the ideological culmination of the entire Symbolist movement. Afterwards, the so-called "crisis of Symbolism" hastened
the disintegration of the movement as such.

Between 1907 and 1910, Ivanov produced two major theoretical essays, "Two Elements in Contemporary Symbolism" ("Dve
stikhii v sovremennom simvolizme," 1908) and "The Testaments
of Symbolism" ("Zavety simvolizma," 1910). Originally written
as lectures, they can be considered belated manifestos, intended
to clarify basic Symbolist positions. In the retrospective "Testaments of Symbolism," Ivanov declared: "[Russian] Symbolism did
not want to be and could not be 'only art.'"[2] This terse statement
expressed a central tenet of Symbolist thought: the insufficiency
of aesthetics. According to Ivanov, art was inextricably linked to
all aspects of human endeavor. Symbolism should therefore seek
to transcend the merely aesthetic and act upon life itself.[3] Such
a goal not only claimed for the artist a position of utmost promi-
nence and even responsibility but also necessitated a redefinition
of traditional notions of art.

Ivanov was by no means the first to make such grandiose
claims for Symbolism. However, he went further than most of
his coevals in offering a consistent philosophical grounding for
his slogans. Following Vladimir Solov'ev, he embraced the notion
of "theurgy," which called upon the artist to "re-create existing
reality" (*peresozdat' sushchestvuiushchuiu deistvitel'nost'*).[4] "Theurgic art" had radical implications, yet Ivanov, in the theoretical
writings, kept his discussion within carefully defined parameters.
In "Two Elements in Contemporary Symbolism," he offered his
strictest delineation of this concept: "We think that the theurgic
principle in art is the principle of the least force and the most
receptivity. The highest testament of the artist is not to impose
his own will on the surface of things, but to see through and
spread the word of the secret will of essences."[5] Ivanov stressed
the necessity of transformation, but only in response to a certain
transcendental imperative. Indeed, Ivanov's entire philosophical

system was predicated on the existence of an omnipresent objective truth. By demanding that the artist recognize this truth and change the world accordingly, Ivanov left no room for the subjective will of the individual artist.

Ivanov's theurgy was thus not as radical as it may at first appear. It was essentially a theory of discovery, not invention.[6] Condemning subjectivity (which he called "idealism"), he praised instead a "fidelity to things" (in his own terminology, "realism"). Since divine will cannot ordinarily be verified empirically, Ivanov attributed to the artist special abilities of perception. He accepted the possibility of mystical experience and coined the term "mystical realism" to designate (approvingly) this basic creative impulse.[7]

On a theoretical level, these ideas are consistent and understandable (once the reader accustoms himself to Ivanov's penchant for creating idiosyncratic terminology).[8] Yet Ivanov did not conceive of his work as being purely theoretical. In addition to elaborating a philosophical system, he sought to offer practical guidelines. In "The Testaments of Symbolism," he discussed the "thesis" of Russian Symbolism, emphasizing the necessity for theory *and* practice: "Artists were confronted with the problem of completely incarnating in their life as well as in their work (absolutely in the 'agon' of life as in the 'agon' of work!) the worldview of 'mystical realism' or (according to Novalis) the worldview of 'magical idealism.'"[9]

This account of Symbolism rests on two important propositions. The first maintains the inseparability of life and work (in a word, *zhiznetvorchestvo*). The second equates "mystical realism" (Ivanov's own term) with "magical idealism" (Novalis's celebrated formulation). It is worth considering why the name Novalis appears in a crucial passage about Russian Symbolism. For Ivanov, the phrase "magical idealism" was synonymous with the entirety of Novalis's thought.[10] In a lecture of 1909, Ivanov stated: "*Novalis* is that *living [element]* which ties us to Romanticism. . . . He calls his worldview *magical idealism*. His ideal is a *theurgic ideal*."[11] By defining "magical idealism" in terms of theurgy, Ivanov identifies Novalis as a proto-Symbolist.

To understand Ivanov's fascination with Novalis, another factor must be considered: biography. Like the Symbolists, the
romantics strongly believed in the indivisibility of life and art.
For more than a century after Novalis's death, numerous "biog-
raphers" consciously transformed his life into myth. The central
role in these life-dramas was played by Novalis's fiancée, Sophie
von Kühn,[12] whose early death inspired his greatest poetry
("Hymns to the Night") and, putatively, his death (from grief).[13]
Such an account, possessing an undeniable appeal to the reading
public, glossed over several significant facts. To name only the
most salient: Novalis became engaged to another woman after
Sophie had passed away. The marriage to this second woman
never took place because of Novalis's own death (of tuberculo-
sis, not grief). Such details lessened the romantic effect of the
Novalis legend and were therefore played down or completely
ignored.[14] In Ivanov's time these mystifications still represented
the reigning tendency in scholarship.

Ivanov, who suffered the unexpected death of his own beloved
(his second wife, Lidiia Dmitrievna Zinov'eva-Annibal) in October 1907, was clearly attracted by the image of a poet devastated
by the death of his great love. It is noteworthy that the first explicit references to Novalis in Ivanov's work occur in 1908 ("Two
Elements"). In 1909, Ivanov's fascination led him to translate
Novalis's entire significant poetic output. In a lecture he gave
shortly afterwards, Ivanov summarized Novalis's biography, repeating the traditional legend: "After the death of his fiancée he
spent the remainder of his life in grief for her and in the joy
of meetings, when it seemed to him that she was with him."[15]
Whether Ivanov was aware of the inaccuracy of this statement
is of little consequence.[16] What is crucial is the fact that this description of Novalis's existence after Sophie's death accurately
depicts Ivanov's own state in 1909.

In the years that followed Lidiia's death, Ivanov went through
a prolonged period of grief. During this time, his literary output
consisted of programmatic and theoretical essays, two books of
poetry—*Love and Death* (*Liubov' i smert*) and *Rosarium*, which were
eventually published as the second part of *Cor Ardens* (1912)—

and the Novalis translations. In addition, Ivanov produced a number of curious biographical writings. These include diaries, which he kept intermittently; many short and mysterious jottings (mostly written in Latin and addressed to Lidiia); and letters to the mystic Anna Rudolfovna Mintslova (which have survived only in fragmentary form). In all of these writings (with the partial exception of the essays), Ivanov's energies were directed toward a single goal: reunification with Lidiia. The notion of theurgy, so carefully elaborated in the essays, becomes central not only in the poetry, but also in the biographical writings. The miserable state of Ivanov's own existence, as it were, forced him to try his hand at *zhiznetvorchestvo*.

The contrast between literary and biographical writings requires explanation. For present purposes, one central distinction should be considered: "literary" texts are produced for publication, while their "biographical" counterparts are intended for a select audience or, conceivably, for no one except the author himself. In terms of style and artistic organization, these two types of texts can be remarkably similar. Like the Symbolists in general, Ivanov actively sought to dissolve the dividing line between personal and public genres. Victor Zhirmunsky's description of German romanticism is in this respect entirely applicable to Russian Symbolism:

The letters of the Romantic poets bear a remarkable resemblance to their creative works. Not only because their works are characterized by psychological naturalism and not simply because these poets wish their works to be a poetic diary of their experiences, but also because in their letters, experience is already stylized in accordance with a literary model. Life and poetry come together; the poet's life resembles his verses.[17]

Ivanov's biographical writings, like the romantics' letters, rely on the same principles as the author's published work.

Before examining biographical writings from the period immediately after Lidiia's death, it will be helpful to turn to a work Ivanov wrote many years later about this period. Though the piece was originally part of a letter of 1939, Ivanov himself chose to publish it as a separate essay in 1946 under the title "An Echo" ("Ein Echo").[18]

It was about thirty years ago: some stars had just become visible on the twilight sky when we sailed out of a mountain ravine onto the coastline of the Black Sea. There I perceived, amidst the chatter of my travel companions, like a soft summons from my hidden tranquility—or was it a spiritual echo of the distant sound of the waves?—some Latin words, so unexpected that I at first could not grasp their meaning. Yet they became all the more meaningful after deeper and deeper meditation. Those words, which impressed on me with gentle insistence something that I had somehow thought about earlier, possessed such a clear palpableness that they had on me the effect of newly attained genuine knowledge. "Quod non est debet esse; quod est debet fieri; quod fit erit"—these were the words. ("What is not, should be; what is, should become; what becomes will be.")

True to my habit of shaping rhythmically what moves me deeply, I attempted to mount my secret jewel on the golden ring of a distich:

> Quod non est, Pater esse iubet fierique creatum,
> Spem iusso fieri Spiritus afflat: "eris." [19]

The continuation of this passage (in which Ivanov replaces "being" with "beauty" and analyzes it in terms of Theodor Haecker's aesthetic theory) has no relevance to present concerns. However, the incident itself reveals salient elements of Ivanov's own theurgic ideal as well as his state of mind after Lidiia's death.

The actual experience Ivanov records can be dated to 1908.[20] Taken at face value, the passage illustrates Ivanov's notion of theurgy based on maximum receptivity. The poet, in the midst of a magnificent natural scene, hears a voice apparently inaudible to his companions.[21] This voice expresses in essence the ideal of *zhiznetvorchestvo*—it prophesies change, promising existence for what does not yet exist. Ivanov's activity is limited to giving poetic form to this message (putting the jewel into the appropriate setting, according to the metaphor he supplies). He thus remains true to his own artistic ideal; rather than forcing his subjective will onto nature, he observes and spreads an insight that originates in nature.

To a reader familiar with the larger context of Ivanov's work, the "echo" motif calls forth a number of important associations. Ivanov's first collection of verse, published in 1903, contains a metapoetic poem called "The Alpine Horn" ("Alpiiskii rog"), which concludes with the line, "Blessed is he who hears the song and the echo."[22] This poem serves as the epigraph for a later essay entitled "Thoughts on Symbolism" ("Mysli o simvolizme," 1912), where Ivanov expounds a theory of Symbolist poetry based on his own conception of echo.[23] Ivanov contends that the true poet must force his audience to respond not in unison but in counterpoint: "If my listener is only a mirror, only an echo . . . then I am not a *symbolist* poet."[24] In short, Ivanov conceives of Symbolism as a process through which a poetic impulse inspires a *complementary* echo in the audience.[25]

On first glance, "An Echo" seems simply another variant on this metapoetic theme. Yet a number of elements differentiate it from both "The Alpine Horn" and "Thoughts on Symbolism." The title itself poses an immediate interpretive problem. The "echo" apparently refers to the mysterious Latin phrase that Ivanov overhears, but does it express a transcendent truth or Ivanov's own convictions? In other words, is the echo's source external (the objective truth in which the Symbolists so firmly believed) or internal (the poet's personal credo)? Ivanov himself makes no effort to resolve this ambiguity: the voice was "like a soft summons from my hidden tranquility—*or* was it a spiritual echo of the distant sound of the waves?"[26] One might seek to reconcile these alternatives by invoking Ivanov's beloved concept of "anamnesis," the Platonic doctrine that external knowledge resides "a priori" within every individual. Yet even "anamnesis" cannot explain why the Latin language is required to transmit transcendent truth. If this voice truly originates in a world beyond, why should it speak Latin? Does the transcendent communicate only with those who have had the benefit of a rigorous classical education?[27]

The message itself demands closer scrutiny: "What is not, should be; what is, should become; what becomes will be." *What* is it that "should be"? *Everything* that is not? Should the poet await further instructions before attempting to interpret these cryptic words? Such questions remain unanswered. In turning the statement into a distich, Ivanov creates his own idiosyncratic echo. Although he claims merely to give the voice poetic form, he actually expands considerably on the original. He adds mystical/religious actants ("Pater," "Spiritus") and, in the pentameter line, a new concept: a spirit breathing hope. This image, a representation of "inspiration" in its most direct sense (the word is etymologically derived from the Latin *inspirare*, "to breathe into") evokes a traditional literary topos, absent in the original statement.

There is no need to decide whether Ivanov's experience was a "mystical initiation"[28] or an instance of self-delusion. It is enough to recognize several details that make the scene paradigmatic for Ivanov's life and work in the period after Lidiia's death. First and foremost, "An Echo" assumes the possibility of contact with the transcendent world. Ivanov frequently posited the existence of this world in his theoretical essays; indeed, it forms an essential tenet of Symbolist (and all Neoplatonic) thought. Yet "An Echo" is not written as philosophical hypothesis; it claims to be a record of actual experience (a scene from the "real life" of Viacheslav Ivanov). A second crucial element is the other world's reliance on Latin. Foreign languages, used frequently in Ivanov's writings, often obtain a symbolic function in this period. They signal an epiphany, Ivanov's temporary escape from his immediate (Russian) surroundings.[29] Finally, one should note that the contact with this other world is directly linked to theurgy, the need to create "what is not," or, in other words, to transform what is.

After the death of Lidiia, Ivanov's desire to achieve contact with the world beyond gained special urgency. He was convinced that his wife had become a part of the transcendent world and, therefore, that it should be possible to communicate with her. For expert spiritual guidance in these matters, he turned to Anna Rudolfovna Mintslova. Mintslova, a devotee of occultism, is one of the most enigmatic and eccentric figures of the period.[30] She appears to have lived in a fantasy world of her own creation, touching base with reality only long enough to post letters and telegrams, an activity she performed with the same indefatigable

fanaticism that she brought to her mystical endeavors. Her volu-
minous letters to Ivanov begin before Lidiia's death and continue
until 1910, when she disappeared from Moscow, never to be
seen or heard from again. These letters concern mystical topics and, in the early period, often summarize Rudolf Steiner's
lectures (without acknowledgment). In the years after Lidiia's
death, the letters become more frequent and less coherent. For
example, Mintslova's side of the correspondence from January 1–
22, 1908, covers 99 pages.[31] On January 21, she seems to have
set a personal record by sending Ivanov three letters (notated
as "morning," "afternoon," and "night," respectively) and two
telegrams. The contents as well as the quantity of these writings
offer ample evidence that Mintslova was not entirely sane. Yet
her considerable influence on Ivanov cannot be disputed. Evgeniia Gertsyk, who spent the summer of 1908 with both of them,
testifies to this in her memoirs.[32] Moreover, in a series of letters
to Mintslova, Ivanov addressed her as "dear teacher" (*dorogoi
uchitel'*), and the tone as well as the subject matter was obviously
serious. These fragmentary letters were written over a two-week
span in January, most probably in 1908.[33] They record Ivanov's
efforts, through occult means, to rejoin Lidiia.

The following passage, dated "The night of January 26" and
quoted in its entirety, can be considered representative:

> Breve aevum separatum
> Longum aevum coniugatum
> In honorem Domini
> Quidquid terram est perpessum
> Veniet tua [vi]ta fessum
> In dies sacramini.[34]

Dear teacher, here is a Latin poem in medieval style that I just heard
from Her during midnight prayer, when I conversed with Her, and She
consoled me in separation, responding to my request "Take me" with
the words "I am already taking you"—and I felt that She was filling my
soul with herself and proclaiming "Let it be your will."[35]

It should be emphasized that this letter could not have been
conceived as an elaborate literary hoax. Ivanov never made any

attempt to publish it. On the contrary, its very survival must be considered fortuitous since it was not among the papers Ivanov took with him when he left Russia in 1924. Yet Ivanov reports such unusual "realia" in such a stylized manner that he forces the reader to understand the letter as a literary text (which, strictly speaking, it is not).[36]

For all of its peculiarities, this passage bears an obvious resemblance to the roughly contemporaneous scene described in "An Echo." In one sense, Ivanov appears even more "receptive" in his letter than in the essay. In "An Echo," he heard a Latin statement and gave it verse form. This time Ivanov hears a Latin poem *directly*. (Ever the scholar, he momentarily interrupts his mystical revelation to make a formal observation—that the poem is medieval in style.) Ivanov presumably does not know the speaker of the Latin words in "An Echo." In the letter to Mintslova, however, he immediately recognizes the voice as that of his recently deceased wife. While Ivanov expresses his individual will ("Take me"), his desire appears to be in complete harmony with that of Lidiia (as reflected in her response: "I am already taking you").

Both passages describe contact with a world beyond. "An Echo" takes place at twilight, the border between day and night. The present scene occurs at midnight, traditionally the time of mystical experience.[37] Once again, Latin serves as the medium through which the world beyond communicates.[38] In both cases, the transcendent voice promises to transform reality. Yet there is a crucial difference. While the "echo" expresses a general philosophical statement, Lidiia's words specifically concern Ivanov.

Did Ivanov truly experience an epiphany (theurgy as receptivity), or did he create this vision in accordance with his own needs (theurgy as an expression of subjective will)? Rather than answering this question directly, it will be helpful to turn to Olga Deschartes's description of this same incident:

Once in the winter of 1908, V.I. sat at his desk, busy with his usual work. Suddenly he heard a voice, slowly and clearly pronouncing some Latin words. Without attempting to understand them, he started to write them down. The voice dictated in a monotone, steadily, and then became silent. V.I. read what he had written down:—verses.

BREVE AEVUM SEPARATUM
LONGUM AEVUM CONIUGATUM
IN HONOREM DOMINI
QUISQUIS TERRAM EST PERPESSUS
VENIET TUA VITA FESSUS
IN DIES SACRAMINI.[39]

This version, presumably transmitted by Ivanov himself, contains a number of departures from the original text. Most striking are the omissions: Deschartes mentions neither Mintslova (Ivanov's "dear teacher") nor Lidiia. The substitutions are also noteworthy. Ivanov, no longer conversing with the dead or reciting midnight prayers, is involved in mundane activities, utterly unprepared for the revelation that occurs.

The difference between these two versions reflects more than a desire to portray Ivanov in a less peculiar light. (Had this been the intention, the entire scene could have been omitted.) Deschartes's account rewrites the letter to Mintslova in order to align Ivanov's biography with his philosophy. By depicting a poet who suddenly and unexpectedly confronts the transcendent, it "corrects" the original version, in which the poet forces this confrontation. Ivanov appears as the astonished recipient of transcendent knowledge, a striking contrast to the letter, where he eagerly participates in occult practices. Attentive editing (whether on the part of Ivanov or Deschartes is secondary) thus brings the entire scene within the parameters of Ivanov's discussion of theurgy.

The significance of the mysterious Latin verses extends beyond the issue of theurgy to the question of genre. Their promise of a long reunification after a short separation has obvious relevance to *Love and Death*, the fourth book of *Cor Ardens*. In this book, a poetic protagonist, bereft of his beloved, repeatedly strives to overcome the separation caused by death. The link between "Breve aevum separatum" and *Cor Ardens* is both thematic and intertextual. The same Latin poem appears—without attribution and with minor textological changes—as the first of two stanzas that open *Love and Death*.[40] Ivanov further accentuated the significance of these verses by concluding *Cor Ardens* with Mikhail Kuzmin's musical setting of this same Latin poem.

The midnight prayers (a "biographical" text) thus left a palpable trace in Ivanov's poetry ("literary" work). However, Ivanov supplied no commentary to these verses—their supernatural origin remains a mystery to the reader of *Cor Ardens*.

The 1909 diaries offer a wealth of supplementary material for an investigation of Ivanov's theurgic practice. In this quintessentially Symbolist document, quotidian reality mixes freely with dreams, visions, and personal intrigue. A knowledge of Ivanov's theoretical positions often clarifies specific diary entries. For example, on August 10, 1909, Ivanov writes, "Kuzmin continues to play Beethoven's Ninth Symphony. During the last movement, one felt the closeness and almost the voice of Lidiia."[41] The mystical role attributed to music in much Symbolist theory renders this event less surprising than it might otherwise be. Yet this passage has a more specific referent; in his philosophy of art, Ivanov accorded a privileged place to Beethoven's setting of Schiller's "Ode to Joy." As early as 1904, in *The Hellenic Religion of the Suffering God* (*Ellinskaia religiia stradaiuschchego boga*), he lauded Beethoven's Ninth Symphony for re-creating in modern times the spirit of the Dionysian dithyramb.[42] Ivanov understood Dionysian myth as a paradigm of death and resurrection (death not as an end but as a means of rebirth). It thus becomes consistent that the modern equivalent of the dithyramb should "resurrect" Lidiia. In regard to the diary entry, one must ultimately question the theurgic power of Beethoven's music since Ivanov's experience appears overdetermined by his prior philosophical convictions.

In the diaries, communication from beyond the grave takes various forms. Lidiia appears in dreams, as an apparition, and as a disembodied voice, and even makes her own diary entries (marked by a change of handwriting and a disregard for punctuation marks and word boundaries). She frequently uses foreign languages, primarily Latin and Italian, and invariably concludes her message with the Italian phrase *ora e sempre* ("now and always"). These words have strong religious overtones since they conclude a number of Italian prayers.[43] In addition, they have direct relevance to Ivanov's poetry. In *Love and Death*, this phrase serves as the epigraph to the introductory sonnet of the cycle "The Blue Veil" ("Goluboi Pokrov").[44] The poem itself is framed by these words. It begins with the line "Byl O r a - S e m p r e tainyi nash obet" ("*Ora-Sempre* was our secret vow") and ends with "Sempre, slyshish'?—Slyshu. Ora" ("Sempre, do you hear?— I hear. Ora"). In this poem, as in the earlier texts, a foreign language signals communication with a transcendent realm. In the context of the poem, the phrase's eschatological implications stand out. The joining of *sempre* and *ora* corresponds to the synthesis of the momentary (*mig*) and the eternal (*vechnost'*). Once again, there is an intertextual relationship between a biographical document (the diaries) and the literature (the poetry). Lidiia's cryptic "signature" (*ora e sempre*) appears to be the subtext for a poem about mystical experience. In short, a phrase with fundamental autobiographical significance becomes an integral part of a poetic text. While a knowledgeable reader of the poem may recognize the phrase's religious dimension and even vaguely sense its autobiographical implications, he cannot possibly understand its full theurgic significance. In the biographical writings, the phrase testifies to Ivanov's conviction that he and his wife have triumphed over death.

This intertextual connection adds a new dimension to Ivanov's poetry. However, one could contend that such details are superfluous. After all, poets frequently rewrite "personal" experience in their works. This criticism would perhaps be valid if the interplay between biographical documents and literary texts were limited to the level of subtextual echoes. In the case of Ivanov's work, however, it extends to the most fundamental sphere of his thought—the symbol. In 1908, Ivanov offered his most precise definition of this crucial concept: "In different spheres of consciousness the same symbol obtains different meaning. . . . Like a ray of sunlight, the symbol cuts through all planes of existence and all spheres of consciousness, signifying in each plane different things, filling each sphere with a different meaning."[45] According to Ivanov, a symbol is not tied to a single meaning, but rather obtains a variety of significations depending on the "plane of existence," or what one could probably call the "context."

In Ivanov's poetry, the "burning heart" (or *cor ardens*) is one of a relatively small number of fundamental symbols. Its most obvious association is biblical (Luke 24:32), where it connotes religious fervor.[46] When, in 1906, Ivanov chose the image as the title of his book, he seems to have had primarily this meaning in mind. However, in the period after Lidiia's death, the burning heart takes on additional significance. In a diary entry from June 15, 1908, Ivanov records a dream: "I saw Lidiia with giant swan's wings. In her hands she held a burning heart, of which we both partook."[47] This scene, as Pamela Davidson has demonstrated, has a literary antecedent. It parallels with astonishing exactitude a passage from Dante's *Vita Nuova* (*New Life*), a work Ivanov knew intimately. In Dante, the burning heart serves as a link between Dante (the poet) and Beatrice (his dead beloved).[48]

The image of Dante and Beatrice, joined by a burning heart, recalls the pairing of Ivanov and Lidiia, also joined by a burning heart. Such an interpretation of the diary entry is supported by other writings of the period. In the dedication to *Cor Ardens*, written after Lidiia's death, Ivanov depicts both himself and Lidiia in terms of this very image. He speaks of his own "burning heart" (*plameneiushchee serdtse*) and Lidiia's "fiery heart" (*ognennoe serdtse*).

A similar usage can be found in extremely obscure biographical writings. Among Ivanov's papers in the Lenin Library there are 83 manuscript pages (written mainly in Latin) of what appears to be automatic writing.[49] As in the letters to Mintslova, Ivanov notes the month and day but not the year. Internal evidence strongly suggests that these jottings date from this same period. They are clearly connected to the automatic writing found in the diaries, often repeating key words and phrases (for example, *ora e sempre*). Like the letters and diaries, they record communication between Ivanov and Lidiia. The entry from August 7 contains the following assertion: "ardor cordis signum victoriae nostrae" ("the heart's flame is the sign of our victory"). Since *ardor cordis* is immediately recognizable as a variant of *cor ardens*, it becomes evident that a literary symbol has obtained personal significance. It is now a "sign of *our* victory," presumably over death.

The burning heart is ubiquitous in Ivanov's work of this period. With each use, the image gains symbolic weight. Simultaneously, it acquires an increasing degree of "reality" since it is inextricably linked to the mystical experiences in Ivanov's personal life. This process is most clearly illustrated when the same burning heart finds its way into the Novalis translations. As has been suggested, Ivanov's sudden interest in Novalis in the period immediately following Lidiia's death was conditioned as much by biography as by poetry. Like the work of Dante and Petrarch (the obvious literary models for Ivanov's *Love and Death*), Novalis's poetry mourns the death of a beloved woman. In his extraordinarily free renditions of Novalis, Ivanov rewrote his own bitter experience of loss.[50] Although the image of a burning heart is foreign to Novalis's poetry, it creeps into Ivanov's translations five times. A single example should suffice to demonstrate the phenomenon. In the concluding stanzas of the fifth of the "Hymns to the Night" ("Hymnen an die Nacht"), Novalis writes of the path to eternal life: "Von innrer Glut geweitet/Verklärt sich unser Sinn." ("Broadened by an inner glow/Our sense is transfigured"). These lines, admittedly obscure, would challenge any translator. Yet Ivanov sidesteps the difficulties by ignoring Novalis's imagery and substituting his own. He writes: "I serdtsa plamen' tlennyi/ Griadushchego zalog" ("And the perishable flame of the heart/ Is the pledge of the future"). Novalis's text might allow for an image of an internal fire (*Von innrer Glut*), but it contains no suggestion of a heart. In the "flame of the heart," one immediately recognizes Ivanov's *cor ardens*. Furthermore, Ivanov interprets his own addition, stating that the burning heart is a "pledge of the future." Novalis's poetry is thus subsumed as part of Ivanov's own personal symbolic system. Ivanov the translator, like Ivanov the theurgist, clearly oversteps the boundary of objectivity. The burning heart, first an image of religious fervor, then a sign of personal victory, now becomes a promise of immortality. These significations are not mutually exclusive, but neither are they identical.

The hermeneutic implications of this phenomenon are considerable. In Ivanov's theory *and* practice, the symbol is a dynamic concept. Each new appearance modifies or broadens previous meanings. To understand the full significance of Ivanov's symbols, it is necessary to trace their usage through all of his writings. As the example of the burning heart indicates, Ivanov's practice does not distinguish between personal texts, lyric poetry, and translations from another poet. All genres of Ivanov's writings, whether biographical or literary, constitute parts of a single, indivisible Symbolist text.

In his writings from the period after Lidiia's death, Ivanov seeks to annul any distinction between the personal and poetic spheres. Moreover, Ivanov's very behavior from this period—insofar as it can be reconstructed from the biographical writings—demonstrates the consequent application of this same principle. Yet this expansion of the symbol's sphere of influence, this coincidence of the personal and the literary, occurs at the expense of Ivanov's theurgic ideal. While Ivanov's theoretical statements demand maximum receptivity from the artist, his other works exemplify a more subjective view of the creative process. The years 1907–10 mark an atypical, particularly tragic chapter in Ivanov's biography. Nevertheless, his writings from this period represent an organic development of (and not a rupture from) his previous work.[51]

From a post-Symbolist standpoint, the behavior that accompanied the Symbolists' attempts to join life and art appears eccentric, at times even ridiculous. Yet this behavior cannot be ignored, for it forms part of a larger pattern. The Symbolists' biographies warrant critical attention because they offer the modern reader access to the movement's fundamental beliefs.

Seven

The Legacy of the Symbolist Aesthetic Utopia: From Futurism to Socialist Realism

IRINA GUTKIN

Futurists as "the New Men of the New Life"

By the early 1910's, when the decline of the Symbolist movement had become apparent to its own members as well as to
outsiders, new aesthetic trends were appearing in the form of
diverse groups and loose associations. Members of this new generation of the artistic avant-garde, who eventually became known
under the name "Futurists," fostered aesthetic tastes that stood
in pointed contrast to the work of their Symbolist predecessors.

Indeed, a cursory comparison between eccentric futurists—
irreverently mischievous and loudly insolent—and their predecessors, the Symbolists, those erudite mystics and refined aesthetes, is bound to evoke an image of striking dissimilarity that
would seem to preclude further analogy. In fact, the Futurists
themselves deliberately emphasized this contrast. The Futurists'
early manifestos, as well as some of their works, are rife with
derisive gibes at Symbolist aesthetics.[1] Thinly veiled innuendos
and overt invectives were aimed at the notion of the eternal feminine, Argonautism, and other tenets dear to the Symbolists. To

give but one example, in their "opera" *Victory over the Sun* (*Pobeda nad solntsem*, 1913) the Futurists, portrayed as *silachi*—titanic athletes or supermen or sorts—bury the sun in apparent negation of the Symbolist worship of that symbol. According to Mikhail Matiushin, the author of the opera's musical score, Futurists thus proclaimed the "victory over the old, accepted concept of the beautiful sun . . . , over romantism and empty verbosity."[2] This strategy worked to obscure an array of affinities that the new generation of visual and verbal experimental artists shared with the aesthetic ideologies of the Symbolist generation.

Like the Symbolists, the Futurists were informed by a sense of impending crisis and of the imminent advent of an ideal world. Consequently, their experiments centered on the creation of new forms, anticipatory of the future life. The Futurist avant-garde, in its early period, was possessed by an all-pervasive revolutionary urge to violence and destruction. It was this spirit that prevailed over constructive aesthetic strategies. The destructive energy was applied to distortion of the customary static forms of representation and perception of reality. Like the Symbolists, the Futurists pitted themselves against the ways of the "old world." They adopted a tactic whose main goal was *épatage*, and *épater le bourgeois* was their slogan. However, from the point of view of the Futurists, the Symbolists also belonged with the camp of the "old" and the "bourgeois." In comparison with the Symbolists, the Futurists chose much louder and more public (i.e., consciously less arcane and esoteric) ways to dramatize their actual lives. The young Futurist avant-gardists were set on casting off all conventions, and they deliberately offered their bohemian whims for public display. Their every action, from their manner of dressing to the language of the manifestos and the very covers and paper of their publications, was a deliberate act of defiance aimed at the rejection of the accepted forms of life.

During 1912 and 1913, David Burliuk, Vladimir Maiakovsky, and several of their artistic friends of the Rayonist persuasion scandalized the public by appearing on a number of occasions with painted faces. In an interview entitled "Why We Are

Painting Ourselves" ("Pochemu my raskrashivaemsia," 1913), the
painter Mikhail Larionov, the leader of the Rayonists, and Ilia
Zdanevich explained this action in the following words:

> The new life requires a new community and a new way of propagation.
> Our self-painting is the first speech to have found unknown truths.
> We have joined art to life. After the long isolation of the artist we
> have loudly summoned life and life has invaded art, it is time for art to
> invade life. The painting of faces is the beginning of the invasion.[3]

In other words, more than a flouting of accepted standards, this
shocking behavior announced an aesthetic program aimed at
subordinating life to art.

Since theater was allotted a very special place in the Symbolist
theories of the life of the future, for the early Futurists theater
became a preferred form of self-expression, which was informed
by the desire for a role in the creation of new forms of future life
and art. In the words of Aristarkh Lentulov, who designed the
sets for Vladimir Maiakovsky's eponymous "tragedy," the poet
was expressing "utopian realism, a kind of dream of the new
life."[4] At one gathering, pompously entitled the First All-Russian
Congress of Singers of the Future,[5] both the "tragedy" *Vladimir
Maiakovsky* and the "opera" *Victory over the Sun* were proclaimed
to be examples of the "theater of the future man."[6] In Victor
Khlebnikov's Prologue to the opera, a Futurist (*Budetlianin*) calls
the audience to take Futurist theater (*sozertsog Budeslavl'*) as a
guide to the fantastic world of the future and speaks of the
theater as a transformational force (*togda-to sozertsavel' budet preo-
brazhavl'*).[7]

Early Futurist manifestos, in spite of their declamatory rheto-
ric, often directed against Symbolism, show in their declarations
on the nature and role of poetic language a kinship to Symbolist
theories. Thus, Futurists emphasized the mythmaking properties of the word. They declared: "We consider the word to be
the creator of the myth; the word, as it dies, gives birth to a
myth and vice versa."[8] Moreover, though they attacked the Symbolists' poetic groping for metaphysical truths, they nevertheless
ascribed to the Futurist poet the power to create the human

soul;[9] indeed, they proclaimed themselves "the new people of the new life."[10]

While rejecting the mimetic method and the decorative function of art, Futurists upheld its futurological character, and therefore recognized a certain applied or utilitarian task in the arts. They believed that art ought to shape life, including human behavior and psyche, in order to mold a "new man." They pictured themselves as the models for that new man, transgressing in their experiments the borders between personal life and art. It is likely, then, that in deriding their predecessors, the Futurists did not merely ridicule Symbolist aesthetic sensibilities, but also sought to assert exclusive rights on the formation of the future.

Benedict Livshits, the chief memoirist of the Futurist movement, acknowledged this fact. He pointed out that rejection of a general doctrine made it easier for the Futurists (and also for the Acmeists) to fight with "hefty, lumbering" Symbolism and "to become a literary school."[11] However, it was much easier to declare the "shattering of syntax," or the creation of new words for "the new people of the new life," than "to put a solid theoretical foundation under these uncertain yearnings, and, in turn, it was still immeasurably more difficult than to make any a priori constructs to justify the declarations by creative production."[12]

The early Futurists applied much of their energy to techniques with which to destroy or distort matter, forcing it to take a new form. The constructive tendencies that actually guided these energies in the creation of the new forms for the new life became predominant a decade later, in the 1920's. After the Bolshevik Revolution many members of the Futurist avant-garde put themselves at the service of the new society striving to realize a utopian vision of the future in the life of the new Soviet state.

"We Shall Build Our New World": Who Is in Charge of the Design?

Futurological perception of aesthetic endeavor was rooted in a certain historical perspective. This historical perspective, prevailing in Russian culture in the first decades of the twentieth century, can be called millenarian.[13] From this point of view, whatever the preferred scheme—be it Marxist (as interpreted by Bogdanov and Lunacharsky, or Lenin and then Stalin) or Christian (as interpreted by Joachim of Fiore, Solov'ev, or Fedorov)— it had its fount in the expectation of the imminent end of history (more often than not perceived in terms of apocalyptic catastrophism) and in the consequent, if not downright immediate, advent of the Millennium. The ideal future was construed as the ideal society in which all historical opposites are reconciled and that has been thus far the property of social and literary utopias. A millenarian conception of history allowed for the fluid eclecticism characteristic of Russian intellectual life in the first two decades of this century. In this cultural environment the doctrines of Vladimir Solov'ev and Karl Marx, Nikolai Fedorov and Friedrich Nietzsche converged as compatible and complimentary "salvation schemes"—that is, approaches to the common cause of building the ultimate future life.[14] This historical perspective informed movements—Symbolist, Futurist, Marxist-communist— whose aesthetic sensibilities were otherwise very diverse.

If a millenarian conception of history served as the common denominator in salvation schemes, the notion of what constitutes the active agent in the realization of salvation may be singled out as the ideological factor that separated them. Influenced by Nietzsche and his idea that in modern society "God is dead," the Symbolists took their cue from Solov'ev and sought a replacement for absent metaphysical authority—that is, a new religion. They considered realization of the divine in man as a condition of the ultimate salvation, and revelation was seen as the primary means for attaining this goal. Hence, there was an emphasis on the role of the individual, and especially the artistic individual, who was endowed with the higher prophetic potential.

Another trend, known as "god-building" (*bogostroitel'stvo*), also took its inspiration from Nietzsche. Instead of a metaphysical search for a new god, however, the "god-builders" in fact eliminated the divine from their scheme by transferring the demiurgic function to the "human collective," identified as the active agent in the creating of future reality. God-building then can be considered an attempt to fuse Marxism with Christianity, in that the god-builders were willing to take from Christianity its symbolic and mythological properties, reckoning that Marxist ideals would be better understood by the masses if presented within the familiar Christian paradigm.[15]

The chief ideologue of god-building, Alexander Bogdanov (real name Malinovsky, 1873–1928), developed a coherent theory of cultural evolution. His "organizational science"—a complex theory that evolved over a period spanning two decades and that lent itself to various interpretations[16]—was from its inception intended as no less than the science of sciences, that is, an attempt to discover a structural law that would establish connections among all the sciences.[17] Combining Darwin with Marx, and Joseph Dietzgen with Ernst Mach and Federov, Bogdanov viewed world history as a progression of "organizational forms of experience"—that is, of various ways that the "human collective" has devised to facilitate labor processes (understood by Bogdanov as a general struggle with nature and, consequently as necessary for the survival of human kind).

According to Bogdanov, the monistic view of the universe that religion—initially a primary force of organization—once offered was gradually lost as the division of labor and specialization in "abstract" sciences splintered knowledge into a multitude of discrete fields. Since the proletarian class, by its very position in the highly organized machine mode of production, constituted the pinnacle of "organized human collective," the time had come for the restoration of the integral monistic view, on the new synthetic basis that Bogdanov thought his techtology could provide. (Bogdanov admitted eventually that such a total organizational science could be realized only "in the future.")[18] His theory emphasized mastery over human biology and psychology with the goal of creating a supreme human being fit to live in the ultimate human collective.[19] Inspired by ideas of Nikolai Fedorov, he contended that science would soon find ways to make this man immortal.[20] He assigned art a privileged role, as the "highest and least understood form of organizational activity."[21] Art's distinctive potential for organization of the human psyche or will lies, he suggested, in the special kind of language that all arts use. Essentially, he argued, words are concepts and as such constitute rudimentary means of organization.[22] Bogdanov defined art as "language plus cognition."[23] Hence, the axiological criteria for the arts: art must not serve a decorative function; it must both express and form the "collective perception of the world" (*kollektivnoe mirooshchushchenie*).

Bogdanov's "organizational science" was intended first of all as a practical philosophy. "Techtology" (from the Greek *tecton*, "builder") was expected to arm the builders of ultimate society with all-encompassing knowledge.[24] After the Bolshevik Revolution, which was perceived as the triumph of the proletariat, Bogdanov's organizational theory served as the theoretical ground for the Proletarian Culture movement (*Proletkul't*)[25] and the Scientific Organization of Labor (*nauchnaia organizatsiia truda*, or N.O.T.).[26] Lenin vehemently criticized Bogdanov's theories precisely because he saw in them a dangerous rival. The Bolsheviks in general, and especially Lenin, recognized "the power of ideas," which inevitably are conveyed through language.

The Bolshevik Revolution, which put forward the immediate task of constituting new culture, created a situation in which the potential for both rivalry and cooperation between the Bolshevik power and artistic avant-garde could be realized. On the one hand, shared orientation toward the ideal future carried a potential for cooperation and distribution of labor in the common task of construction of the new reality. On the other hand, different forces presented alternative models of the "new man" as the leader in transforming reality. Moreover, Marxist revolutionaries, ultimately the Bolsheviks, considered themselves the vanguard of the vanguard historical class, the holders of the "true scientific knowledge" that enabled them to predict the historical future. Therefore, they claimed the role of avatars of the new man and political organizers of the "elemental" (*stikhiinye*) and "unconscious" (*nesoznatel'nye*) masses. After the Bolshevik Revolution the question of who would have the leading role in designing a new life became paramount.

The acceptance of the revolution by the artistic avant-garde was conditioned, among other things, by their millenarian conception of history, which went hand in hand with apocalyptic leanings. That is to say, while some cultural pundits focused on the horror of the revolution and the fratricidal civil war, others read the revolution as a sign of the advent of the new era, the beginning of the expected Millennium. They shared the euphoric feeling that the time had come to realize millenarian goals—that is, to implement new forms of life.

As early as 1918 an editorial in the gazette *Art of the Commune* (*Iskusstvo kommuny*), a mouthpiece for the Futurist avant-garde, called for dictatorship of the Futurists in the sphere of the arts in order to bring about "the victory over matter in the sense of achieving perfect mastery of it."[27] This declaration, which clearly emulated the Bolshevik slogan demanding the dictatorship of the proletariat, apparently expressed the prevailing sentiment that the Bolshevik coup had opened a new historical era in which the avant-garde artists would be the power brokers in building the beautiful society of the future.

The Bolshevik leaders, some of whom regarded with suspicion the experiments of the artistic avant-garde (or Futurists, as they were called summarily), nevertheless depended on the avant-garde in matters of "cultural construction." In this sense the image of the future world, offered in Leon Trotsky's consequential book *Literature and Revolution* (*Literatura i revoliutsiia*, 1923) may serve as a compelling example. In the concluding pages of the first part, in the section entitled "The Undoubted and the Projected" ("Nesomnennoe i predpolagaemoe"), Trotsky, then a people's commissar in the Bolshevik government, expounded his image of the world of the future. The following quotations are selected to give an overview of Trotsky's comprehensive plan for the transformation of reality:

Man will get used to regarding the world as an obedient clay for molding increasingly perfect forms of life. The wall between art and production will fall. The future monumental style will not be decorative, it will give form. In this, the Futurists are right. . . . But not only the wall between art and production will fall; simultaneously the wall between art and nature will also fall. This is not meant in the sense of Jean-Jacques

[Rousseau], that art will become closer to a state of nature; but on the contrary, nature will become more "artificial." The present position of mountains and rivers, of fields, of meadows, of steppes, of forests and seashores, cannot be considered final. . . . If faith only promised to move mountains, then technology, which takes nothing "on faith," is able to lift up mountains and move them. Up till now this was done for industrial purposes; . . . in the future it will be done on an incomparably larger scale, in accordance with a general industrial-artistic plan. . . . In the end man will rebuild the earth, if not in his own image, then to his own taste. . . . Socialist man, by way of machine, wants to and will command nature in its entirety, with its grouse and sturgeon. He will designate where the mountains should be, and where they should open for passes. He will change the course of the rivers and will lay down rules for the oceans.[28]

Although Trotsky took a cautious approach to Futurism, chiding the Futurists' ideas as outlandish and divorced from "life," his sweeping picture of future society is based on the key notions of the life-building programs, in which, it will be remembered, "life" was to be subordinated to art. First of all, aesthetic criteria clearly eclipse utilitarian concerns in Trotsky's landscape of the future. He argues that in the past alterations in the surface of the planet were made "for industrial purposes," but in the Future this will be done at man's will—that is, man will organize the face of the earth as the Futurist artist organizes his painting, and nature will become more "artificial" (*iskustvennee*).

Trotsky's conception of the world of the future is informed by sensibilities akin to those of the Futurists. He seems to have been inspired by the same transformational urge as Maiakovsky in his desire to "mess up the map of everyday."[29] That is to say, Trotsky's approach to physical matter was akin to the Futurist conception of the revolutionary treatment of artistic material. It is virtually a proposition to remake the face of the earth like a work of nonrealist art, changing its surface and structure to an unrecognizable degree by means of machines and technology.

Much attention was given in Trotsky's vision to the struggle with the forms of "everyday life" (*byt*)—a component essential also to the avant-garde. In planning the future reconstruction of *byt* and of man himself, Trotsky took concrete artistic experiments as his launching point. For instance, he started expounding his views on the new man with a reference to Vsevolod Meyerhold's conception of the theater as a model for life and praised the producer's innovative method of actor training ("stage biomechanics"), which emphasized efficient use of the body through rhythmic organization of movement: "What a few enthusiasts are dreaming about now, not always coherently, with regard to the theatricalization of *byt* and rhythmicalization of man himself, fits well and firmly into this perspective."[30] Lest *byt* become stagnant and petrified again, Trotsky emphasized introduction of the dynamic principle into daily life—that is, the concept of life as constant change, envisioned as a sort of artistic "perpetual revolution" (*permanentnaia revoliutsiia*):

Man, who will learn how to move mountains and rivers, how to erect peoples' palaces on the summit of Mont Blanc and at the bottom of the Atlantic, will, of course, be able to add to his mundane life not only richness, brilliance, and intensity but also the highest dynamism. The new-formed shell of everyday life will hardly have taken shape before being again shattered under the pressure of new technical-cultural inventions and achievements.[31]

As in the avant-garde theories, in Trotsky's plan overall transformation of reality includes a new family structure, which "will liberate the woman from the condition of half-slavery" and which includes new approaches to the rearing of children: "Care for the nourishment and upbringing of children, which weighs down the present-day family like a gravestone, will be removed and will become the subject of communal initiative and inexhaustible collective creativity."[32] Trotsky's locution suggests that application of the creative principle ("collective creativity") to the routine forms of family life is a struggle with death.

Finally, Trotsky envisions the creative reconstruction of man himself—emotions, psyche, and even physiology. From Meyerhold's organization of movement in accordance with aesthetic principle, man will go on to transform psycho-physiological processes:

Man will finally take seriously the task of harmonizing himself. He will take on the task of bringing into the motion of his own organs—in working, walking, or playing—the utmost precision, functionality, economy, and, consequently, beauty. He will want to master the half-unconscious and then unconscious processes of his own organism—[such as] breathing, blood circulation, digestion, reproduction.[33]

Ultimately, the fear of death, and possibly death itself, will be overcome. The future new man of Trotsky's vision—in his words, "a higher social-biological type, a Superman, if you will"[34]—is also a figure familiar to us from Symbolist and Futurist theories:

Man will become immeasurably stronger, more intelligent and subtle; his body will become more harmonious, his movements more rhythmic, his voice more musical. The forms of everyday life will take on dynamic theatricality. The average human type will rise to the heights of an Aristotle, a Goethe, or a Marx. And above this ridge new peaks will perpetually rise.[35]

Overall, Trotsky's design is informed by the idea that the artist-messiah, through the act of his creative will, can bring about an instant transformation of reality. But in the context of the 1920's the demiurgic role of the artist was transferred to the toiling masses, whose creative energy was expected to serve as the major force in the transformational scheme. Nevertheless, creative spirit and aesthetic principle remained the active forces of transformation. As in Bogdanov's theory of "organizational art," in Trotsky's vision Marx's notion of "man made whole" was fused with avant-garde aesthetic concepts. He expressed the belief that in the future everyone would be able to fulfill the role of the individual creative genius, and creative activity would be carried out by the working collective.

Trotsky's design could hardly be called practical. Nevertheless, his essay contains a blueprint for a communist utopia that has been guiding the Soviet mentality to the recent collapse of the Soviet system—a fact suggesting in turn that the legacy of modernist life-creating theories is more long lasting than is generally granted.[36]

"Art into Life": Aesthetics of Constructivism and Production Art

After the Bolshevik Revolution those modernist theories and practices that had projected the life of the future became the property and concern of nascent Soviet society at large. This is apparent in the destructive tendencies of the incipient Soviet culture, which were first focused on the elimination of those "old"—that is, "stagnant" and "bourgeois"—forms of life that had already been targeted by the artistic avant-garde. Revolutionary society tried to supplant the bourgeois family with the commune, bourgeois marriage with free associations between men and women, the family kitchen with "kitchen-factories." It is quite obvious now that the society on the whole was possessed by a revolutionary constructivist euphoria: nothing seemed impossible—space travel, flying cities, and immortality all seemed immediately attainable.[37]

The artistic avant-garde, nevertheless, was making a conscious effort to remain at the forefront of the offensive against old *byt* as well as of the struggle to institute new forms. This is why it is not accidental that the avant-garde artists who united under the banner of "Left Art" were the first ones to seek cooperation with the new political regime.[38] Basically, the avant-garde artists who sought a place and a role in the revolution and who espoused a congruent aesthetic program gathered under this banner. The orientation toward forging the future art and life can be seen as the unifying factor in Left Art aesthetics. In this respect it is indicative that the erstwhile "Futurists" formed the core of the Left Art movement and that the journal *Lef* served as its organizational center and forum. Left Art harbored the Constructivism and, perhaps to a lesser extent, Production Art (*proizvodstvennoe iskusstvo*) movements, whose theories and praxes reflected the general utopian striving to realize the future by aesthetic means.[39]

Production Art, which originated in part as a response to the Marxist theory that accorded the proletariat the role of the ultimate historical class, was an attempt to fuse avant-garde aes-

thetics with certain strands of Marxist thought, such as Bogdanov's theory of "organizational art." Avant-garde artists fan-
cied themselves akin to the members of the ultimate class in
that they claimed to be producers as well. Maiakovsky best captured this aesthetic mood in his poem "Poet-Worker" ("Poet-
rabochii," 1918), where he compared poetic art to various kinds
of menial labor:

> I too am a factory. . . .
> Aren't we woodworkers? . . .
> Of course, fishing is an honorable profession,
> But poet's labor is still more honorable:
> To be fishers of men, not fish. . . .
> We polish brains with the file of language. . . .
> Hearts are just like motors.
> The soul is just like an engine.
> We are equals.
> Comrades among working masses.
> Proletarians of flesh and spirit.[40]

Referring to poets as "fishers of men" by way of a gospel metaphor, Maiakovsky in fact reinterpreted in terms of a production
trope a tenet that the task of the verbal artist lay in shaping the
consciousness of the new man.

Constructivism, which began as a nonobjective art movement
of abstract experimenting with the organization of planes, soon
evolved into experimentation in broader spheres traditionally
outside the beaux arts, such as industrial design and architecture,
with a practical goal of instituting the life forms of the future. In
January 1921, at the time when heated debates on the place of the
experimental artist vis-à-vis Marxist political power were tearing
apart the Institute of Artistic Culture, which served as the center
for Constructivists, Vladimir Tatlin, reporting to the Eighth Congress of Soviets on behalf of his fellow Constructivists, explained
their program:

What happened from the social aspect in 1917 was realized in our
work as pictorial artists in 1914 when "materials, volume and construction" were accepted as our foundations. . . . In this way an opportunity
emerges of uniting purely artistic forms with utilitarian intentions. . . .

The results of this ... stimulate us to inventions in our work of creating a new world, and . . . call upon the producers to exercise control over the forms encountered in new everyday life.[41]

Linking the Bolshevik Revolution with the Futurist revolution in the arts, Tatlin went on to name his *Monument to the Third International* as a model of just such a practice. In other words, in Tatlin's interpretation, the principle of utility was still seen in terms of stimulus for further experimentation, and "life"—even though he already called it "new life"—remained subordinate to art.

In response to the all-pervading cult of technology in the 1920's, the prevailing model of the artist became that of an engineer, a master craftsman, who forges new forms out of old matter. Although the creative process could no longer be perceived as the property of individual artist-messiahs and was instead extended to the whole "society of producers," the Production Artists saw their role as somewhat similar to that of the "bourgeois specialists" (*spetsy*)—that is, to help the masses acquire technological know-how in organizing the new reality. Under Production Art and, especially, Constructivism, abstract theoretical projections into the future gave way to projects with applied character, such as producing practical objects suitable for the new everyday life (*byt*). From the point of view of their workable utility, two types of projects may be distinguished in the varied praxis of the experimental artists of the 1920's: those meant for a more distant, altogether indefinite future and those with more immediate "utilitarian" or practical designations.

To the first category belong such celestial projects as "flying cities."[42] However, even in such projects the artists were guided by the earnest belief that their work was based on the principle of functional utility measured in terms of "new *byt*." For instance, Boris Arvatov, a Left Art critic and sociologically minded theoretician bent on wedding the Formalist notion of "art as a device" with Production Art for the masses, defended the sketchy plan for an airborne city by the Constructivist sculptor-designer A. Lavinsky, claiming that it was not "just some kind of eccentricity" but "simply *maximal expediency*": "[It is] in the air in order to free the earth. [It is made] of glass so that it will be filled with light. Asbestos [is used] in order to make the construction lighter. It is on shock absorbers for balance."[43] To the inevitable question of whether such systems are technically possible he gave a dismissive answer:

I am ready to assume the worst—that a literal realization of the plan in all its details is inconceivable, either under present technological conditions or under any conditions. "My business is to propose," . . . so Maiakovsky said to the angels. Lavinsky does this same thing since [in this project] he was preoccupied primarily with the social side of the venture—[that is to say], with the *forms of new everyday life*.[44]

Apart from the fact that this essay, entitled "Materialized Utopia" ("Oveshchestvlennaia utopiia," 1923), cogently illustrates the general aesthetic principles guiding the model of the future "New Jerusalem," it is interesting in yet another respect. Its argument, couched in dialogic form, reveals the author's attempts to separate contemporary Constructivist practices from those of previous, prerevolutionary Futurism. The author emphasizes the functional principle (or what the author calls *tselesoobraznost'*, "expediency"). The turn toward serving the needs of everyday life did, in fact, constitute a watershed in the history of life-creating aesthetics. The aesthetic utopian ideal of art creating life, which took shape at the beginning of the twentieth century, was fused with the utilitarian tradition of the 1860's.

In the category of artistic endeavors intended for use in the present, and hence endowed with unquestionably practical qualities, one may list the models of convertible furniture, such as folding beds, shown at an exhibit organized in 1923 by a group of young Constructivist designers.[45] The new Constructivist furniture was simple and "light" (devoid of decorative embellishments); moreover, each piece was designed for multiple functions, so as to emphasize the dynamic principle of the new life.[46] In this experiment the designers were guided by opposition to the stolid quality of old *byt*, symbolized by household possessions—epitomized in Maiakovsky's poetry, for example, by the bedroom with the much-hated conjugal double bed and by bourgeois family dinners.[47] Similar projects by members of the Left Art group included the clothes and textile designs of Liubov'

Popova and Varvara Stepanova.[48] Vladimir Tatlin too, though renowned rather for his less feasible projects such as the famous "Letatlin"—a winged device for individual flying, or the *Monument to the Third International*—did not shun clothing design. Such unavoidable necessities of everyday life as dishes the artists decorated with Malevich-inspired Suprematist motifs or with Soviet themes, apparently with an intention to transform these traditional objects of "bourgeois" life style by endowing them with a new, edifying function. Eventually, literature too started offering overt role models for the new Soviet men and women— for example, Maiakovsky, in his poem "Good!" ("Khorosho!," 1927), glorified the revolutionary Bolshevik leaders in general, and especially the founder of the security organs, Felix Dzerzhinsky, whom the poet recommended "to a youth, thinking about life, deciding on whose model to make his life," as the most suitable ideal.[49]

As in earlier stages, artists continued to style themselves as models of the new reality by practicing in their own lives what they proclaimed in theory. With the growing tendency toward functionality, Constructivist artists offered themselves to the masses as living models in yet another, more practical sense— that is, by becoming the promoters and first consumers of their own designs. Their experimental work was now intended for popular consumption. Tatlin's coat design, with the pattern and a photograph of Tatlin himself sporting his stylish parka-like creation, appeared in a newspaper under the heading "New Lifestyles" ("Novyi byt").[50] Varvara Stepanova and Liubov' Popova also modeled and wore novel clothes based on their own Constructivist patterns and often made from fabrics of their own design as well. The architect Konstantin Mel'nikov devised a model for a dormitory called poetically *Sleepy Sonata: A Laboratory of Sleep* (*Sonnaia sonata: Laboratoriia sna*, 1929). Intended to organize the physiological process of sleep of a workers' commune, the Laboratory was meant to accommodate some six hundred residents. As one researcher noted, this project was replicated on the level of Mel'nikov's own household, where "sleep was a collective activity"—the whole family slept in one room, divided only by slight angular partitions.[51]

The experimental theater of Vsevolod Meyerhold (1874–1940) of the 1920's, especially his method of stage biomechanics (*teatral'naia bio-mekhanika*), was interpreted by its contemporary critics as a part of the Constructivist and Production Art movements. They also underscored the practical side of Meyerhold's method vis-à-vis the task of creating the new life. In his programmatic essay "Under the Sign of Life-Building" ("Pod znakom zhiznestroeniia," 1923), Nikolai Chuzhak endorsed biomechanics as a form of "Constructivism in theater" and, with typical dictatorial enthusiasm, commended Meyerhold's theater as a laboratory for "cultivating skills, *necessary for the man involved in the production process.*"[52] Likewise, Sergei Tret'iakov, reporting in the magazine *Lef* on the twentieth anniversary of Meyerhold's work in theater, praised the director's achievements as extending "beyond the limits of the theater stage into those of an organizer of the expressive movements of the masses" and therefore as an agent in the construction of the new reality.[53]

The experiments of the revolutionary director, whose productions were milestones of the history of avant-garde theater in Russia, evolved in close relation to the conception of the "new theater" that featured in the life-creating ideologies of Russian Symbolism.[54] The Symbolist program for a "theater of the future" pledged to cast off mimetic conventions and envisioned instead a synthetic act that would combine the various types of theatrical expression. It would erase barriers between the audience and the actors on stage to achieve "liturgical" or "collective" creativity (*sobornoe deistvo*), whereby "the viewer and the performer both become active partakers in the mystical act" (*souchastnikom deistva*), whose purpose is to create new myths, a new consciousness, and, ultimately, a new man.[55]

When in 1920 Meyerhold took charge of the theater department of the People's Commissariat of Enlightenment, he used his post to promote "October in Theater"—a program of reforms that measured up to the Symbolist conception of the "theater of the future." On the one hand, Meyerhold's productions in the genre of "mystery plays" were committed to introducing a new historical mythology into the mass consciousness. On the other hand, whatever the contribution of his biomechanical method to the innovation of the stage art might have been, its application was meant to shape life.

In the narrow sense, biomechanics was a method of actor training that emphasized efficient use of body language as the principle means of expression. Eclectic in its conception, it was a search for a synthetic technique that would enable the actor to reorganize his body. Hence, it made use of such diverse ideas as Dalcroze's eurhythmics, Pavlov's reflexology, and Bogdanov's theory of organizational art via Alexei Gastev's Taylorist models of labor process (from the last the term "biomechanics" itself is said to have been borrowed).[56] As Meyerhold himself explained in a polemical essay, a performance staged according to the principles of biomechanics was a means of "creating a new reality":

Today's new viewer (I am speaking of the proletariat) is the most capable, in my view, of freeing himself from the hypnosis of illusoriness [i.e., imitation of reality], precisely on the condition that he must know that he watches a play; and I am certain he will; [and he] will accept this play consciously, since through this play he will want to express himself as a collaborator and *as a creator of a new reality* because for this living man—[i.e.,] for the new man already reborn under communism—every theatrical reality serves only as a pretext to express from time to time, by ways of reflective response, *the joy of the new existence*.[57]

It is noteworthy that Meyerhold perceived the future reality as already achieved: for him, the new man had already been "reborn under communism."

Meyerhold's experimental methods of actor training found applications in various spheres of life: there were projects devoted to general "theatricalization" of military training as well as to the implementation of rhythmic movement in the production process and in mass physical education.[58] In the longer run, the reverberations of biomechanics may be found in the so-called "sports parades" (*parady fizkul'turnikov*), a distinctive feature of Soviet culture in the 1930's.

From Life-Creation to Life-Building:
Nikolai Chuzhak's Theories

Within the brew of Left Art aesthetics, the concept of art as building life forms received its own theorist in the person of Nikolai Chuzhak (real name Nikolai Nasimovich, 1896–1937), a new figure on the Moscow scene, who came to the Soviet capital in 1922 from exile in Siberia. Chuzhak introduced a term that replaced the Symbolist *zhiznetvorchestvo* (life-creation), namely, *zhiznestroitel'stvo* (life-building). Chuzhak's was an attempt at Marxist validation of avant-garde aesthetics. Certain tenets of his theory provide a viable link between the Symbolist notion of art and the doctrine of socialist realism.

Chuzhak's theoretical endeavors are concentrated in three relatively short articles, each of them representing a new phase in the development of his theory of "new art."[59] The first, "Toward Marxist Aesthetics" ("K estetike marksizma"), was initially written in 1912.[60] The importance of this work is underscored by the fact that he quotes from it in his next programmatic piece, "Under the Sign of Life-Building: Essay in Understanding the Art of the Day" ("Pod znakom zhiznestroeniia: Opyt osoznaniia iskusstva dnia"), published in the first issue of the journal *Lef*, in 1923. Later, after Chuzhak, a member of the editorial board of *Lef*, dissented from the other members, notably Maiakovsky (the journal thereafter folded), he was instrumental in instituting the journal *New Lef* (*Novyi Lef*). There in 1928 he publicized his new "factographical" platform in the essay "The Literature of Life-Building" ("Literatura zhiznestroeniia"),[61] which was reprinted subsequently in the collection *Literature of Fact* (*Literatura facta*, 1929), a symposium on the theory of "factographical" aesthetics.[62]

As the title of Chuzhak's first theoretical essay suggests, he set about the task of instituting Marxist aesthetics. This sets him apart from most other members of the Left Art movement, even though many of them were toying with Marxism in one way or another. As the guiding principle of his critical method he took the idea of dialectics, according to which at any given moment every phenomenon represents a contradiction, and thus contains the vestiges of its own past as well as the seeds of its future. Professing a class approach to aesthetics, Chuzhak predicated the need for a new art that would represent the dialectics of the proletarian class. He spoke of "some kind of new special [art] form" that would express the dialectical collision between "what is" and "what will be": "To expose the sprouts of the future, ripening in the visible reality, to expose new reality, hiding in the depths of contemporaneity, to cast off the dying, the temporarily domineering—such is the true goal of art, regarded from the dialectic point of view."[63] Chuzhak proposed to call the new artistic method "ultra-realism," admitting the imperfections of such a term. By contending that this ultra-realistic art was supposed to be separate from "everyday life," or *byt*, he adhered to the main tenet of avant-garde aesthetics. He underscored the fact that this new form had nothing to do with traditional realism—"with the exception of conditional acceptance of reality as the base," the materialist in Chuzhak made him add promptly. Reconciliation was found in assigning art a transformational function vis-à-vis reality and giving the artist the prerogative to be the creator of future life: "To transform reality in its distant perspective, to perceive it in all its chaos, to illuminate it with the far-off light and to create future reality—such is the thorny, but joyful, path of the genius."[64] Chuzhak's conception of ultra-realism is obviously reminiscent in diction and structure of Symbolist discourse on life-creation, particularly Bely's essays in the section "The Creation of Life" ("Tvorchestvo zhizni") in *Arabesques* (*Arabeski*, 1911). For instance, section 7 of Chuzhak's essay is entitled "Seekers of the Heavenly City" ("Vzyskuiushchie grada"), referring to the New Jerusalem, the Christian metaphor of the ideal millenarian society. Chuzhak underscores, however, that the proletariat is impatient in striving to attain the heavenly kingdom here on earth, and artists must hurry to show him "this future." Also, the closing section of the essay, entitled "To the Sun" ("K solntsu") and devoted to the artist-creators of the future, contains references both to Tommaso Campanella's *Civitas solis* (1623) and to Solness, the hero of Henrik Ibsen's drama *The Master Builder*. These are similarly linked in Andrei Bely's "Theater and Contemporary Drama" ("Teatr i sovremennaia drama," 1907) as the symbols of ideal society.[65] It is difficult, however, not to recognize in Chuzhak's conception of ultra-realism the incipient source of the subsequent official formula of socialist realism, which purported "to show life truthfully . . . not just as 'objective reality,' but to depict reality in its revolutionary development."[66]

In point of fact, the dialectic principle served to validate in Marxist terms the theurgical aesthetics of Vladimir Solov'ev. As his theoretical foundation Chuzhak took the statement of Karl Marx (made in the Foreword to the second edition of the first volume of *Das Kapital*) that "the dialectics, in its mystified form, transfigures and illuminates existing reality" (*preobrazhaet i prosvetliaet sushchestvuiushchee*), while "in its rational form" it also provides the understanding of the future negation of what is— that is, it offers a dynamic view of reality, which in turn allows one to see its ultimate end. Chuzhak then indicated that it was Solov'ev who revealed best the kind of dialectics that "*transfigures and illuminates reality.*"[67] Chuzhak proposed a futurological function for the arts, quoting directly from Solov'ev's programmatic treatise on aesthetics "The General Meaning of Art" ("Obshchii smysl iskusstva," 1890): "representation of any object or phenomenon *from the point of view of its ultimate state or in the light of the future world.*"[68] Chuzhak proposed that Solov'ev's conception, divested of idealistic and mystical notions of "eternal beauty" and of "future otherworldly life," becomes "perfectly acceptable for Marxists."[69]

Declaring current artistic practice to be "at a dead end" (*v tupike*), Chuzhak turned his searching attention to Futurism. In answer to the question "Which art is really closer to the proletariat?" (*Kakoe zhe iskusstvo blizhe proletariatu?*), posed in an essay of 1919 that took this question as its title, he suggested that Futurism was "the closest artistically to the emotions and psychology of the rising class."[70] "Is not Futurism the needed ultra-realism?," asked Chuzhak. He predicted that Futurist experimentation with linguistic forms would be needed "tomorrow"—"when iron necessity will put it [Futurism] face to face with the need for a new iron language required for a new Sermon on the Mount."[71]

When in 1922 Chuzhak came to Moscow, he assumed an active role in grafting his Marx-cum-Solov'ev blend of aesthetics onto the current practices of the avant-garde.[72] His treatise "Under the Sign of Life-Building" was clearly meant to have programmatic significance: it appeared in the section of the first issue of *Lef* devoted expressly to theory, thus putting the whole Left Art movement under the sign of life-building. Quoting generously from his previous work, Chuzhak promoted his earlier idea of ultrarealist art.[73] Some quotations, however, were altered to better fit the ambience of the day. He effaced, for instance, his previous emphasis on the role of the individual artist as the "genius" in the transformation of reality.[74] This alteration reflects the fact that in life-building perceptions after the revolution the creative spirit of the collective replaced the figure of artist-superman. This was in line with the massist spirit and with Bogdanov's organizational theory.

It is in this essay that the new aesthetics received its name— "life-building."[75] Addressing the issue of the genesis of life-building aesthetics in Russian art, Chuzhak now distinguished three stages: first, Symbolism, the "formal construction of concepts of tomorrow"; then Futurism, "the intensification of contemporary contradictions" with "the break-through into the Future"; and finally, the current synthetic stage, at which art actually joins new life and begins to produce "new things." Thus, Futurism once again is made the artistic representative of the working class. As Chuzhak put it, quoting himself, "The Russian proletariat objectively, by virtue of its own progressive march in step with history, happened to be the Pygmalion who brought to life the Galatea of Futurism and turned the evolutionary tasks of art into the task of creating revolution."[76] According to Chuzhak, the dialectical principle dictates, however, that Futurism cannot remain "the only fixed and absolute form of art necessary to the proletariat." Therefore, Futurism should not be considered the "permanent and ultimate form of the art": art must continue to march in step with the ultimate historical class.

This meant first of all that the artist, although alien to the proletariat in its origin, must "create in art new yet unseen life in the image of the working class" (*po obrazu i podobiiu rabochego klassa*). In more practical terms, this requirement amounted to sanctioning the artist's further engagement in serving "life" and, more specifically, to the endorsement of Constructivism and Production Art. Obviously, in Chuzhak's current view, "life" gained back its supremacy over the arts because the new life launched by the revolution was, as he saw it, "immeasurably larger than art." This explains why, for instance, at the beginning of his essay Chuzhak downgrades the Constructivist and Production Art efforts,[77] calling them "only timid sophomoric studies" in comparison to "life," where one can witness "a whole uprising of things, resulting from a process of dialectically developing matter, created by an unknown collective artist-demiurge."[78] Toward the end, however, these very same projects are praised, because, Chuzhak argues, however unfledged they may seem relative to the grandeur of "unfolding new life," they are *useful* to this life.[79]

The current stage of life-building was defined by Chuzhak as the "production of new material and ideological values"—such, he wrote, "is the only reliable criterion with which the dialectician approaches art."[80] Besides, Chuzhak found fault with the fact that emerging aesthetic ventures were splintering and going in different directions, each claiming to be the ultimate method. The cure, he suggested, could be found in a universal "guiding philosophy of art, [construed] *as one of the methods of life-building*," and it is to this end that all ideologues of the artistic front must direct their efforts.[81] Needless to say, Chuzhak took this task upon himself.

In his attempts to organize Left Art under a unified life-building theory, Nikolai Chuzhak was not alone. His program found support in Sergei Mikhailovich Tret'iakov (1892–39), a one-time Ego-Futurist and a close associate of Chuzhak's since the period of their collaboration in the Far Eastern Futurist journal *Creation* (*Tvorchestvo*). Tret'iakov's essay "Whence and Whither? (The perspectives of Futurism)" ("Otkuda i kuda? [Perspektivy futurizma]," 1923),[82] published in the first issue of *Lef*, complimented Chuzhak's "Under the Sign of Life-Building" by bringing into relief some cardinal components that we discerned in the earlier theories of both Symbolists and Futurists but that were missing or understated in Chuzhak's program. In addition, Tret'iakov's essay contains ideas that anticipate certain tenets of socialist realist doctrine.

In general, Tret'iakov's theory on the role of art in the construction of the future communist reality is rooted in Bogdanov's organizational theory. Thus, Tret'iakov stated that the revolution had put forward new goals for the artist—namely, the shaping of the masses' psychology and the organization of class will. According to Tret'iakov, the Futurists were the artistic task force best suited to fulfill this mission, because "since its infancy Futurism was concerned not so much with the creation of new paintings, poetry, and prose but with the propagation of a conception of the new man." Tret'iakov supported the idea of Production Art and defined it as art in which "the artist's creativity serves not the tasks of decorative work of all sorts but is applied to all production processes." The new artist belongs not to the cast of "demiurges" but to an appropriate trade union. He creates useful products. The criterion of usefulness, however, he defined as "artistic organization in a progressive direction"—that is, the artist organizes mass energy for the task of building "the most organized form of human society—the commune." Instead of "content" the new artist must be concerned with the "purpose" (naznachenie) of his art. Along the same lines, Tret'iakov postulated that the task of the verbal artists was to create a new "live language, necessary for his time," because "next to the man of science, the 'artistic worker' must become a psycho-engineer, a psycho-constructor." [83] Evidently, this ideation prefigured the formula "Writers are the engineers of human souls," which became the official tenet of socialist realism's conception of the artist and whose coinage has been attributed to Stalin.

Tret'iakov emphasized that the new artist was characterized by a creative or life-building attitude toward reality. He could not be given to a reflective love of nature. His concept of beauty should rest on the notion of nature organized by human will:

It is difficult for him to love nature in the old way of a landscape painter, tourist, or pantheist. The thicket, the untilled steppes, the unused waterfalls, the rain and snow that fall without being commanded to, the avalanches, the caves, and the mountains—all this is repulsive to him. Beautiful is everything that bears the signs of the organizing human hand; splendid is every product of human manufacture, directed toward the goal of conquering and mastering the elemental forces and inert matter.[84]

In redefining the notion of beauty, Tret'iakov followed the strategy used by Chernyshevsky in his dissertation *The Aesthetic Relations of Art to Reality* (*Esteticheskie otnosheniia iskusstva k deistvitel'nosti*, 1853). Tret'iakov's picture of the beautiful future reality, which is rooted in Futurist sensibilities, is close to Trotsky's both in content and in time.

In promoting transformational aesthetics, Tret'iakov perpetuated the distinction between two antithetic modes of reality (*byt*, or everyday reality, and *bytie*, or existence in a metaphysical sense, corresponding to *realia* and *realiora*), a distinction that had been propounded by the Symbolists and maintained, albeit with modifications, by the next generation of the avant-garde. He specified in what kind of reality the revolutionary artist must be involved: "Not *byt* in its inertia and dependence on an established pattern of things, but *bytie*—a dialectically perceived reality that is in the state of perpetual formation, reality understood as the advancement toward the commune, which [as the ultimate goal] is not to be forgotten for a single minute."[85] In this opposition, the principal opposition of the Russian modernist mentality, Tret'iakov too rejected the inertia of *byt* and supported the implicit notion of dynamic transformation of physical matter. However, he redefined its second member: the indefinite "realiora" of the Symbolists or the "future" of the Futurists was replaced by a more definite "commune," or communism. In so doing he, too, came very close to the formulation of socialist realism as the depiction of reality in its revolutionary development, as it was spelled out a decade later, in line with the total mobilization of society's efforts toward communist construction.

Tret'iakov reiterated the slogan "To bring art into life until art is fully dissolved in it,"[86] which had been one of the principle precepts of life-creating theories since the concept was inaugurated by the Symbolists. Yet in his interpretation the slogan became a call for art's return to reflection of everyday life, since life is already "new": contemporary Futurist art was expected to show "the new man in reality, in everyday actions, in the system of his material and psychological life."[87]

The aesthetic axiology whose goal was "joining art with life" and that was once relegated to the distant future was now considered subject to realization in the present. The tenet of making life like art was translated into the principle of functionality.

Vestiges of Life-Building Ideas in the Origins of Socialist Realism

The preceding analysis demonstrated that certain notions of life-building, especially those spelled out by Nikolai Chuzhak and Sergei Tret'iakov, who grafted avant-garde theories onto Marxism, approximated closely, even language-wise, the principal formulaic tenets of the socialist realist doctrine—a fact that has not received scholarly consideration.[88]

The polemics connected with the preparation of the First Congress of Soviet Writers, in which certain key formulas of socialist realism attained categorical shape, manifest the role of life-building vestiges in Soviet culture. In the pre-congress debates and in the speeches at the congress, one can see that the rejection of "formalism" goes hand in hand with the reappropriation of those avant-garde ideas that formed the core of life-building theories. For instance, Maxim Gorky proclaimed that the destiny of true revolutionary art was the creation of "new reality." The writer Fedor Gladkov supported this principle and called for art that would be an instrument for the transformation of reality.[89] The idea was echoed in the speeches of other writers, critics, and bureaucrats. From the congress podium resounded also the idea that the dramatic arts especially constitute a major transformational force.

The question arises: how do we account for the fact that the appropriation of avant-garde ideas accompanied the loud campaign against avant-garde art and the flagrant denunciation of experimental artists that resulted in eventual imprisonment and physical annihilation of a great number of them (the long list of names includes Chuzhak and Tret'iakov)? Any answer to this question is subsumed by a larger problem that received different designations—Stalinism, the "purges" or Great Terror, totalitarianism. No attempt is made here to answer that larger question, which has obviously eluded solution.[90] We may recall, however, that there existed an inherent rivalry between the Bolsheviks and the avant-garde artists with regard to who should be in charge of designing the future reality. Or, as Boris Groys suggested: "There would have been no need to suppress the avant-garde if its black squares and transrational poetry confined themselves to artistic space, but the fact that it was persecuted indicates that it was operating on the same territory as the state."[91]

It is also germane to consider the historical perspective that prevailed in Soviet culture by the mid-1930's. It will be remembered that the modernist aesthetics of life-building was guided by the millenarian conception of history. This perspective was characterized by the rejection of the past and the striving out toward the ideal future. The present was perceived as more akin to the past than to the future. From the first days after the Bolshevik Revolution cultural discourse was dominated by the pathos of the absolute break with the past. A historian cannot fail to notice, nevertheless, the eagerness with which the makers of the new culture strained to discern in present-day reality some features of the "new life." By the time the socialist realist aesthetic doctrine was taking shape, however, the historical outlook was thoroughly invested with the Marxist conception of history, and especially with the notion of socialism as "the first stage of communism." The time frame projected for completion of "the first stage," which was unfeasible from the outset, with the adoption of the "general line" in 1929 grew progressively shorter, until in 1936 socialism was ultimately pronounced "achieved and won." The haste with which the march toward communism was drummed up reflected upon the historical status of the present in Soviet culture. It was increasingly stressed that present-day "socialist" life in a sense already constituted the future life that was sought for. To give but one example, in his speech at the First Congress of Soviet Writers Gorky gave the following lesson in the new perception of new reality:

> We still do not see reality adequately. Even the landscape of our country has drastically changed: its particolored character has disappeared—a bluish strip of oats, a black patch of plowed land next to it, a golden ribbon of rye, a greenish one of wheat, strips of land overgrown with weeds, altogether—the multicolored sorrow of overall scatteredness [and] disunity. Today huge expanses of land are colored mightily, with one color.[92]

Reality has changed and must be seen differently, postulated Gorky. Characteristically, this vision is monochromatic and unified—because now the picture of grandiose life was guided by a unified monistic view of reality and history.

Consequently, rejection of everyday life, or the new Soviet *byt*, became inappropriate. On the ideological plane, it was the peculiar schizophrenia with regard to historical perspective that created the situation in which calls for further efforts toward the communist future were matched by equally resourceful efforts to maintain the status quo.[93] Hence, the exclusion of the "formalist" or "Decadent" because historically they were associated with the rejection of existing empirical reality and as such constituted, in the parlance of Soviet aesthetics, an "escape from reality" (*ukhod ot deistvitel'nosti*). For the same reason so-called *critical* realism—that type of nineteenth-century realism that adopted an acrid view of reality—was also unsuitable for aesthetic representation of the new life.

Thus, in this new historical perspective two central life-building principles—the idea that art must be separate from "everyday life" in the present and the idea that art must be merged with "life" in the future—became subject for reconsideration. Art had to assume the task of reflecting or, at best, decorating the new life, which in itself was declared to be of unprecedented beauty. Thus, art became increasingly subordinate to the needs of everyday life as read in the light of the party program. The life-building program was taken over by the party and state.

At the same time, since the quest for the communist future had not been completed, the pursuit for the ultimate form of the future and the artist's central role in this process remained operative in socialist realist culture. As an aesthetic doctrine, socialist realism combined fatefully the principal modernist idea of the transformational relation of art to life with the idea that the experimental artist must subordinate his art and his personality to "life." To summarize, the following affinities can be distinguished between modernist "life-building" and the aesthetics of socialist realism:

The futurological character of aesthetic endeavor, which was adopted by the Symbolists and modified in Marxist terms in Chuzhak's theory of dialectical "ultra-realism," translated into the socialist realist tenet mandating that art show reality "in its revolutionary development"—mandating, that is, that art not merely reflect life "as it is" but show it "as it ought to be."

The conception of the artist as a creator of "new man," which was shared by Symbolists and Futurists, was also accepted and modified by socialist realism into the concept of the artist as an "engineer of human souls." The highly privileged status of artists in general and writers in particular in Soviet society suggests that the notion of the transformational or demiurgic power of art was recognized by official Soviet culture. The idea of art's transformational function was expressed in the requirement that the artist take an "active stance toward reality" (*aktivnoe otnoshenie k deistvitel'nosti*). The official formulation of socialist realist aesthetics decreed by the First Congress of Soviet Writers prescribed, however, that "the truthfulness and historical concreteness in artistic representation of reality must be combined with the task of the ideological conversion and education of the working people in the spirit of socialism."[94] As the very language of the formulation suggests, the task of "psychic engineers" was conceived in definite and narrow terms—namely, as ideological indoctrination. Modernist life-builders thought of creating the "new man" in terms of a breakthrough into a new form: Symbolists dreamed of "transfiguration" of man, the Futurists took up the task of "reforging" (*perekovka*) of man. Socialist realism abandoned the emphasis on form, but assumed the task as a process of gradual ideological inculcation (*ideinoe vospitanie trudiashchikhsia*).

Nevertheless, under socialist realism, the artist was still revered as a seer and creator of the new reality. In practice that meant that the criterion of artistic talent was conceived as ability to perceive and present at any given moment the direction of history in its progression toward the communist future—that is to say, the veering party line accepted by the Soviet culture as the expression of that direction. Such a requirement kept artists in the spotlight as well as in trouble. They themselves were expected to be the models for the new socialist man. Next after the party leaders, artists—and writers especially—were accorded the highest place in the social hierarchy. The criterion of self-exploration and experimentation in the sphere of personal life championed by the avant-garde artists was translated into grotesque rites of public self-laceration when the artists denounced "deviations" from the correct historical course, their own as well as those of their colleagues.

In conclusion it seems appropriate to quote the view of Nikolai Valentinov, a contemporary of the Symbolists who was actively involved in Marxism and the revolutionary movement, expressed in his memoirs *Two Years with the Symbolists* (*Dva goda s simvolistami*, published in 1969):

Strange as it may seem, there is a great deal of similarity between Bely's view on art at that time [1907] and present views of the people in the Kremlin. Like him, they reject art for art's sake. For them art is only a means of "transformation of life" in accordance with that absolutely true philosophy—or, if you will, materialistic religion—which they, the Kremlin theurgists, claim to possess. Artists are "engineers of souls." Stalin was the hierophant over the theurgists and his every word had to be incarnated in works of art and in life. Now Khrushchev, Bulganin, and Mikoian are the theurgists. They command "daring creative endeavors" of Soviet art (see address of the Party Central Committee to the Congress of Soviet Writers on December 15, 1954).[95]

Appendix

The Russian Texts

Listed below are the original Russian texts of quotations found in the book in translation. Included are all substantial quotations from primary sources, as well as those brief quotations that are idiosyncratic in style or language. All appendix entries are keyed to endnote numbers for the given essay.

Paperno: Introduction

1. Символизм не хотел быть только художественной школой, литературным течением. Все время он порывался стать жизненно-творческим методом, и в этом была его глубочайшая, быть может, невоплотимая правда, но в постоянном стремлении к этой правде протекала, в сущности, вся его история. Это был ряд попыток, порой истинно героических, — найти сплав жизни и творчества, своего рода философский камень искусства.

8. Здесь пытались претворить искусство в действительность, а действительность в искусство. События жизненные, в связи с неясностью, шаткостью линий, которыми для этих людей очерчивалась реальность, никогда не переживались как **только** и **просто** жизненные; они тотчас становились частью внутреннего мира и частью творчества. Обратно:

написанное кем бы то ни было становилось реальным, жизненным событием для всех. Таким образом, и действительность, и литература создавались как бы общими, порою враждующими, но и во вражде соединенными силами всех, попавших в эту необычайную жизнь, в это «символистическое измерение». Это был, кажется, подлинный случай коллективного творчества.

15. Человек не произведение только природы, но и дело или создание искусства. Последний акт Божественного творчества был первым актом человеческого искусства.

16. Учение о воскрешении есть истинный позитивизм, позитивизм в отношении к действию . . . такой позитивизм, который устраняет всякую возможность агностицизма, т.е. чего-либо недоступного знанию.

22. от мысли и от художественного творчества русские образованные люди всегда ждали преображения жизни; в этом отношении у нас сходятся такие антиподы как Писарев с его утилитарным взглядом на искусство и Достоевский с его лозунгом «красота спасет мир».

27. именно жизнь, — то есть движение вперед, наростание новых и новых событий, — только она одна — творчество.

28. Искусство наших дней утверждает жизнь, как творческий процесс. . . . и не приемлет жизни, коснеющей в оковах быта.

29. Искусство есть временная мера: это — тактический прием в борьбе человека с роком. Как в ликвидации классового строя нужна своего рода диктатура класса (пролетариат), так и при упразднении несуществующей, мертвой, роковой жизни нужно провозгласить знаменем жизни мертвую форму. . . . Но, как знать, не должна ли взорваться, исчезнуть, не быть и вся наша жизнь, подвластная року? Тогда-то новое творчество сольется с новой жизнью.

One / Paperno: The Meaning of Art

3. преображение материи чрез воплощение в ней другого, сверхматериального начала.

5. превращение физической жизни в духовную, т.е. в такую, которая . . . способна внутренно преображать, одухотворять материю или истинно в ней воплощаться.

6. при непосредственном и нераздельном соединении в красоте духовного содержания с чувственным выражением, при их полном взаимном проникновении материальное явление, действительно ставшее пре-

красным, т.е. действительно воплотившее в себе идею, должно стать таким же пребывающим и бессмертным, как сама идея.

7. По гегельянской эстетике красота есть воплощение универсальной и вечной идеи в частных и преходящих явлениях, при чем они так и остаются преходящими, исчезают, как отдельные волны в потоке материального процесса, лишь на минуту отражая сияние вечной идеи. Но это возможно только при безразличном, равнодушном отношении между духовным началом и материальным явлением. Подлинная же и совершенная красота, выражая полную солидарность и взаимное проникновение этих двух элементов, необходимо должна делать один из них (материальный) действительно причастным бессмертию другого.

8. не менее реально и гораздо более значительно (в космогоническом смысле) нежели те материальные стихии, в которых она воплощается.

13. всякое ощутительное изображение какого-то бы ни было предмета и явления с точки зрения его окончательного состояния, или в свете будущего мира.

17. творчество, проведенное до конца, непосредственно переходит в религиозное творчество — теургию.

19. вселение Господа в человеческую личность.

26. художник должен стать собственной формой: его природное «я» должно слиться с творчеством; его жизнь — должна стать художественной. Он сам «слово, ставшее плотью».

28. Подобно реалистам, мы признаем единственно подлежащим воплощению в искусстве: жизнь, — но тогда как они искали ее вне себя, мы обращаем взор внутрь. . . . Пусть поэт творит не свои книги, а свою жизнь.

Two / Matich: Symbolist Meaning of Love

5. Для [Соловьева] Богочеловечество . . . есть . . . единственное *дело,* которое человек призван делать на земле. Призвание человека есть прежде всего теургия, т.е. осуществление *дела* Божья . . . как в личной, так и в общественной жизни.

6. Быть может, никто после Платона, не сказал столь глубокого и жизненного о любви и поле, увенчивая первую и восстанавливая человеческое достоинство и богочеловеческое назначение второго, . . . как Вл. Соловьев.

9. Жена, облеченная в солнце, уже мучается родами: она должна явить истину, родить слово, и вот древний змий собирает против нее свои последние силы . . . в конце Вечная красота будет плодотворна, и из нее выйдет спасение мира, когда ее обманчивые подобия исчезнут, как та морская пена, что родила простонародную Афродиту. *Этой мои стихи не служат ни единым словом.*

Cited in text: понятие андрогинизма, духовной телесности и богочеловечности . . . Первое — в мифе, вложенном в уста Аристофана («Пиршество»), второе — в определении красоты («Федр»), и третье — в самом понятии Эрота, как посредствующей силы между Божеством и смертною природой (речь Диотимы в «Пиршестве»). . . . Он не связал их вместе и не положил в реальное начало высшего жизненного пути, а потому и конец этого пути — воскрешение мертвой природы для вечной жизни — остался для него сокрытым, хотя логически вытекал из его собственных мыслей. . . . Платонов Эрот . . . не совершил . . . своего назначения, не соединил неба с землею и преисподнею, не построил между ними никакого действительного моста, и равнодушно упорхнул с пустыми руками в мир идеальных умозрений («Жизненная», 235).

11. Наше личное дело . . . [и] общее дело всего мира . . . — одухотворение материи. Оно подготовляется космическим процессом в природном мире, продолжается и совершается историческим процессом в человечестве.

12. Только при этом, так сказать, химическом соединении двух существ однородных и равнозначительных, но всесторонне различных по форме, возможно (как в порядке природном, так и в порядке духовном) создание нового человека, действительное осуществление истинной человеческой индивидуальности.

13. В эмпирической действительности человека, *как такового,* вовсе нет — он существует лишь в определенной односторонности и ограниченности, как мужская или женская индивидуальность. . . . истинный человек . . . не может быть только мужчиной, или только женщиной, а должен быть высшим соединением обоих. Осуществить это единство или создать истинного человека, как свободное единство мужского и женского начала, сохраняющих свою формальную обособленность, но преодолевших свою существенную рознь и распадение, это и есть собственная *задача* любви.

14. превращение или *обращение внутрь* той самой творческой силы, которая в природе, будучи обращена наружу, производит дурную бесконечность физического размножения организмов . . . . духовно-телес-

ные токи, которые постепенно овладевают материальной средой, [оду-
хотворяют ее и воплощают в ней те или другие образы всеединства,]
— живые и вечные всеподобия абсолютной человечности.

15. Упразднение деторождений — упраздняют и акт, совершенно
естественно, не по закону, а просто в силу . . . а-законности. . . . Иначе
нужно . . . утверждать *здесь* феноменальное . . . преображения тела.

16. каким-то другим, равным по силе ощущения соединения и плот-
скости; другим общим, единым . . . актом.

19. Платон называл любовью «земной» — любовь к другому полу,
а «небесною» любовью называет вовсе не филантропическую, но чув-
ственную любовь и только к одинаковому с собою полу. Он называет
при этом и цитирует поэтессу Сафо . . . это так бесспорно, что в этом
невозможно сомневаться.

22. Мне нравится тут обман возможности: как бы намёк на двупо-
лость, он кажется и женщиной и мужчиной.

26. пионер грядущего века, когда с ростом гомосексуальности, не
будет более безобразить и расшатывать человечество современная эс-
тетика и этика полов, понимаемых как «мужчины для женщин» и «жен-
щины для мужчин».

Cited in text: Мы — эллины: нам чужд нетерпимый монотеизм иуде-
ев, их отвертывание от изобразительных искусств, их, вместе с тем,
привязанность к плоти, к потомству, к семени («Крылья», 218/32).

Cited in text: по еврейской же легенде чадородие и труд — наказание
за грех, а не цель жизни. И чем дальше люди будут от греха, тем дальше будут уходить от деторождения (ibid., 218/32).

Cited in text: Мы — эллины, любовники прекрасного, вакханты гря-
дущей жизни. Как виденье Тангейзера в гроте Венеры, как ясновидения
Клингера и Тома, есть праотчизна, залитая солнцем и свободой, с пре-
красными и смелыми людьми, и туда, через моря, через туман и мрак,
мы идем, аргонавты! И в самой неслыханной новизне мы узнаем древ-
нейшие корни, и в самых невиданных сияниях мы чуем отчизну! (ibid.,
220/33).

Cited in text: Бедные братья, только я из взлетевших на небо остался
там, потому что вас влекли к солнцу гордость и детские игрушки, а
меня взяла шумящая любовь, непостижимая смертным (ibid., 320/109).

48. Современная критика имеет тенденцию рассматривать Кузмина
как *проповедника*, считать его носителем опасных каких-то идей. Так,
мне пришлось слышать мнение, будто «Крылья» для нашего времени
соответствуют роману «Что делать?» Чернышевского.

59. Наш день прошел, как вчерашний. Мы с Д. С. продолжали чи-

тать в моей комнате вчерашнюю книгу. Потом обедали. . . . Дм. С. ушел к себе в гостиницу довольно рано, а я легла спать и забыла, что замужем.

70. Мы не можем быть двое, не должны смыкать кольца. . . . Океану любви наши кольца любви!

Notes

5. [Он рассматривал] историю как процесс становления богочеловечества, имеющего объединить сынов Божиих на земле и самое Землю в одно божественное Тело Жены, облеченной в Солнце.

16. Акт обращён назад, вниз, в род, в деторождение.

Three / Masing-Delic: The Living Work of Art

15. Cited partially:

Скульптор

Евгений Баратынский

Глубокий взор вперив на камень,
Художник нимфу в нем прозрел,
И пробежал по жилам пламень,
И к ней он сердцем полетел.

Но, бесконечно вожделенный,
Уже он властвует собой:
Неторопливый, постепенный
Резец с богини сокровенной
Кору снимает за корой.

В заботе сладостно—туманной
Не час, не день, не год уйдет,
А с предугаданной, с желанной
Покров последний не падет,

Покуда, страсть уразумея
Под лаской вкрадчивой резца,
Ответным взором Галатея
Не увлечет, желаньем рдея,
К победе неги мудреца.   (1841)

33. Cited partially:

Три подвига

Владимир Соловьев

Когда резцу послушный камень
Предстанет в ясной красоте,
И вдохновенья мощный пламень
Даст жизнь и плоть твоей мечте,
У заповедного предела
Не мни, что подвиг завершен,
И у божественного тела
Не жди любви, Пигмалион!
Нужна ей новая победа:
Скала над бездною висит,
Зовет в смятенье Андромеда
Тебя, Персей, тебя, Алкид!
Крылатый конь в пучине прянул,
И щит зеркальный вознесен.
И опрокинут в бездну канул
Себя увидевший дракон.
Но незримый враг настанет,
В рог победный не зови —
Скоро, скоро тризной станет
Праздник счастья и любви,
Гаснут радостные клики,
Скорбь и мрак и слезы вновь ...
Евридики, Евридики
Не спасла твоя любовь.
Но воспрянь! Душой недужной
Не склоняйся пред судьбой.
Беззащитный, безоружный
Смерть зови на смертный бой!
И на сумрачном пороге,
В сонме плачущих теней
Очарованные боги
Узнают тебя, Орфей!
Волны песни всепобедной
Потрясли Аида свод,
И владыка смерти бледной
Евридику отдает.   (1882)

43.   Свет из тьмы. Над черной глыбой
         Вознестися не могли бы
         Лики роз твоих,
         Если б в сумрачное лоно
         Не впивался погруженный
         Темный корень их.

51. Cited partially: На вязаном покрывале кровати, фасонными каблуками прямо на вошедшего, в гладкой, черной юбке, широко легшей напрочь, праздничная и прямая, как покойница, лежала навзничь миссис Арильд. Ее волосы казались черными, в лице не было ни кровинки.

Анна, что с вами? — вырвалось из груди у Сережи, и он захлебнулся потоком воздуха, пошедшим на это восклицание.

Он бросился к кровати и стал перед нею на колени. Подхватив голову Арильд на руку, он другою стал горячо и бестолково наискивать ее пульс. Он тискал так и сяк ледяные суставы запястья и его не доискивался. «Господи. Господи!» — громче лошадиного топота толклось у него в ушах и в груди. Тем временем как взглядываясь в ослепительную бледность ее глухих, полновесных век, он точно куда-то стремительно и без достижения падал, увлекаемый тяжестью ее затылка. Он задыхался, и сам был недалеко от обморока. Вдруг она очнулась.

— You, friend? — невнятно пробормотала она и открыла глаза (Boris Pasternak, *Proza*, 180).

Four / Lavrov: Andrei Bely.

2. В то время, когда каждый думал, что он один пробирается в темноте, без надежды, с чувством гибели, оказалось — и другие совершали тот же путь.

4. С. М. Соловьев рассказывает мне о своем новом знакомом Л. Л. Кобылинском, яром марксисте и одновременно ницшеанце, деятельно работающем в рабочих организациях и одновременно сходящем с ума при чтении Ницше; он начинает меня сильно интересовать.

5. я, Батюшков, Эртель одно время составили как бы *трио;* другой группой была группа: Соловьевы, Петровский, я; наконец, в университете я все более сходился с моим гимназическим товарищем В. В. Владимировым; около него группировались Печковский и С. Л. Иванов.

6. происходит он — в университетском коридоре, под открытым не-

бом: в Кремле, на Арбате, в Новодевичьем монастыре или на лавочке Пречистенского бульвара.

8. в «аргонавтах» ходил тот, кто становился нам близок, часто и не подозревая, что он «аргонавт»; не подозревал о своем «аргонавтизме» Рачинский, еще редко меня посещавший и не бывавший у Эллиса; не подозревал Э. К. Метнер, весной 1902 года не живший в Москве, что и он — сопричислен.

10. аргонавтический центр обрастал партером из приходивших на Эллиса, Челищева, Эртеля.

13. Наши юношеские устремления к заре, в чем бы она не проявлялась — в идеологии, в жизни, в личном общении, были как бы планом совместной жизни в новых пространствах и в новых временах.

15. душою кружка — толкачом-агитатором, пропагандистом.

16. Символ — веха переживаний, это условный знак, говорящий: «Вспомни о том, что открылось тебе тогда-то, о чем *грех* рассуждать и *смешно* спорить...». Иногда символ говорит: «Я помогу тебе вспомнить и снова пережить это».... Так я смотрю и на свой собственный символ — золотое руно. Это условный знак, это рука, указывающая, где вход в дом, это фонограф, кричащий: «встань и иди» ... Но содержание этого символа дает мне мой интеллект и моральный инстинкт, к[ото]рый развит раньше, чем я придумал символ руна.

17. Кстати: я и один молодой человек (Л. Л. Кобылинский) собираемся учредить некоторое негласное общество (союз) во имя Ницше — союз *аргонавтов:* цель экзотерическая — изучение литературы, посвящ[енной] Шопенгауэру и Ницше, а также их самих; цель эзотерическая — путешествие сквозь Ницше в надежде отыскать *золотое руно*. . . . Эмилий Карлович — чувствуете Вы, что звучит в этом сочетании слов, произнесенном в XX столетии русскими *студентами* — *аргонавты сквозь Ницше* за *золотым руном*!! . . . для других это уплывание за черту горизонта, которое я хочу предпринять, будет казаться гибелью, но пусть знают и то, что в то время когда парус утонет за горизонтом для взора *береговых* жителей, он все *еще* продолжает бороться с волнами, плывя ... к неведомому Богу ...

20.   Он встал, как водопад, бурлящий в пене белой,
Кивающий, как призрак в тьме ночной,
Как хмурый горный кряж в броне обледенелой,
Что держит свод небес безбрежно-голубой.

22.   С силой мрака вступивши в борьбу,
            Среди тьмы ты бесстрашно огонь свой зажег
            И России святую судьбу
            Ты предрек, духом Божьим горевший пророк.

23. Положение бакунинского кружка было проще: он имел Гегеля позади себя, нами чаемый Гегель был впереди нас, — его мы должны были создать, потому что Вл. Соловьев был для нас лишь звуком, призывающим к отчаливанию от берегов старого мира.

24. был только импульсом оттолкновения от старого быта, отплытием в море исканий, которых цель виделась в тумане будущего.

25.   Пожаром склон неба объят...
            И вот аргонавты нам в рог отлетаний
            трубят...
            Внимайте, внимайте...
            Довольно страданий!
            Броню надевайте
            из солнечной ткани!

            Зовет за собою
            старик аргонавт,
            взывает
            трубой
            золотою:
            «За солнцем, за солнцем, свободу любя,
            умчимся в эфир
            голубой!..»
            Старик аргонавт призывает на солнечный пир,
            трубя
            в золотеющий мир.

            Все небо в рубинах.
            Шар солнца почил.
            Все небо в рубинах
            над нами.
            На горных вершинах
            наш Арго,
            наш Арго,
            готовясь лететь, золотыми крылами
            забил.

26. Мое желание солнца все усиливается. Мне хочется ринуться сквозь черную пустоту, поплыть сквозь океан безвременья; но как мне осилить пустоту? . . . Стенька Разин все рисовал на стене тюрьмы *лодочку*, все смеялся над палачами, все говорил, что сядет в нее и уплывет. *Я знаю, что это*. Я поступлю приблизительно так же: построю себе солнечный корабль — Арго. Я — хочу стать аргонавтом. И не я. Многие хотят. Они не знают, а это — так.

Теперь в заливе ожидания стоит флотилия солнечных броненосцев. Аргонавты ринутся к солнцу. Нужны были всякие отчаяния, чтобы разбить их маленькие кумиры, но зато отчаяние обратило их к Солнцу. Они запросились к нему. Они измыслили немыслимое. Они подстерегли златотканые солнечные лучи, протянувшиеся к ним сквозь миллионный хаос пустоты, — все призывы; они нарезали листы золотой ткани, употребив ее на обшивку своих крылатых желаний. Получились солнечные корабли, излучающие молниезарные струи. Флотилия таких кораблей стоит теперь в нашем тихом заливе, чтобы с первым попутным ветром устремиться сквозь ужас за золотым руном. Сами они заковали свои черные контуры в золотую кольчугу. Сияющие латники ходят теперь среди людей, возбуждая то насмешки, то страх, то благоговение. Это рыцари ордена Золотого Руна. Их щит — солнце. Их ослепительное забрало спущено. Когда они его поднимают, «*видящим*» улыбается нежное, грустное лицо, исполненное отваги; невидящие пугают[ся] *круглого черного пятна*, которое, как дыра, зияет на них вместо лица.

Это все аргонавты. Они полетят к солнцу. Но вот они взошли на свои корабли. Солнечный порыв зажег озеро. Распластанные золотые языки лижут торчащие из воды камни. На носу Арго стоит сияющий латник и трубит отъезд в рог возврата.

Чей-то корабль ринулся. Распластанные крылья корабля очертили сияющий зигзаг и ушли ввысь от любопытных взоров. Вот еще. И еще. И все улетели. Точно молньи разрезали воздух. Теперь слышится из пространств глухой гром. Кто-то палит в уцелевших аргонавтов из пушек. Путь их далек . . . Помолимся за них: ведь и мы собираемся вслед за ними.

Будем же собирать *солнечность*, чтобы построить свои корабли! Эмилий Карлович, распластанные золотые языки лижут торчащие из воды камни; солнечные струи пробивают стекла наших жилищ; вот они ударились о потолок и стены . . . Вот все засияло кругом . . .

Собирайте, собирайте это сияние! Черпайте ведрами эту льющуюся светозарность! Каждая капля ее способна родить море света. Аргонавты да помолятся за нас!

29. Были недавно ужасы, явление грозящего в молнии, который потребовал от меня под угрозой немедленной гибели подтверждение моей готовности к борьбе. Я дал подтверждение. И на время *они* отступили от меня.

30. по газетам: на небе вспыхивает новая звезда (она вскоре погасла); печатается сенсационное известие, будто эта звезда — та самая, которая сопровождала рождение Иисуса младенца; Сережа прибегает ко мне возбужденный, со словами: «Уже началось».

31. Почти *у всех членов нашего кружка с аргонавтическим налетом были ужасы — сначала мистические, потом психические и, наконец, реальные.*

32. Более отвратительного животного, чем какое я видел на небе в 7 часов вечера 25 авг[уста], я никогда не видал. . . . Громадная мутная, как промасленный лист бумаги, зелено-желтая (я избегаю более точных эпитетов, которые вертятся у меня в голове, чтобы ... «гусей не раздразнить») луна поднималась на ужас земнородным, предвещая, по меньшей мере, какую-нибудь из казней египетских, чуму и т.п. . . . Атмосфера, липкая, удушливая, была насыщена злокачественным туманом и дрянными испарениями Цветного бульвара. Желто-шафранный закат довершал картину. Мне нужно было пройти на Сретенку, и я ясно почувствовал, что несдобровать, — и действительно захворал бессонницей и проч.; но духом бодр и спокоен.

33. О Астра, началось .... Дымка превратилась в черт знает что. Многое гораздо ближе, чем можно ближе ожидать. Приходите, пожалуйста, на минуту. Имею нечто сообщить. Инспектор Лунаков.

34.   Иосиф быстро шел по улицам крутым,
          Среди крутых домов и площадей безлюдных;
       Горела в нем душа предчувствием святым,
          До дна раскрытая для откровений чудных ...

35.   Стать блаженно-счастливыми
                 Наступила пора ...
            Зацветает оливами
                 Голубая гора ...
            Ангел с крыльями белыми
                 Просиял из угла,
            Лучезарными стрелами
                 Перерезана мгла ...

37. Над речами Карено и Терезиты у Гамсуна неугасимое северное сияние ... Неугасимое северное сияние ... Падает ласковый снег. Останавливаешься. Закрываешь глаза. Пусть весь мир пронесется, умчится — мягко, мягко. И это настроение провожает сквозь ужасы в ласковую тишину. А ужасов не мало. Плещутся оргийные волны жизни ... . . . А на душе мягкая грусть — вечное мелькание снежных хлопьев, вечный отдых после долгой бури, блеск золотого, пьянящего шампанского на горизонте, белесоватая тишина ... Герои Гамсуна — это люди, которые раз прислушались к внутренне прозвучавшей музыке и узнали что-то такое, после чего им не стоит волноваться.

38. еще один шаг — и любимое существо становится лишь бездонным символом, окном, в которое заглядывает какая-то Вечная, Лучезарная Подруга.

39. Брезжит надежда, что русская поэзия приблизится к великой задаче организации хаоса для окончательной победы над ним.

40. Задача теургов сложна. Они должны идти там, где остановился Ницше, — идти по воздуху.

43. Трагедия «аргонавтизма»: не сели конкретно мы вместе на «Арго»; лишь побывали в той гавани, из которой возможно отплытие; каждый нашел свой корабль, субъективно им названный «Арго».

45. «Среды» Астрова длились несколько лет, здесь являлись впоследствии разнообразные люди: проф. И. Озеров (с нами беседовавший на тему «Общественность и искусство»), проф. Громогласов (из Академии), прив.-доц. Покровский, Бердяев и В. И. Иванов: П. Д. Боборыкин однажды прочел здесь доклад. Многообразные темы докладов сменяли друг друга; в сезон 904–905 годов мне запомнились рефераты: мои («О пессимизме», «Психология и теория знания», «О научном догматизме», «Апокалипсис в русской поэзии»), Эллиса (2 доклада «О Данте»), М. Эртеля («О Юлиане»), Сизова («Лунный танец философии»), Шкляревского («О Хомякове»), П. Астрова («О свящ. Петрове»); В. П. Поливанов читал свою повесть, поэму «Саул», Соловьев — им написанную поэму «Дева Назарета» и т.д.

46. я ради повинности появлялся в астровском кружке преть в аргонавтическом разглагольствовании.

52. Вечное проявляется в линии времени зарей восходящего века. Туманы тоски вдруг разорваны красными зорями совершенно новых дней. . . . Срыв старых путей переживается Концом Мира, весть о новой эпохе — Вторым Пришествием. Нам чуется апокалиптический ритм времени. К Началу мы устремляемся сквозь Конец.

53. *единственный год в своем роде: переживался он максимальнейшим напряжением*. . . . наши ожидания какого-то преображения светом максимальны. . . . все лето 901 года меня посещали благие откровения и экстазы; в этот год осознал я вполне веяния Невидимой Подруги, Софии Премудрости.

54. было ясно сознание: этот огромный художник — наш, совсем наш, он есть выразитель интимнейшей нашей линии московских устремлений.

56. Мы все переживаем зорю ... Закатную или рассветную? Разве Вы ничего не знаете о великой грусти на зоре? Озаренная грусть перевертывает все; она ставит людей как бы вне мира. Заревая грусть — только она вызвала это письмо ...

Близкое становится далеким, далекое — близким; не веря непонятному, получаешь отвращение к понятному. Погружаешься в сонную симфонию ...

Разве Вы ничего не знаете о великой грусти на зоре? . . . .

Но все изменилось... Я нашел живой символ, индивидуальное знамя, все то, чего искал, но чему еще [не?] настало время совершиться. Вы — моя зоря будущего. В Вас — грядущее событие. Вы — философия новой эры. Для Вас я отрекся от любви. Вы — запечатленная! Знаете ли Вы это?..

57. впервые начинается для меня культ «*солнечного золота*» и настроений, связанных с ним; нота женственной зари сменяется нотою мужественности. . . . Тон зорь лета 1901 года — розовый; тон зорь 902 года — ослепительно золотой.

59. все «*апокалиптическое*», понятое исторично, начинает быть для меня лишь символическим восхождением молитвенным ко Христу; «*Апокалипсис*» есть «*Апокалипсис*» души: путь посвящения в тайну Христова Имени; «она» становится лишь вратами ко внутреннему Христу во мне: София становится Христософией: ризой Христовой.

60.   Летим к горизонту: там занавес красный
            сквозит беззакатностью вечного дня.
            Скорей к горизонту! Там занавес красный,
            весь соткан из грез и огня.

61. Во всех стихотворениях этого периода звучит явственно нота «*срыва*» надежд . . . лейтмотив этого лета — «*не то*», «*не те*», я уже не ощущаю в себе того живительного тока духовности, который окрылял меня эти два года.

68. случайный обрывок, почти протокольная запись той подлинной, огромной симфонии, которая переживалась мною ряд месяцев в этом году.

69. Я *хочу подвига, долга, счастья,* а не слов «о».

70. Когда это будущее станет настоящим, искусство, приготовив человечество к тому, что за ним, должно исчезнуть. Новое искусство менее искусство. Оно — знамение, предтеча.

71. Третью часть «Симфонии» я писал, оказавшись в деревне, у матери, в Серебряном Колодце, меж первым и пятым июнем, нося́ся целыми днями галопом в полях на своем скакуне и застрачивая в седле: сцену за сценой.

73. «Золото в лазури» — в своем роде то же, что «Разбойники» Шиллера, который считал гениальность (чью? — конечно, *своего* типа) трудно совместимую со вкусом. . . . В этой гениальности есть нечто шиллеровское, слегка надломленное, чересчур стремительное: отсюда недостаток вкуса или, правильнее, недостаточное подчинение своих порывов своему вкусу.

74. Язык Белого — яркая, но случайная амальгама; в нем своеобразно сталкиваются самые «тривиальные» слова с утонченнейшими выражениями, огненные эпитеты, огненные метафоры с бессильными прозаизмами: это златотканая царская порфира в безобразных заплатах . . . Белый ждет читателя, который простил бы ему его промахи, который отдался бы вместе с ним безумному водопаду его золотых и огнистых грез, бросился бы в эту вспененную перлами бездну.

75. Если бы Флобер был жив и знаком с ним, то он, может быть, посоветовал бы г. Андрею Белому предать сожжению *почти* все им написанное, как по его совету поступал с своими юношескими опытами Мопассан.

76. не может быть исчерпана творческая личность автора «симфоний». Дело в том, что Белого никак нельзя втиснуть в строго литературные рамки. . . . Он постоянно выплескивается за борт пластических пределов, постоянно нарушает цельность формы и вдается в отнюдь не литературного характера пророчества. Это знамение времени. В этом повинен не один Белый.

77. Светозарна философия зорь. Пелена за пеленой спадает на горизонте, и вот, пока небо темно над головой, у горизонта оно жемчужное. Да.

Если в Вас воплощение Души Мира, Софии Премудрости божией, если Вы Символ Лучесветной Подруги — Подруги светлых путей, если, наконец, зоря светозарна, просветится и горизонт моих ожиданий. Моя сказка, мое счастье. И не мое только. Мое воплощенное откровение, благая весть моя, тайный мой стяг. Развернется стяг. Это будет в день Вознесения.

78. Весной 1903 г. я купила в книжном магазине небольшую книжку поэта Андрея Белого «Вторая симфония драматическая», так как я о ней слышала от многих. Приехав домой, я раскрыла книжку и была поражена тем, что нашла в ней буквально выраженья из этих писем рыцаря, и поняла, что под именем Сказки в этой симфонии он говорит обо мне.

79. Дети Солнца сквозь бездонную тьму хотят ринуться к Солнцу. Как бархатные пчелы, что собирают медовое золото, они берегут в сердцах запасы солнечного блеска. Сердце их вместит полудневный восторг: оно расширится, как чаша, потому что душа их должна стать огромным зеркалом, отражающим молнии солнц. . . .

81. В Москве уже потому центр, что уж очень просится в сердце то, чему настанет когда-либо время осуществиться. Открывается с поразительной ясностью, легко дается. Недавно был в Девичьем монастыре. Восторг снегов превышал все меры. Снега заметали границу между жизнью и смертью. Сквозная сосна вопила о том, что тайно подкралось к душе.

83. В символизме к пяти чувствам прибавляется и шестое — чувство Вечности: это коэффициент, чудесно преломляющий все.

84.   Бывало: за Девичьим Полем
    Проходит клиник белый рой;
    Мы тайну сладостную волим,
    Вздыхаем радостной игрой:
    В волнах лучистого эфира
    Читаем летописи мира.

85. время наших прогулок — закат; мы особенно отдаемся вечерней заре. [с А. С. Петровским] мы забирались на балкон, озирали сонный Арбат и смотрели, как начиналось на востоке порозовение.

86. два раза в небе произошло нечто неизъяснимо-отрадное, выразившееся в своем «*внешнем*» как синтез несовместимых (или редко совместимых) закатов: синтез розового, религиозного, мистического, женственного заката, символизирующего св. Церковь, Душу Мира, Софию, Lumen Coeli Sancta Rosa (Мережковский) с золотым, ницшеанским, человекобожеским, самоутверждающимся закатом.

88. Новодевичий Монастырь — цель прогулок, заходим туда, посещаем могилы отца, Поливанова, Владимира Соловьева, М. С. и О. М. Соловьевых, совсем еще свежие . . . часто среди утонченнейших разговоров о гробе и Вечности мы начинаем молчать, наблюдая тишайшее бирюзоватое небо; оно розовеет к закату. . . . Помолчавши, бывало, опять вызываем слова из молчанья: слова о последнем, о тихом, о нашем, о вовсе заветном.

89. Бегу сюда отдаться негам.

91. Приблизилось небо. Я радовался над могилой Соловьевых. . . . Он принял свое несчастие героически — иначе быть не могло. Еще в день смерти своих родителей он говорил мне, что ко всему приготовлен (казалось, он уже знал, что и мать не будет жива, — он *все* знал). Он готовился к ужасу, зачитываясь «*Чтением о богочеловечестве*». Говорил: «Во мне поднялась волна мессианических чувств, и она вынесет меня» ...

92. Сами же мы набрасывали покров шуток над нашей заветной зарей . . . и начинали подчас дурачиться и шутить о том, какими мы казались бы «непосвященным» людям и какие софизмы и парадоксы вытекли бы, если бы утрировать в преувеличенных схемах то, что не облекаемо словом, т.е. мы видели «Арлекинаду» самих себя.

93. Бугаев заходил ко мне несколько раз. Мы много говорили. Конечно, о Христе, Христовом чувстве ... Потом о кентаврах, силенах, о их бытии. Рассказывал, как ходил искать кентавров за Девичий монастырь, по ту сторону Москва-реки. Как единорог ходил по его комнате ... Мои дамы, слушая, как один это говорит серьезно, а другой серьезно слушает, думали, что мы рехнулись.

94. «кентавр», «фавн» для нас были в те годы не какими-нибудь «стихийными духами», а способами восприятия.

95. Если то, что *по-нашему* так прекрасно, если оно безумие, да здравствует безумие: посшибаем очки трезвости с близоруких носов!

97. Виндалай Левулович Белорог. Единорог. Беллендриковы поля, 24-й излом, № 31.

Огыга Пеллевич Кохтик-Рогиков. Единорот. Вечные боязни. Серничихинский тупик, д. Омова.

Поль Ледоукович Θαθυββα. Миус. Козни. Роговатая улица, д. Шажранова.

98. Недавно Бугаев наделал переполох своим Огыгами, Единорога-

ми и т.д. К нему чуть не призвали психиатра, и много было тяжелого и для него самого и для нас.

100. не . . . шуткой, а желанием создать «атмосферу», — делать все так, как если бы эти единороги существовали.

101. я убегаю из Москвы [в] Нижний Новгород [где] оправляюсь несколько от ряда [жестоких] ударов, нанесенных моим утопиям о мистерии.

103.　　　　　Сквозь пыльные, желтые клубы
　　　　　　　Бегу, распустивши свой зонт.
　　　　　　　И дымом фабричные трубы
　　　　　　　Плюют в огневой горизонт.
　　　　　　　　　　　　«На улице» (1904)

104. Заговорили сущности. Сдернута маска — повсюду удивленные, удивляющие, незамаскированные лица.

105. из боязни, что Вы превратно поймете мою любовь, — я объявляю, *что совсем не люблю Вас*. . . . Мне не надо Вас знать, как человека, потому что лучше я Вас узнал, как символ, и провозгласил великим прообразом.

Мне не нужно ни лично Вас знать, ни знать, как Вы ко мне относитесь. Мое блаженство в том, что *я* Вас считаю сестрой в духе.

106. Я не с небом, и я не с Вами, я с *собой*, с собой говорю: я зову себя, я влюблен в себя самого — вон там за гранью времен я зову самого себя, я зову Вас, я всех зову: «Пора, пора ...»

107. всегда подходил ко мне, и мы немного и отрывочно беседовали на самые общие темы. Я его пригласила к нам, и он заходил раза два или три и при этом никогда ни одним словом, ни одним жестом не давал понять, что он мне писал.

108. Я очень сильно сомневаюсь (относительно Бугаева), был ли я когда-либо действительно понят и любим и не является ли «старинный друг», как меня называет Андрей Белый, просто одним из персонажей «Симфонии», а я сам, живая личность, — просто моделью.

109. было трудно сразу взять настоящий тон по отношению друг к другу. . . . не знали, что друг с другом делать, о чем говорить: о погоде не стоит, а о Прекрасной Даме невозможно.

111. Я садился на диван, опершись рукою на край стола. А. А. садился в кресло перед столом, а выходившая к нам Л. Д. очень часто

забиралась с ногами на кресло около окна, и начинались наши молчаливые многочасовые сидения, где разговора-то, собственно, не было, где он был лишь случайными гребешками пены какого-то непрерывного душевного журчания струй, а если и был разговор, то вел его главным образом я, а А. А. и Л. Д. были ландшафтом перерезавших их ручей слов.

112. Верю, мы связаны для Вечности. — Верю, что нет нас, отдельных, обособленных, а все мы, поскольку обращены к вечности, обращены к Единому источнику, давшему нам единый закон свой, исполняя который приближаемся с верой, надеждой, любовью к нему — Источнику всякой любви.

113. Во мне звучат «фальшивые ноты с точки зрения религиозной любви»? . . . Я знаю ее одну *святую и безгрешную* всегда, даже в ее яркой земной красоте. . . . Я не думаю, что мы с тобой «как-то особенно во Христе». У Него — все равны. . . . Ты же разрываешь, нарушаешь, делишь вместо того, чтобы принять ее святую полноту.

114. в обыденном действии показать необыденность значения его.

115.   Проповедуя скорый конец,
         я предстал, словно новый Христос,
         возложивши терновый венец,
         разукрашенный пламенем роз.

117. У Вас есть такие прозрения, богоощущения, которых нет ни у кого из нас.

118. Если Вы будете иногда писать мне, я смогу опять взять сосуд алавастровый и сесть при дороге.

Сидящая при дороге с алавастровым сосудом.

119.   Да, ты не знал любви, но, полный умиленья,
         Не сладостной мечты ты жаждал, но виденья,
         И радостно порой на жизненном пути
         Ты жаждал не в слезах, но в звуках изойти,
         И много ты страдал, от грезы пробужден,
         И мыслью ко кресту не раз был пригвожден;
         Но в *купол вечности* впубояя взор лучистый,
         Ты горних ангелов внимал напев сребристый,
         В полете горлинок и в шуме сизых крыл
         Ты очертания иной страны ловил,

В напевах слышал ты в сердечном замиранье
И шепот райских струн и райских струй журчанье,
Ты видел перламутр на райских небесах
И бога светлый лик, встающий на водах.

120. Наш мистический опыт этого времени, узнание апокалиптических переживаний в связи с «белым» цветом; смеясь, мы говорили друг другу, что мы исследуем «белые начала» жизни; в них — веяние наступающей великой эры пришествия Софии Премудрости и Духа Утешителя.

121. В его присутствии все словно мгновенно менялось, смещалось или озарялось его светом. И он в самом деле был светел.

122. Он был как бы бестелесен, не-физичен.

123. Был светлоглазый красивый поэт, деликатнейший, стал же «неистово шумящий на помосте» крикливый журналист.

Notes

33. Спустились тени. Мятежные больные сумерки, как беспокойные сны, спустились на землю. Вдали за лесом засыпает заря, золотой закат, как Вы говорите. Розовое золото заката трепещущим заревом тускнело, бледнело, умирало ... Лес засыпал ... В купах дерев словно шептал кто-то быстрым, тревожным шепотом, словно ворожил какими-то тайными чарами.

86. Метаметереологическое наблюдение: в Дедове от 11 мая до 11 июня всего чаще бросалось мне в глаза следующее: фон заката хороший, совсем майский — розовое золото, но на этом фоне очень нехорошее — длинная чернильно-синяя туча с багровыми краями. Вообще мая почти совсем не было, а было что-то странное, скорее июль, но не июль. В Гапсале закатов до сих пор было мало, а когда были, то нехорошие — оранжево-красные.

Five / Grossman: Briusov and Petrovskaia

9. Достаточно было быть влюбленным — и человек становился обеспечен всеми предметами первой лирической необходимости: Страстью, Отчаянием, Ликованием, Безумием, Пороком, Грехом, Ненавистью и т.д. ... Символисты хотели питаться крепчайшими эссенциями чувств.

12. или стать спутницей его «безумных ночей», бросая в эти чудовищные костры все свое существо, до здоровья включительно, или перейти в штат его «жен мироносиц», смиренно следующих по пятам триумфальной колесницы.

18. я в себе ощущал в то время потенции к творчеству «*ритуала*», обряда; но мне нужен был помощник или, вернее говоря, помощница — *sui generis* гиерофантида; ее надо было найти; и собственно подготовить; мне стало казаться, что такая родственная душа — есть: Нина Ивановна Петровская. Она с какой-то особою чуткостью относилась ко мне. Я часто к ней стал приходить; и — поучать ее.

19. Моя тяга к Петровской окончательно определяется; она становится мне самым близким человеком, но я начинаю подозревать, что она в меня влюблена; я самое чувство влюбленности в меня стараюсь претворить в мистерию ... Я не знаю, что мне делать с Ниной Ивановной; вместе с тем: я ощущаю, что и она мне нравится как женщина; трудные отношения образуются между нами.

25. с плачем, с револьвером в руке, с ядом в шкапчике и с уплотнением «символов» до материальной реальности требовала, чтобы из «*ада извел*».

29. белые, холодные залы, белые одежды, белые цветы, белыми слезами истекающие непорочные свечи, и мы, слиянные в таинстве служения новому Христу. ... самого Белого — «лжепророка».

38. высшую ступень человеческого развития и даже нечто выше ее, что он одной половиной своего существа проник уже в новый период развития, что центр тяжести развития его организма переместился в мозг.

таинственный закон природы, в силу которого роковым образом гибнут все такие соединительные «мосты». .... Но именно то, что послужило причиной гибели Ницше, составляло одновременно и его могущество.

46. В моем понимании, любовь, ... — это космическая стихия, это рок, тяготеющий над человечеством, это благодатная сила, охраняющая человека от вымирания.

... любовь это — неведомая сила, возрождающая, воскрешающая жизнь все сызнова, сызнова — до бесконечности.

... любовь — это неудержимое стремление (оно же может стать и источником неутолимых страданий) к полному слиянию двух полов, дабы род человеческий стал лучше и мог достичь Совершенства.

Во имя этой-то любви и этого стремления к Совершенству человек страдает, работает, мучится, борется, убивает один другого, результатом чего является прогресс и совершенствование человеческой породы.

В эту-то сущность жизни пытался я проникнуть . . . Я изучал все проявления любви, чтобы создать себе таким образом полное миросозерцание. Путь далекий, очень далекий.

49. Для меня это был год бури, водоворота. Никогда не переживал я таких страстей, таких мучительств, таких радостей.

53. Вл. Соловьеву финляндское озеро Сайма служило источником вдохновений о Ней: в стихиях воды видел он Ее лик.

57. Я упоен — ! мне ничего не надо! / О, только б длился этот ясный сон.

60. И Ты дала мне увидать последние глубины, последние тайны моей души.

61. И вдруг пришла ты, как что-то новое, неожиданное, несбыточное, о чем мечталось давно и что вдруг осуществилось. Пришла любовь, о которой я только писал в стихах, но которой не знал никогда; пришла женщина, о которых я только читал в книгах (в твоем Пшибышевском), но не видал никогда. Ты мне часто говорила, что тот год был воскресением для тебя; но он был и для меня воскресением. У меня вдруг открылись глаза, сделались в сто раз более зоркими; в руках я почувствовал новую силу. Я вдруг увидал вокруг вновь сокровища.

62. Любовь и стремление к чему-то лучшему, высокому . . . одни являются источником вдохновения для истинного художника.

И мужчина и женщина, скованные узами такой любви, безотчетно стремятся вперед, вперед — в лучезарное будущее . . . веря в великую силу вечно возрождающей ко все совершеннейшей жизни — Любви.

63. Есть два пути восхождения человеческого духа. Один — спокойное самоутверждение, блаженная олимпийская ясность, ровный и торжественный подъем могучего вдохновения. Это — образ «мудреца и поэта» на высокой горной вершине, в розовых утренних лучах. И другой — via dolorosa человеческой души, идущей сквозь хаос, сквозь трагический саморазлад, страшный путь в глубокой тьме при свете синих молний на черном небе отчаяния.

64. И любовь . . . приходит залитая жертвенной кровью. . . . Это упоительная евхаристия, жертвоприношение тела и крови, Дионисов божественный экстаз.

65. Да, я все же не знаю страсти, т.е. слепящей, безумной; я не могу вступить в ее область. Я только стою у ее тяжелых ворот. . . . Судьба мне отказала в лучшем из даров — в блаженстве страдания!

66. Страсть — прежде всего тайна. Любовь — чувство в ряду других чувств, возвышенных и низких. . . . Страсть не знает своего родословия, у нее нет подобных. . . . Страсть в самой своей сущности загадка; корни ее за миром людей, вне земного, нашего. Когда страсть владеет нами, мы близко от тех вечных граней, которыми обойдена наша «голубая тюрьма», наша сферическая, плывущая во времени, вселенная. Страсть — та точка, где земной мир прикасается к иным бытиям, всегда закрытая, но дверь в них.

70.   Неколеблемой истине
    Не верю я давно,
    И все моря, все пристани
    Люблю, люблю равно.

71. мне было смешным наше стремление к единству сил или начал или истины. Моей мечтой всегда был пантеон, храм всех богов.

72. Мысль — вечный Агасфер, ей нельзя остановиться, ее пути не может быть цели, ибо эта цель — самый путь.

76. В январе этого года подступила к сердцу такая невыносимая тоска, что я решила умереть. . . .

Он . . . спросил:

— А ты найдешь второй револьвер? У меня нет. . . .

— А зачем же второй?

— А ты забыла обо мне? . . .

— Ты хочешь умереть? Ты ... ты? Почему?

Он сказал:

— Потому что я люблю тебя.

79. Стремление к чему-то небывалому, невозможному на земле, тоску души, которой хочется вырваться не только из всех установленных норм жизни, но и из арифметически точного восприятия пяти чувств — из всего того, что было его «маской строгой» в течение трех четвертей его жизни, — носил он в себе всегда.

80. Что же отметил тогда во мне Валерий Брюсов. . . . ? Он угадал во мне органическую родственность моей души с одной половиной своей, с той — «тайной», которой не знали окружающие, с той, которую он в себе любил и, чаще, люто ненавидел.

82. Он и она должны соединиться в общее лоно, чтобы слиться в

одно пламя, в одно священное солнце. Там совершится чудо, — великое неземное чудо. . . . Он — Она. Андрогина!

83. что любовь не всегда безумие, и что безумие не всегда любовь!

84. Ты говоришь «спуск», вершина миновала, . . . я этого не чувствую. . . . Нет, верь, дорогой, это не спуск, *это начало.*

Верь в чудо!

85. Но в душе моей нет больше ответов на то, что Ты опять ищешь. . . . каков я теперь: без безумия, с упрямой, с ненасытной жаждой работать, но с бессмертной любовью к Тебе.

87. Я не могу более жить изжитыми верованиями, теми идеалами, через которые я перешагнул. Не могу более жить «декадентством» и «ницшеанством», в которые верю я, верю.

88. Есть какие-то истины — дальше Ницше, дальше Пшибышевского, дальше Верхарна, впереди современного человечества. Кто мне укажет путь к ним, с тем буду я.

89. то был жестокий удар для меня. Ты не знаешь, сколько нитей оборвала ты тогда между моей душой и твоей.

90. Книга стихов должна быть не случайным *сборником* разнородных стихотворений, а именно *книгой,* замкнутым целым, объединенным единой мыслью.

97.   Уголь — я, ты — маргерит.
        Но мой лик преображенный
        Пред твоей душой горит!

98.   Полно! изведано счастье!
        Кубок пустой опрокинут.
        Слаще, чем дрожь сладострастья
        Вольные волны нас ринут.

100. вся душа целиком, в оргийной радости страданья, не брошена в костер. . . . не узнать этой тайны, этого чуда им, изнемогающим в противоречии чувства и долга, — им, отравленным жалостью, которая хуже смерти для тех, кому дают ее они, как драгоценный дар.

101. блаженства распятья, сладострастно-покорной муки во имя Любви.

105. — О чем вы думаете? . . .
     — . . . о любви . . .
. . . Тайна чужой неизвестной души.
     — . . . Я бродяга, скитаюсь по душам и все жду встречи с той любовью, что вижу только во сне. . . .

— Моя любовь то, что называют «безумием». Эта бездонная радость и вечное страдание. Когда она придет, как огненный вихрь, она сметет все то, что называется «жизнью». В ней утонет все маленькое, расчетливое, трусливое, чем губим мы дни. Тогда самый ничтожный станет богом и поймет навсегда великое незнакомое слово «безпредельность».....

— Та любовь, о которой ты говоришь — чудо, и я чувствую, — оно уже коснулось моей души.

107. я хочу умереть ... чтобы смерть Ренаты списал ты с меня, чтобы быть моделью для последней прекрасной главы.

108. как та Рената, которую ты создал, а потом забыл и разлюбил. ... пережила всю нашу жизнь минуту за минутой.

109. Мое новое и тайное имя, записанное где-то в нестираемых свитках San Pietro — Рената.

110. Не кому-либо из знаменитых людей, прославленных в искусствах или науках, но тебе, женщина светлая, безумная, несчастная, которая возлюбила много и от любви погибла, правдивое это повествование, как покорный служитель и верный любовник, в знак вечной памяти посвящает автор.

111. Но со стороны уверенностью могу я здесь дать клятву, перед своей совестью, что в будущем не отдам я никогда так богохульственно ... во власть одного из его созданий, какой бы соблазнительной формой оно ни было облечено.

Notes

13. Бальмонт был для меня неким берегом в юности, от которого я скоро отчалила. Не был он для меня ни теургом, осиянным свыше, как А. Белый, ни мэтром, достойным поклонения и глубокого добровольного подчинения, как В. Брюсов.

Six / Wachtel: Viacheslav Ivanov.

5. Мы думаем, что теургический принцип в художестве есть принцип наименьшей насильственности и наибольшей восприимчивости. Не налагать свою волю на поверхность вещей — есть высший завет художника, но и прозревать и благовествовать сокровенную волю сущностей.

9. Художникам предлежала задача цельно воплотить в своей жизни и в своем творчестве (непременно и в подвиге жизни, как в подвиге

творчества!) миросозерцание мистического реализма или — по слову Новалиса — миросозерцание «магического идеализма».

15. После смерти невесты он проводит остальное время жизни в грусти по ней и радости свиданий в то время, когда ему казалось, что она с ним.

35. Вот латинское стихотворение, в средневековом стиле, которое я только что услышал от Нее, дорогой учитель, во время полночной молитвы, когда я беседовал с Ней, и Она меня утешала в разлуке, говоря, на мою просьбу: «Возьми меня,» — «Уже беру,» — и чувствовал, как она наполняет собою мою душу, возвещает «Воля твоя».

41. Кузмин продолжает играть 9-ую симфонию. Чувствовались близость и почти голос Лидии при последней части.

45. В разных сферах сознания один и тот же символ приобретает разное значение. . . . Подобно солнечному лучу, символ прорезывает все планы бытия и все сферы сознания и знаменует в каждом плане иные сущности, исполняет в каждой сфере иное назначение.

47. Лидию видел с огромными лебедиными крыльями. В руках она держала пылающее сердце, от которого мы оба вкусили.

Notes

26. [похожи] порой на изначальное воспоминание . . . порой на далекое, смутное предчувствие, порой на трепет чьего-то знакомого и желанного приближения.

36. я получила Ваше заказное письмо. *Все* Ваши виденья до того стройны, ясны и безусловны, что трудно говорить о них, и лишь слова Благодарения возможны здесь, слова радости Великой ——— Все они, эти видения, гласят *одно* — что Она Сама хочет вести Вас, и что с каждым днем растут силы Ваши.

Seven / Gutkin: From Futurism to Socialist Realism

12. [Конечно, в тысячу раз легче оглашать воздух такими призывами,] чем подводить под эти смутные тяготения прочную теоретическую базу, и, в свою очередь, неизмеримо труднее всяких априорных построений — оправдание деклараций творческой продукцией.

28. человечество будет . . . привыкать смотреть на мир, как на покорную глину для лепки все более совершенных жизненных форм. Стена между искусством и промышленностью падет. Будущий большой

стиль будет не украшающим, а формирующим. В этом футуристы правы. . . .

Но не только между искусством и производством, — одновременно падет стена между искусством и природой. Не в том, жан-жаковском, смысле, что искусство приблизится к естественному состоянию, а в том, наоборот, что природа станет «искусственнее». Нынешнее расположение гор и рек, полей и лугов, степей, лесов и морских берегов никак нельзя назвать окончательным. . . . Если вера только обещала двигать горами, то техника, которая ничего не берет «на веру», действительно способна срывать и перемещать горы. До сих пор это делалось в целях промышленных . . . , в будущем это будет делаться в несравненно более широком масштабе по соображениям общего производственно-художественного плана. . . . В конце концов (человек) перестроит землю, если не по образу и подобию своему, то по своему вкусу. . . . Социалистический человек хочет и будет командовать природой во всем ее объеме, с тетеревами и осетрами, через машину. Он укажет, где быть горам, а где расступиться. Изменит направление рек и создаст правила для океанов.

29. Cited partially:

> Я сразу смазал карту будня,
> плеснувши краску из стакана;
> я показал на блюде студня
> косые скулы океана.
> На чешуе жестяной рыбы
> прочёл я зовы новых губ.
> А вы
> Ноктюрн сыграть
> могли бы
> на флейте водосточных труб?

30. О чем отдельные энтузиасты не всегда складно мечтают ныне — по части театрализации быта и самого человека, — хорошо и плотно укладывается в эту перспективу.

31. Человек, который научится перемешать реки и горы, воздвигать народные дворцы на вершине Монблана и на дне Атлантики, сумеет уж конечно придать своему быту не только богатство, яркость, напряженность, но и высшую динамичность. Едва сложившись, оболочка быта будет лопаться под напором новых технико-культурных изобретений и достижений.

32. Заботы питания и воспитания, могильным камнем лежащие на нынешней семье, снимутся с нее и станут предметом общественной инициативы и неистощимого коллективного творчества.

33. Человек примется, наконец, всерьез гармонизировать себя самого. Он поставит себе задачей ввести в движение своих собственных органов — при труде, при ходьбе, при игре, — высшую отчетливость, целесообразность, экономию и тем самым красоту. Он захочет овладеть полубессознательными, а затем бессознательными процессами в собственном организме: дыханием, кровообращением, пищеварением, оплодотворением.

35. Человек станет несравненно сильнее, умнее, тоньше; его тело — гармоничнее, движения ритмичнее, голос музыкальнее. Формы быта приобретут динамическую театральность. Средний человеческий тип поднимется до уровня Аристотеля, Гете, Маркса. Над этим кряжем будут подниматься новые вершины.

40.   Я тоже фабрика. . . .
         А мы не деревообделочники разве?
         Конечно — почтенная вещь — рыбачить.
         Но труд поэтов — почтенней паче —
         людей живых ловить, а не рыб. . . .
         Мозги шлифуем рашпилем языка. . . .
         Сердца — такие же моторы.
         Душа — такой же хитрый двигатель.
         Мы равные
         Товарищи в рабочей массе.
         Пролетарии тела и духа.

43. В воздухе, — чтоб освободить землю. Из стекла, — чтоб наполнить светом. Асбест, — чтоб облегчить стройку. На рессорах, — чтобы создать равновесие. . . .

44. Готов предположить худшее — буквальная реализация плана во всех его деталях немыслима ни при нынешнем, ни при каком угодно состоянии техники. «Мое дело предложить» ... так заявил ангелам Маяковский. То же самое делает и Лавинский, так как Лавинского занимала главным образом социальная сторона дела — *формы нового быта.*

57. Теперешний новый зритель (я говорю о пролетариате), наиболее способный, на мой взгляд, освободиться от гипноза иллюзорности, и именно при том условии, что он должен (и я уверен, будет) знать, что перед ним игра, пойдет на эту игру сознательно, ибо через игру он

хочет сказать себя как содействующий и *как созидающий новую сущ-ность*, ибо для его живого (как для нового, в коммунизме уже переро-дившегося человека) всякая театральная сущность лишь предлог время от времени провозглашать в рефлекторной возбудимости *радость но-вого бытия*.

63. Вскрыть зреющие в видимой реальности ростки грядущего, вскрыть новую действительность, прячущуюся в недрах современно-сти, отбросить отживающее, временно-господствующее — вот истин-ная цель художества, рассматриваемая при свете диалектики.

64. Претворить действительность в далекой перспективе, осознать ее во всей ее разрухе, озарить далеким светом и создать грядущую действительность — таков тернистый, но радостный путь гения.

71. Для создания нового железного языка, когда железная необходи-мость поставит его перед необходимостью новой нагорной проповеди.

76. Российский пролетариат объективно, самым ходом поступатель-ных своих шагов в истории, явился Пигмальоном, оживившим Гала-тею футуризма, обратившим эволюционные задания искусства в твор-чество революции.

84. Трудно ему любить природу прежней любовью ландшафтника, туриста или пантеиста. Отвратителен дремучий бор, невозделанные степи, неиспользованные водопады, валящиеся не тогда, когда им при-казывают, дожди и снега, лавины, пещеры и горы. Прекрасно все, на чем следы организующей руки человека; великолепен каждый продукт человеческого производства, направленный к целям преодоления, под-чинения и овладения стихией и косной материей.

85. Не быт в его косности и зависимости от шаблонного строя ве-щей, но бытие — диалектически ощущаемая действительность, находя-щаяся в процессе непрерывного становления. Действительность — ни на минуту не забываемый ход к коммуне.

92. Мы еще плохо видим действительность. Даже пейзаж страны резко изменился, исчезла нищенская пестрота, голубоватая полоска овса, рядом с нею — черный клочок вспаханной земли, золотистая лента ржи, зеленоватая — пшеница, полосы земли, заросшей сорными травами, а в общем — разноцветная печаль всеобщего раздробления, разорванности. В наши дни огромные пространства земли окрашены могуче, одноцветно.

94. правдивость и историческая конкретность художественного изо-бражения действительности должны сочетаться с задачей идейной переделки и воспитания трудящихся людей в духе социализма.

95. Сколь это ни странно, между взглядами в это время на искусство Белого и нынешними взглядами людей Кремля очень много сходства. Они, как и он, отрицают чистое искусство. Искусство для них только средство «преобразовать жизнь» в согласии с той абсолютно-верной философией, или, если хотите, материалистической религией, которой, по их уверению, обладают они, теурги Кремля. Художники — это «инженеры душ». Сталин был иерофантом над теургами и каждое его слово требовало воплощения в произведениях искусства и в жизни. Теперь теургами — Хрущев, Булгарин и Микоян; это они руководят «смелыми творческими дерзаниями» советского искусства (см. обращение 15 декабря 1954 г. ЦК партии к съезду советских писателей).

Notes

Notes

Paperno: Introduction

1. V. Khodasevich, "Konets Renaty," in his *Nekropol'* (Paris, 1976), p. 8.

2. The word *zhiznetvorchestvo* appears in Viacheslav Ivanov's "Zavety simvolizma," in his *Borozdy i mezhi* (Moscow, 1916), p. 139; and in Andrei Bely's *Vospominaniia o A. A. Bloke* (1922–23) (Munich, 1969), p. 275. Bely also uses the phrases *zhiznennoe tvorchestvo* and *tvorchestvo zhizni*; see, e.g., Andrei Bely, "Teatr i sovremennaia drama," in idem, *Arabeski* (Moscow, 1911), pp. 22, 35. The term *zhiznetvorchestvo* is widely used by students of Symbolism.

3. I am indebted to Michael Wachtel for the analysis of the meaning of the concept and its possible English equivalents. Wachtel commented that another ambiguous aspect concerns the very notion of "life," which means "human existence," "living matter," and "the individual life of the artist."

4. On the story of the relations between Blok, Liubov' Blok, and Bely see V. N. Orlov, "Istoriia odnoi druzhby-vrazhdy," in his *Puti i sud'by* (Moscow and Leningrad, 1963); for information in English, see Avril Pyman's *The Life of Aleksandr Blok* (Oxford, 1979). See also the following documents: Andrei Bely, *Vospominaniia ob A. A. Bloke* (Munich, 1969);

V. N. Orlov, ed., *Aleksandr Blok and Andrei Bely. Perepiska* (Moscow, 1940); Aleksandr Blok, "Pis'ma k zhene," in *Literaturnoe nasledstvo*, vol. 89 (Moscow, 1978); L. D. Blok, *I byl', i nebylitsy o Bloke i o sebe* (Bremen, 1979). In the words of Khodasevich, "the story of this love played an important role in the literary life of the epoch, in the lives of many people, including those who have not been directly involved in it, and, in the long run, in the whole history of Symbolism." See V. Khodasevich, "Andrei Bely. Cherty iz zhizni," *Vozrozhdenie*, February 13, 1934.

5. See Z. G. Mints, "Poniatie teksta i simvolistskaia estetika," in *Materialy vsesoiuznogo simpoziuma po vtorichnym modeliruiushchim sistemam*, vol. 1, no. 5 (Tartu, 1974), pp. 134–41.

6. Lidiia Ginzburg described *zhiznetvorchestvo* as "deliberate construction of artistic images and aesthetically organized plots in life." See her *O psikhologicheskoi proze* (Leningrad, 1977), p. 27; English translation: Lydia Ginzburg, *On Psychological Prose* (Princeton, N.J., 1991), p. 20. For a recent example, see Svetlana Boym, *Death in Quotation Marks: Cultural Myths of the Modern Poet* (Cambridge, Mass., 1991), where *zhiznetvorchestvo* is defined as "imaginative self-stylization" (p. 5).

7. Khodasevich, "Konets Renaty," pp. 9 and 13.

8. Ibid., pp. 10–11. On this issue see also V. Khodasevich, "O simvolizme," in his *Izbrannaia proza* (New York, 1982).

9. Khodasevich, "Konets Renaty," p. 8.

10. See Malcolm Bradbury and James McFarlane, "The Name and Nature of Modernism," in Malcolm Bradbury and James McFarlane, eds., *Modernism: 1890–1930* (Middlesex, Eng., 1976), pp. 19–55, for the discussion of the concept.

11. See Irina Paperno, *Chernyshevsky and the Age of Realism: A Study in the Semiotics of Behavior* (Stanford, Calif., 1988), p. 7.

12. Olga Matich was the first to appreciate and reveal the importance of the heritage of the 1860's for Russian Symbolists. See her "Dialectics of Cultural Return: Zinaida Gippius's Personal Myth" (1987), in Boris Gasparov, Robert P. Hughes, and Irina Paperno, eds., *Cultural Mythologies of Russian Modernism: From the Golden Age to the Silver Age* (Berkeley, Calif., 1992), pp. 53–60, and her essay in the present volume.

13. John Malmstad, Preface, in John Malmstad, ed., *Andrey Bely: Spirit of Symbolism* (Ithaca, N.Y., 1987), p. 9.

14. The first volume of Fedorov's *Filosofiia obshchego dela* appeared in 1907 (marked 1906) in Vernyi, in a limited edition (volume 2 was published in 1913 in Moscow); accounts of Fedorov's philosophy appeared in 1904 in *Vesy*, *Istoricheskii vestnik*, and *Russkii arkhiv*. On Fedorov see

the pioneering work by S. Grechishkin and A. Lavrov, "Andrei Bely i N. F. Fedorov," in *Tvorchestvo A. A. Bloka i russkaia kul'tura dvadtsatogo veka. Blokovskii sbornik III* (Tartu, 1979), and comprehensive studies by Michael Hagemeister, *Nikolaj Fedorov* (Munich, 1989), and S. Semenova, *Nikolai Fedorov: Tvorchestvo zhizni* (Moscow, 1990).

15. Fedorov, *Filosofiia*, 2: 239.   16. Ibid., 1: 2.

17. Ibid., p. 421.   18. Ibid., 2: 241–42.

19. The concept "theurgy" is borrowed from patristic and Neoplatonic sources, where it is used to mean "divine action." Solov'ev (and, following him, other Symbolists) freely reinterpreted and expanded the concept.

20. ". . . realizatsiia chelovekom bozhestvennogo nachala vo vsei empiricheskoi, prirodnoi deistvitel'nosti." Vladimir Solov'ev, *Kritika otvlechennykh nachal*, in his *Sobranie sochinenii* (St. Petersburg, 1911–14), 2: 352.

21. See Vladimir Solov'ev, "Tri rechi v pamiat' Dostoevskogo. Pervaia rech'", in his *Sobranie sochinenii*, 3: 189; and idem, "Obshchii smysl iskusstva," ibid., 6: 80–81.

22. Evgeny Trubetskoy, "Svet Favorskii i preobrazhenie uma," *Russkaia mysl'*, no. 5 (1914): 27. A concrete attempt to read the Symbolist theory of art as a program of political action was undertaken by Georgy Chulkov in his theory of "mystical anarchism," initially supported by Ivanov. See Georgy Chulkov, *O misticheskom anarkhizme* (St. Petersburg, 1906), with an introduction by Viacheslav Ivanov.

23. Zinaida Gippius, *Literaturnyi dnevnik 1899–1907* (Munich, 1970), pp. 48 and 191. The original reads: "tvorit' zhizn' vmeste," "pervyi, samyi estestvennyi i prakticheskii zhiteiskii vykhod," "nachinaet 'myslit'' o 'voprose pola.'"

24. Ivanov, "Zavety simvolizma," p. 139.

25. "Iskusstvo est' tvorchestvo zhizni." Andrei Bely, "Pesn' zhizni," in his *Arabeski*, p. 43.

26. "Zhizn' i est' tvorchestvo." Andrei Bely, "Teatr i sovremennaia drama," in his *Arabeski*, p. 20.

27. Gippius, *Literaturnyi dnevnik*, p. 288.

28. Fedor Sologub, "Iskusstvo nashikh dnei," *Russkaia mysl'*, no. 12 (1915): 62.

29. Andrei Bely, "Teatr i sovremennaia drama," in his *Arabeski*, p. 21.

30. Irene Masing-Delic reviewed the ideas on immortality in Russian and early Soviet fiction in her *Overcoming Death: The Myth of Immortality in Twentieth-Century Russian Literature* (Stanford, Calif., 1992).

31. See Richard Stites, *Revolutionary Dreams: Utopian Vision and Experimental Life in the Russian Revolution* (Oxford, 1989). Stites sees a clear connection between the prerevolutionary artistic avant-garde and the utopianism of the Bolshevik Revolution and Bolshevik state (p. 6); he sets a limit for the utopian period at about 1932, when Stalin (and totalitarianism) took over. Boris Groys views Stalinism and totalitarian art as a stage in the development of the avant-garde culture. See Boris Groys, "Stalinism kak esteticheskii fenomen," *Sintaksis*, no. 17 (1987): 98–110, and his *The Total Art of Stalinism: Avant-Garde, Aesthetic Dictatorship, and Beyond* (Princeton, N.J., 1992). The author of the essay on Russian modernism ("Modernism in Russia 1893–1917") in the comprehensive guide on modernism, Bradbury and McFarlane's *Modernism: 1890–1930*, claimed, "we know for certain that [modernism in Russia] ended in 1917" (p. 134). This statement is an anachronism.

32. See Fedor Stepun, *Vstrechi* (New York, 1968), pp. 144 and 151; Nikolai Valentinov, *Dva goda s simvolistami* (Stanford, Calif., 1969), p. 127 (quoted in Irina Gutkin's essay in this volume); N. Ia. Mandelshtam, *Vtoraia kniga* (Paris, 1972), pp. 449–58.

One / Paperno: The Meaning of Art

1. Vladimir Solov'ev, *Sobranie sochinenii* (St. Petersburg, 1911–14), 6: 76.

2. See ibid., p. 82.   3. Ibid., p. 41.

4. Ibid., p. 40.   5. Ibid., p. 84.

6. Ibid., p. 82.   7. Ibid.

8. Ibid., p. 43.   9. Ibid., p. 33.

10. On Chulkov, see also note 22 for the Introduction.

11. Vladimir Solov'ev, "Pervyi shag k polozhitel'noi estetike," in his *Sobranie sochinenii*, 7: 75; on this issue see James West, *Russian Symbolism: A Study of Vyacheslav Ivanov and the Russian Symbolist Aesthetics* (London, 1970), p. 37.

12. On Christological doctrine, see Jaroslav Pelikan, *The Christian Tradition. A History of the Development of Doctrine*, vol. 1 (Chicago, 1971), p. 233.

13. Solov'ev, *Sobranie sochinenii*, 6: 85.

14. Ibid., 3: 189–90.

15. Aspects of Bely's theory of *zhiznetvorchestvo* were reviewed by Maria Carlson, in chap. 2 ("The Silver Dove") of John E. Malmstad, ed., *Andrey Bely: Spirit of Symbolism* (Ithaca, N.Y., 1987), pp. 60–95, and

by L. K. Chursina, in "K probleme 'zhiznetvorchestva' v literaturno-esteticheskikh iskaniiakh nachala XX veka (Bely i Prishvin)," *Russkaia literatura*, no. 4 (1988): 186–99.

16. See Andrei Bely, *"Problema kul'tury,"* Simvolizm (Moscow, 1910), p. 10.

17. Andrei Bely, "Bal'mont," in his *Lug zelenyi* (Moscow, 1910), p. 230; see also his article entitled "O teurgii," in which Bely used the word to mean divine action, mystical translation of word into deed (*Novyi put'*, no. 9 [1903]: 102).

18. Bely develops the theme of the deification of man in "Liniia, krug, spiral' simvolizma," *Trudy i dni*, no. 4–5 (1912): 20; on this issue see Robert A. Maguire and John E. Malmstad, "Petersburg," in Malmstad, *Bely*, p. 100.

19. Andrei Bely, *Arabeski* (Moscow, 1911), p. 236.

20. Andrei Bely, "Fridrikh Nitsshe," in his *Arabeski*, pp. 66, 68, 65.

21. Friedrich Nietzsche, *"The Birth of Tragedy" and "The Genealogy of Morals"* (New York, 1956), pp. 9–10.

22. Solov'ev, *Sobranie sochinenii*, 10: 29. See the interpretation of Nietzsche's aestheticism by a present-day scholar who argues, "Nietzsche looks at the world in general as if it were a sort of artwork; in particular, he looks at it as if it were a literary text." Alexander Nehamas, *Nietzsche: Life as Literature* (Cambridge, Mass., 1985), p. 3.

23. Bely, *Arabeski*, p. 217.

24. Bely, *Arabeski*, p. 90.

25. Viacheslav Ivanov, "O Vladimire Solov'eve," in his *Borozdy i mezhi* (Moscow, 1916), pp. 111–12.

26. Bely, *Lug zelenyi*, p. 28.

27. Dolgopolov claims that Briusov's "Sviashchennaia zhertva" was written "s ogliadkoi na Belogo" ("having Bely in mind") and that it had "a magic significance" for Briusov. See L. Dolgopolov, *A. Belyi i ego roman "Peterburg"* (Leningrad, 1988), pp. 20–21. A revealing comment on Briusov's attitude is found in Valentinov's book: "Reading Bely, Briusov would write on the margins: 'Every word is unclear. What is a creative transfiguration of reality?'" Nikolai Valentinov, *Dva goda s simvolistami* (Stanford, Calif., 1969), p. 132.

28. Valery Briusov, *Sobranie sochinenii v semi tomakh* (Moscow, 1973–75), 6: 97, 99.

29. For this information I am indebted to Michael Wachtel.

30. On Bely's philosophy of language and its theological sources see Steven Cassedy, "Bely's Theory of Symbolism as a Formal Iconics of

Meaning" and "Bely the Thinker," in Malmstad, *Bely*, pp. 285–335; the further development of theological metaphors in discussions of poetic language is traced in Irina Paperno, "O prirode poeticheskogo slova. Bogoslovskie istochniki spora Mandelshtama s simvolizmom," *Literaturnoe obozrenie*, no. 1 (1991): 29–36; English translation in *Christianity and the Eastern Slavs*, vol. 2: Robert P. Hughes and Irina Paperno, eds., *Russian Culture in Modern Times* (Berkeley, Calif., forthcoming), and Steven Cassedy, "Icon and Logos: The Role of Orthodox Theology in Modern Language Theory and Literary Criticism," in Hughes and Paperno, *Russian Culture*.

31. Ivanov, *Borozdy i mezhi*, p. 139.

32. Victor Zhirmunsky, in *Nemetskii romantizm i sovremennaia mistika* (German Romanticism and Contemporary Mysticism) (Petrograd, 1914), points out the importance of the heritage of realism for Symbolism, which he treats as neoromanticism. In Zhirmunsky's words, the age of positivism and naturalism that separates the last romantics from the Symbolists enriched Symbolism. The experience brought about "a new love for real life" and led to the establishment of "such mysticism that accepted the deification of any earthly matter" (p. 190).

33. The metaphor "incarnation," in application to aesthetics, metaphysics, and social programs, was used by many Symbolists. See, for example, Gippius's "Khleb zhizni" (1901). According to Pachmuss, Gippius shared Bely's idea that the meaning of art lies in the incarnation of the word into flesh. See *Between Paris and St. Petersburg: Selected Diaries of Zinaida Hippius*, ed. and trans. Temira Pachmuss (Urbana, Ill., 1975), p. 5. According to Gippius, Merezhkovsky focused his thoughts "on the *incarnation* of Christianity, on the Christianization of the earthly flesh of the world, on bringing heaven down to the earth." Zinaida Gippius, *Dmitry Merezhkovsky* (Paris, 1951), p. 99. Sologub echoes Bely's metaphor in Fedor Sologub, "Iskusstvo nashikh dnei," *Russkaia mysl'*, no. 12 (1915): 35–62.

34. Metaphors derived from the Christological doctrine informed discussions of "the man and poet" issue in Pushkin studies; see Irina Paperno, "Pushkin v zhizni cheloveka Serebrianogo veka," in Boris Gasparov, Robert P. Hughes, and Irina Paperno, eds., *Cultural Mythologies of Russian Modernism: From the Golden Age to the Silver Age* (Berkeley, Calif., 1992), pp. 19–51.

35. Andrei Bely, "Teatr i sovremennaia drama" in his *Arabeski*, p. 21.

36. Andrei Bely, "Realiora," *Vesy*, no. 5. (1908): 59. Following Solov'ev, the Symbolists used the word "realism" in the meaning ascribed to

it in the Platonic theory of universals (as opposed to nominalism). Thus, many polemical arguments concerning "realism" rested on a rhetorical operation of substituting the word with its homonym. An illustration can be found in Nikolai Berdiaev's article "Decadence and Mystical Realism" ("Dekadentstvo i misticheskii realism," *Russkaia mysl'*, no. 6 [1907]: 114–23). Berdiaev argues that the "mystical realism" propagated by the Symbolists is opposed both to positivistic "naturalistic realism" and to modernist "decadent aesthetism." Nineteenth-century realism and classicism, he states, are "pseudo-realisms," whereas the true, or "real," realism is Symbolism. It is quite clear from the context that by "realism" in the "real" sense Berdiaev means the mystical doctrine of the objectification of the word, or idea, expressed in the theological concept of the incarnation of the Word. In application to art, "realism" means art that creates (not reflects) life.

Two / Matich: Symbolist Meaning of Love

1. The most undisguised, radical expression of the antiprocreative bias of nineteenth-century utopian culture was Fedorov's project of resurrecting the dead, which proscribed the reproductive impulse. The wheel of history and laws of nature were to be reversed; "progress" would be defined by the act of giving new birth to one's fathers, who would then live forever, instead of to children, who were destined to die. For a discussin of the antiprocreative tendency in Russian utopianism, see Olga Matich, "The Merezhkovskys' Third Testament and the Russian Utopian Tradition," in *Christianity and the Eastern Slavs*, vol. 2: Robert P. Hughes and Irina Paperno, eds., *Russian Culture in Modern Times* (Berkeley, Calif., forthcoming).

2. In the words of Fedor Stepun, Ivanov's life practice was a unique combination of Slavophilism and Westernization, paganism and Christianity, philosophy and poetry, philology and music, ancient studies and journalism. Fedor Stepun, "Viacheslav Ivanov," in his *Vstrechi* (Munich, 1962), p. 141.

3. Evgeny Trubetskoy described Solov'ev's "The Meaning of Love" as an "erotic utopia"; see V. Zenkovsky, "Utopizm russkoi mysli," *Novyi zhurnal*, 42 (1955): 233.

4. Vladimir Solov'ev, "Smysl liubvi," in his *Sobranie sochinenii* (St. Petersburg, 1911–14), 7: 40.

5. Evgeny Trubetskoy, "Vladimir Solov'ev i ego delo," in *Sbornik per-vyi. O Vladimire Solov'eve* (Moscow, 1911), p. 84. In the same collection,

Viacheslav Ivanov describes Solov'ev's vision of history in utopian terms: "[He perceived] history as the making of godmanhood, whose goal was to unite the sons of God on this earth and the Earth itself in one divine Body of the Woman clothed in the Sun." ("O znachenii Vl. Solov'eva v sud'bakh nashego religioznogo soznaniia," p. 42.)

6. Ivanov, "O znachenii Solov'eva," p. 42.

7. Related to his teaching of Sophia, Solov'ev's image of the androgyne also came from Jakob Boehme and Franz Baader, not only from Plato.

8. Plato, *The Symposium*, trans. W. Hamilton (Baltimore, Md., 1967), pp. 46–47. Further references are given in the text.

9. Vladimir Solov'ev made this statement in 1900 in the third edition of his book of poetry. I am quoting it from Vladimir Solov'ev, *Stikhotvoreniia i shutochnye p'esy* (Leningrad, 1974), p. xiii.

10. Vladimir Solov'ev, "Zhiznennaia drama Platona," in his *Sobranie sochinenii*, 9: 235. Further references are given in the text.

11. Solov'ev, "Smysl liubvi," p. 52.

12. Ibid., p. 19, quoted from Vladimir Solov'ev, "The Meaning of Love," in *A Solovyov Anthology*, ed. S. L. Frank, trans. N. Duddington (Westport, Conn., 1974), p. 160.

13. Ibid., p. 24, quoted from *A Solovyov Anthology*, p. 164.

14. Ibid., p. 60, quoted from *A Solovyov Anthology*, p. 179.

15. Temira Pachmuss, *Intellect and Ideas in Action: Selected Correspondence of Zinaida Hippius* (Munich, 1972), p. 67.

16. Ibid., p. 64. "The [sex] act is directed backwards, downwards, into generation, childbirth," wrote Gippius to Filosofov (p. 67). As a substitute for the generic urge to propagate, Gippius suggested the Christian kiss, containing God's spark. Premised on the partners' androgynous identity, in Solov'ev's sense, it represented the union of "the two in one" that preserved each individual's uniqueness. "I love kisses. In a kiss both are equal," wrote Gippius in *Contes d'amour* (Zinaida Hippius, *Contes d'amour*, in her *Between Paris and St. Petersburg: Selected Diaries of Zinaida Hippius*, ed. and trans. Temira Pachmuss [Urbana, Ill., 1975], p. 71).

17. Elaine Showalter, *Sexual Anarchy: Gender and Culture at the Fin de Siècle* (New York, 1990), pp. 172–73.

18. V. V. Rozanov, *Liudi lunnogo sveta: Metafizika khristianstva* (Petersburg, 1911), p. 111.

19. V. V. Rozanov, "Krotkii demonizm," in his *Religiia i kul'tura* (Petersburg, 1899), p. 162.

20. Hippius, *Contes d'amour*, pp. 73–74.

21. Ibid., p. 77. (The Russian original and English translation of *Contes d'amour* exist only in expurgated versions, but the omissions are not the same in both instances. For the passage just cited the Russian is unavailable.) Gippius's androgynous position was reflected in the male lyrical persona of her poetry and the male pen names under which she wrote philosophical essays and literary criticism.

22. Ibid., p. 74.

23. Unlike her counterpart in the Ivanov circle, Lidiia Zinov'eva-Annibal, Gippius seems to have neglected the ideological connotations of lesbian love, perhaps to conform with the male Platonic ideal. Apparently in 1900, Gippius had an affair with Baronness Elizabeth von Overbach, an English composer. "Can both of us be equal in our love? For I cannot be happy otherwise," she wrote in reference to that relationship (ibid., p. 78).

24. Pachmuss, *Intellect and Ideas*, pp. 71–72.

25. Like Plato, Ivanov was a practitioner of maieutics, or the midwifery of thought, a dialectical method involving question and answer and mutual criticism in arriving at the truth.

26. Viacheslav Ivanov, *Sobranie sochinenii* (Brussels, 1971–), 2: 750.

27. According to Bely, Shestov gave Ivanov the epithet Magnificent (Andrei Bely, *Nachalo veka* [Moscow-Leningrad, 1933], p. 322). It resembles the reference to Gippius as Zinaida Prekrasnaia (Zinaida the Fair), by analogy with Elena Prekrasnaia (Helen of Troy).

28. Stepun, "Ivanov," p. 143.

29. Ibid.

30. In a typical case of cultural syncretism, they also evoked Christ's Last Supper and the Passion of Christ, which the Ivanovs reenacted, combining them with the agony and ecstasy of Dionysus.

31. Bely, *Nachalo veka*, p. 316.

32. For a discussion of Plato and Greek homosexuality, see K. J. Dover, *Greek Homosexuality* (Cambridge, Mass., 1978), and Anthony Price, *Love and Friendship in Plato and Aristotle* (Oxford, 1989).

33. Olga Deschartes, "Vvedenie," in Ivanov, *Sobranie sochinenii*, 1: 104. Like Plato, Ivanov believed that the spirit is born of beauty and that each person he loved represented the path *de realibus ad realiora*.

34. The image of the adolescent also evokes Pushkin's homoerotic "Imitation of Arabic" ("Podrazhanie arabskomu"), which begins with the verse "Tender youth, gentle youth" (*Otrok milyi, otrok nezhnyi*).

35. Deschartes, "Vvedenie," p. 98.

36. Ivanov, *Sobranie sochinenii*, 2: 753. The image of Gorodetsky before the mirror as the high point of his Platonic relationship with Ivanov may also be compared to Kuzmin's narcissistic mirror motif, symbolizing separation from as well as merging with the beloved. In *Wings*, Vania Smurov admires his own reflection in the water after he is told by another youth that he has a beautiful body. See Irina Paperno, "Dvoinichestvo i liubovnyi treugol'nik: Poeticheskii mif Kuzmina i ego pushkinskaia proektsiia," in John E. Malmstad, ed., *Studies in the Life and Works of Mixail Kuzmin (Wiener Slawistischer Almanach*, 24 [1989]), pp. 59–61.

37. Ivanov, *Sobranie sochinenii*, 2: 759.

38. Perhaps the first Symbolist reference to the *Phaedrus* and the myth of the winged soul occurred in the 1901 novel *Leonardo da Vinci*, by Merezhkovsky; later it appeared in his study of Tolstoy and Dostoevsky. Discussing Plato's metaphor of love, Merezhkovsky emphasizes the association of pain and fever with feelings of love, symbolized by the regeneration of wings in the lover's soul, which Plato compares to the pain of teething and of boils and wounds.

39. Vania Smurov is the name of one of the young boys around Alesha in *The Brothers Karamazov*.

40. Mikhail Kuzmin, *Kryl'ia*, in his *Proza*, ed. V. Markov (Berkeley, Calif., 1984), 1: 319; quoted from Mikhail Kuzmin, *Wings*, trans. and ed. Neil Granoien and Michael Green (Ann Arbor, Mich., 1972), p. 108. Further references to both—first to the Russian, then to the English— are given in the text. For a discussion of the *Phaedrus* and *Wings*, see Donald Gillis, "The Platonic Theme in Kuzmin's *Wings*," *Slavic and East European Journal*, 22, no. 3 (1978): 336–47.

41. See Lavrov's essay in this volume.

42. Max Klinger and Hans Thoma were German painters associated with the Decadence.

43. Ivanov's Platonic feelings were extended to the sons of his wife, Lidiia. In his diary he speaks of moments when he is in love with Kostia (Ivanov, *Sobranie sochinenii*, 2: 797) and with Serezha (ibid., p. 745).

44. Ibid., p. 744.

45. For a discussion of the Hafiz Society, see N. A. Bogomolov, "Epizod iz Peterburgskoi kue'turnoi zhizni, 1906–1907 gg.," *Blokovskii sbornik*, no. 8 (Tartu, 1988), pp. 95–111.

46. Temira Pachmuss, Preface, in Hippius, *Between Paris and St. Petersburg*, p. viii.

47. Ivanov, *Sobranie sochinenii*, 2: 749–50.

48. Alexander Blok, "O drame," in his *Sobranie sochinenii v vos'mi tomakh* (Moscow, 1962), 5: 185.

49. For a discussion of courtly love vs. marriage, see Denis de Rougemont, *Love in the Western World*, 2nd ed., trans. M. Belgion (Princeton, N.J., 1956), pp. 32–35, 275–311.

50. For a discussion of Blok's marriage, see Vl. N. Orlov, "Istoriia odnoi liubvi," in his *Puti i sud'by* (Leningrad, 1971), pp. 636–743.

51. Andrei Bely, *Arabeski* (Moscow, 1911), p. 125.

52. Andrei Bely, *Vospominaniia ob Aleksandre Bloke* (Letchworth, Eng., 1964), p. 21.

53. "He liked the 'almond' eyes of Asia, in whose smile were fused the Gioconda and infant" (Nikolai Valentinov, *Dva goda s simvolistami* [Stanford, Calif., 1969], p. 14).

54. The Blok and Bely marriages contained elements of populist marital practice as well.

55. Irina Paperno, *Chernyshevsky and the Age of Realism: A Study in the Semiotics of Behavior* (Stanford, Calif., 1988), p. 136. On fictitious marriage in the 1860's, see ibid., pp. 31–36, 133–36.

56. For a discussion of Gippius as Cleopatra, see Olga Matich, "Dialectics of Cultural Return: Zinaida Gippius' Personal Myth," in Boris Gasparov, Robert P. Hughes, and Irina Paperno, eds., *Cultural Mythologies of Russian Modernism: From the Golden Age to the Silver Age* (Berkeley, Calif., 1992), pp. 53–60.

57. The biography was written in the 1940's, at a time when the polemics with utilitarian critics were no longer significant, which may help explain the seemingly undisguised Chernyshevskian subtext.

58. For a discussion of the Pygmalion myth in Russian Symbolism, see Irene Masing-Delic's essay in this volume.

59. Zinaida Gippius, *Dmitry Merezhkovsky* (Paris, 1951), p. 34. After Vera Pavlovna and Lopukhov first discuss their marital plans, they shake hands and part as usual. When they get secretly engaged, she feels that they had already been married for a long time, as if nothing had changed.

60. For a discussion of the Merezkhovsky marriage in terms of *What Is to Be Done?*, see Matich, "Dialectics of Cultural Return," pp. 60–66.

61. For a discussion of the radical triple union and collectivity in love, see Paperno, *Chernyshevsky*, pp. 29–36, 133–53, 156–58.

62. Zinaida Hippius, "About the Cause," in her *Between Paris and St. Petersburg*, p. 102.

63. Pachmuss, *Intellect and Ideas in Action*, p. 71.

64. Vladimir Zlobin, *Tiazhelaia dusha* (Washington, D.C., 1970), p. 54; quoted from Vladimir Zlobin, *A Difficult Soul: Zinaida Gippius*, ed. Simon Karlinsky (Berkeley, Calif., 1980), p. 85.

65. Anton Kartashev was president of the Religious Philosophical Society in Petersburg and was the last procurator of the Holy Synod. He was also a close collaborator of the Merezhkovskys.

66. Temira Pachmuss, *Zinaida Hippius: An Intellectual Profile* (Carbondale, Ill., 1971), p. 90.

67. Pachmuss, *Intellect and Ideas*, pp. 652–53, 662.

68. Ivanov, *Sobranie sochinenii*, 1: 34–35.

69. Ibid., 2: 796.

70. Ibid., p. 755.

71. Ibid., p. 756.

72. Margarita Woloschin, *Die Grüne Schlange, Lebenserinnerungen* (Stuttgart, 1954), p. 191.

73. Ivanov, *Sobranie sochinenii*, 2: 777–78.

74. Lidiia Zinov'eva-Annibal's doubts about the triple union were reflected in her 1906 novel, *Thirty-three Monstrosities* (*Tridtsat' tri uroda*), published in 1907.

75. Ivanov, *Sobranie sochinenii*, 2: 758.

76. Ibid., p. 762.

Three / Masing-Delic: The Living Work of Art

1. Hermann Schlüter, *Das Pygmalion-symbol bei Rousseau, Hamann, Schiller* (Zurich, 1968), p. 5.

2. Rousseau's Pygmalion perceives all reality not created by him as so alien that he must produce a creature of his own imagination. The "belle âme" that he is needs a partner, "an other," but this "other" can only be "another self" (*un autre moi-même*). For Rousseau's treatment of the Pygmalion motif, see Schlüter, *Pygmalion-symbol*, pp. 11–44.

3. Quoted from J. L. Carr, "Pygmalion and the *Philosophes*," *Journal of the Warburg and Courtauld Institutes*, 23 (1960): 239. It is this assumed transmutability of matter perceived as essentially one and the same in all its manifestations that allowed Denis Diderot to assert that "flesh can be made from marble, and marble from flesh" and that marble (as any other type of inorganic matter) had "inactive sensitivity," which could be stimulated and become active. Quoted from Lester G. Crocker's *Diderot: The Embattled Philosopher* (New York, 1966), p. 312.

4. Mathias Mayer, "Midas statt Pygmalion," *Deutsche Vierteljahrsschrift für Literaturwissenschaft und Geistesgeschichte*, 64, no. 2 (1990): 290–91.

5. Elsie B. Adams, *Bernard Shaw and the Aesthetes* (Columbus, 1971), p. 133.

6. Carr, "Pygmalion," p. 255. These ideas had logical repercussions for pedagogics. A good teacher should fill the blank space of the mind within the purely material shell of the body with valid consciousness—that is, he should act as a kind of Pygmalion (as Shaw's Professor Higgins does). A good pedagogue makes learning, or the acquisition of consciousness, a pleasurable experience.

7. Alexander Lavrov's article in this volume deals in detail with the development of the term and concept "life-creator."

8. Adams, *Bernard Shaw*, p. 137.

9. In fact, Nietzsche views the creation of the superman in Pygmalionesque terms. His Zarathustra (in *Thus Spoke Zarathustra*, 1885) perceives "an image sleeping in stone" that he cherishes above all else (as "Bild meiner Bilder") because it is the image of the future dynamic and beautiful superman hidden in the rough stone of the amorphous contemporary man. See Friedrich Nietzsche, *Also sprach Zarathustra, Sämtliche Werke* (Stuttgart, 1964), 6: 92–93. Bergson, in his *Creative Evolution* (1907), seems to perceive a basic "transmutability of matter" (Carr's term) that would allow for wondrous transformations.

10. Liudmila's erotic fantasies in Sologub's *Mel'kii bes* (1907) are Ovidian. Thus she envisions herself as lying naked on a lake shore while a white swan approaches on the dark calm waters, i.e., as Leda. Liudmila also constantly changes the image of her boy lover, Sasha, in dressing-up games and make-believe play. Her creativity, however, is limited to the pursuit of erotic pleasure and aesthetic play and therefore does not acquire the ontological validity of theurgical creativity.

11. Roman Jakobson, "Stikhi Pushkina o deve-statue, vakkhanke i smirennitse," in A. Kodjak and K. Taranovsky, eds., *Alexander Pushkin. A Symposium on the 175th Anniversary of His Birth* (New York, 1976), p. 10. It may also owe something to Diderot's close friend Étienne Maurice Falconet (1716–91), who created a well-known sculpture on the motif in 1763. Falconet's Pygmalion watches his nymph come to life "in rapt adoration" (Carr, "Pygmalion," p. 247). As is well known, Falconet is also the creator of the equestrian statue of Peter the Great, which, of course, is the subject of Pushkin's *The Bronze Horseman* (*Mednyi vsadnik*, 1833). It could be argued that this equestrian monument contains an element of the Pygmalion myth in that the posture of the "proud steed," as it prepares for its leap, is so active as to be nearly animated. Also, according to a popular anecdote of the times, Peter the Great purportedly once embraced a statue of Richelieu with great passion, begging it/him to share some of its/his statesman's wisdom with him. This anecdote was used by the German philosopher Johann Hamann (1730–88) to present Peter

as a noble "Scythian" who had faith in miracles and therefore could become the "creator of his people" (see Schlüter, *Pygmalion-symbol*, pp. 45–71). Pushkin may have known this anecdote, which well illustrates the Enlightenment creed of "natural miracles," performed by men believing in man's endless potential both as malleable raw material and as Promethean creator.

12. Turgenev certainly knew the myth. His "Three Meetings" ("Tri vstrechi," 1852), for example, likens the disillusioned heroine to a Galatea who has returned to her pedestal to remain there forever after her excursion to the realm of love and life. For a detailed discussion of Bazarov as utopian scientist, see Irene Masing-Delic, "Bazarov pered sfinksom. Forma i dissekcija v romane Turgenva *Otcy i deti*," *Revue des études slaves*, 57, no. 3 (1985): 369–83.

13. Boris Bukhshtab, "Predislovie," in Afanasy Fet, *Stikhotvoreniia* (Leningrad, 1959), p. 30.

14. Fet, *Stikhotvoreniia*, p. 227.

15. Evgeny Baratynsky, *Polnoe sobranie sochinenii* (Leningrad, 1957), pp. 187–88, my translation. The emphasis in the quoted passages is mine. Choosing the designation "sage" (*mudrets*) for his sculptor, the poet indicates his affinity with the romantic "lovers of wisdom" group (*liubomudry*). His artist is a philosopher who perceives creativity as a process of cognition as well as a refinement of feeling. Galatea too must "grasp" the meaning and purpose of the passion to which she is subjected (*strast' urazumeia*). It is worth noting that, while in Ovid Pygmalion's nymph was nameless and Galatea belonged to another myth, she was by this time firmly ensconced in the Pygmalion story. The wisdom-lover Dmitry Venevitinov saw "self-cognition" as the driving force behind artistic creativity. The artist, he wrote, "animates canvas and marble solely to realize his own feeling, to convince himself of his own power; the poet betakes himself by means of art into combat with nature, with fate, in order to test his own spirit." Quoted from Lauren G. Leighton, *Russian Romantic Criticism. An Anthology* (New York, 1987), p. 111.

16. According to some Ovid scholarship, *The Metamorphoses* presents the notion that artists are capable of surpassing the Creator Deity, for in a "competition of beauty art comes out ahead" of nature. See Joseph B. Solodow, *The World of Ovid's Metamorphoses* (Chapel Hill, N.C., 1988), p. 219.

17. There is some similarity between Baratynsky's poem and one of Marquis de Saint-Lambert's on the same motif. Although this eighteenth-century poet was mainly interested in the erotic aspects of

the sculptor's work with his "ciseau voluptueux," Lockean notions are also discernible in his vision of the statue awakened to life by "des desirs." See Carr, "Pygmalion," pp. 248–49. In Baratynsky's poem the "insidious chisel" clearly has erotic implications, but eroticism is subordinated to aesthetics in a romantic vein that anticipates Solov'evian views on love sublimated to art.

18. Gogol's *Dead Souls* (*Mertvye dushi*, 1842) may be seen as based on a kind of Pygmalion principle, since the author is faced with the task of transforming grotesque Russian landowners and bureaucrats (these "bears," "cucumbers," "boxes," and "samovars") into human beings by stripping them of their deformities and revealing a hidden, if not beauty, then at least humanity. It was presumably the immensity of this theurgical metamorphosis that prevented Gogol from completing the trilogy of which *Dead Souls* was to form the first part. Ovid is mentioned in the novel in a jocular context. Satirizing Russian bureaucrats' consciousness of rank, the author states that a man who is a veritable Prometheus when with his subordinates undergoes "a metamorphosis such as even Ovid could not contrive" when faced with his superiors. Then he becomes "a mere fly, less even, no more than a grain of sand." Nikolai Gogol, *Dead Souls*, trans. George Reavey (New York, 1985), p. 49.

19. Goncharov was prone to reversals of this type within the context of "sculptural myths." Thus young Alexander Aduev, in *A Common Story* (*Obyknovennaia istoriia*, 1847), on coming to St. Petersburg is at first deeply disappointed in the city. But he "freezes" into admiring immobility before the statue of Peter the Great, unlike Pushkin's "poor Evgeny," who runs away in terror, as the author emphasizes. This reverse reaction to the *Bronze Horseman* was pointed out to me by Ms. Liudmila Yevsukov, graduate student in the Ohio State University Slavic Department.

20. The passages are from Ivan Goncharov, *Oblomov*, trans. David Magarshack (Harmondsworth, Eng., 1986), pp. 233, 413, 447, 455, 455.

21. Konstantin Mochulsky speaks of Solov'ev's "eroticism of thought" (in his *Vladimir Solov'ev. Zhizn' i uchenie* [Paris, 1951], p. 244). S. N. Trubetskoy calls Solov'ev's theories of androgyny and Sophia an "erotic utopia" (quoted from V. V. Zenkovsky, *A History of Russian Philosophy* [London, 1967], 2: 515). Solov'ev's aesthetics seems indebted to the erotic-animation theories of French *philosophes*, as well as to German romantic *Naturphilosophie*, which linked transformation to a "total eroticization of reality" (*Gesamterotisierung*). See Kurt Lüthi, *Feminismus und Romantik* (Vienna, 1985), p. 34.

22. *Oblomov*, pp. 456–57.

23. Stolz is often perceived, by both Soviet and Western critics, as a mediocre man who lacks ideological daring. A notable exception is Vsevolod Setchkarev, who sees Stolz as an entirely positive character, a commonsense person 'who, because of his sobriety and unwavering love for Olga, is able to help her overcome her *taedium vitae*, caused by the loss of youthful illusions about life and by adult realization of the limitations of any human existence. Goncharov was not enamored of radicalism of either a materialist or an idealist type. Stolz represents the "golden mean." See Vsevolod Setchkarev's "Andrej Štol'c in Gončarov's *Oblomov*: An Attempted Reinterpretation," in *To Honor Roman Jakobson* (The Hague, 1967), 3: 1799–1805.

24. See Irina Paperno's *Chernyshevsky and the Age of Realism: A Study in the Semiotics of Behavior* (Stanford, Calif., 1988).

25. The (phonetically orchestrated and hence foregrounded) expression "dlia vsekh vechnaia vesna" (N. G. Chernyshevsky, *Chto delat'?* [Leningrad, 1967], p. 405) seems to imply something other than generic immortality in the Feuerbachian sense. Rather it intimates a real conquest of death achieved by omnipotent mankind. Olga and Stolz also live in a state of "eternal spring," but without the utopian overtones implied in Chernyshevsky's novel.

26. Chernyshevsky's theory of rational egotism is heavily indebted to the French Enlightenment, for example, Rousseau's vision of a "sensibilité morale" that demands the moral pleasure of making others happy, for entirely egotistical reasons (Schlüter, *Pygmalion-symbol*, p. 32), since seeing others in a happy state affords the perceiver undiluted pleasure.

27. According to Zenkovsky, Solov'ev was "inspired by the ideas of N. F. Fyodorov" (*Russian Philosophy*, 2: 516), at least when writing "Smysl liubvi," where immortalization is presented as natural, logical, and, hence, fully feasible.

28. Nikolai F. Fedorov, *Filosofiia obshchego dela*, vol. 2 (Moscow, 1913), p. 226; Vladimir Solov'ev, "Obshchii smysl iskusstva," in his *Sobranie sochinenii* (St. Petersburg, 1911–14), 6: 90.

29. See, for example, Fedorov's "Iskusstvo, ego smysl i znachenie," in his *Filosofiia*, 2: 224–38.

30. Ibid., pp. 225–26.

31. Solov'ev, *Sobranie sochinenii*, 6: 45.

32. There is the possibility, of course, explored more in Solov'ev's poetry than in his philosophy, that beauty may side with deception and evil, after all. In Dostoevskian and Blokian terms, the Beautiful Lady

may "change her appearance," leaving her noble knight in despair at the transformation from the "ideal of the Madonna" to the "ideal of Sodom."

33. Vladimir Solov'ev, *Stikhotvoreniia i shutochnye p'esy* (Munich, 1968), pp. 77–78. It is of interest that Solov'ev seems to be following a Gogolian hierarchy of the arts in the structure of his poem. Gogol's "Sculpture, Painting and Music" ("Skul'ptura, zhivopis' i muzyka," 1831) declares music to be supreme among the "three marvelous sisters" named in the title, since sculpture is limited to the sensual, painting incorporates the spiritual, and music is spirit manifest. Solov'ev perhaps shared Gogol's concern that "if even music abandoned us, what then would become of the world?" For Orpheus's art form came closest to conquering death. Or was it the Word that synthesized (plastic) imagery with (musical) rhythm that was to free the world from death forever?

34. As a Christian thinker Solov'ev naturally acknowledged that Christ had "overcome death by His death." But he did also argue that His spiritual conquest should be followed by an elimination of the physical phenomenon, this to be accomplished by mankind (the ideal lovers) in obedience to Christ's own wishes. Fedorov too argued that God (Christ) Himself wanted mankind to abolish death as a physical phenomenon.

35. In his 1898 article "Plato's Life Drama" ("Zhiznennaia drama Platona," in his *Sobranie sochinenii*, 9: 194–241), Solov'ev claims that Plato formulated the idea of life-creation, postulating that "the task of Eros was to give birth in beauty" (p. 228) by immortalizing the flesh. Plato's mistake, his "life drama," was not to take his own idea seriously enough to realize it in life.

36. Gnostic thought establishes parallels between the "seeds of the Spirit" and sperm (see Jacques Lacarrière, *The Gnostics* [New York, 1977], pp. 84–89). Such parallels seem to be intimated also by both Fedorov and Solov'ev. Clearly, sperm is an inferior materialization of the fiery sparks of the creative spirit, just as procreation is an inferior substitute for creation. It should therefore be metamorphosed back to its origins in a higher spiritual realm where Eros is supreme creation.

37. Non-Symbolist writers within the modernist camp could be wary of theurgical aesthetics, as seems to have been the case with Leonid Andreev, who includes a kind of anti-Pygmalion motif in his story "Eleazar" (1906). In dealing with the spiritually unsuccessful resurrection of Lazarus, the story presents a Roman sculptor (of sculptural beauty) who is dissatisfied with his marble and bronze sculptures, although his contemporaries call them immortal. He yearns to imbue his art works with light, but is unable to do so, and herein lies "the noble

[*svetloe*] suffering of his life" (Leonid Andreev, "Eleazar," in his *Povesti i rasskazy* [Moscow, 1971], 1: 636). Upon meeting the resurrected Lazarus, the epitome of the nonsculptural man, disfigured as he is by four days of decay, the artist loses his ability to create even the lifeless beauty of his heavy bronze and marble statues. He has lost confidence, as it were, in the human form, seeing how easily it is dissolved, as well as in the dead immortality of stone. The only work of art he subsequently creates is a butterfly placed in the midst of some grotesque shapes. The implication seems to be that only the butterfly of the soul survives the material body, and that the latter should be left to decay in its native realm of shapeless matter.

38. Trirodov may well combine other archetypes also, such as the Faust of Goethe's *Faust II*, who wanted to become a wise king in order to create an earthly paradise.

39. In his experiments with plants, Merezhkovsky's da Vinci seems to be "preempting" Goethe and his experiments with the morphology of plants. He unwittingly helps discover laws that show that reproduction need not involve traditional progenitors; instead, a small material component proves sufficient to recreate an entelechy, a total form.

40. This expression is taken from Merezhkovsky's "Deti nochi," in D. S. Merezhkovsky, *Sobranie stikhov 1883–1910* (Letchworth, Eng., 1969), p. 7.

41. All quotes are from Dmitri Merejcovski, *The Romance of Leonardo da Vinci*, trans. Bernard Guilbert Guerney (New York, 1954). The quote here is from p. 67. Subsequent page numbers from this edition are given in parentheses in the text.

42. Yet he himself creates statues that are but a step from the divine, such as the model for the Colossus, showing Francesco Sforza on a rearing "gigantic steed" that tramples a "warrior under its hooves" (p. 69). This model is destroyed, but the ultimate reason for da Vinci's failure to create a god is not mob destructiveness but the subject matter of his work of art. His "bronze horseman" is not trampling on death, but on a man subject to death. The artist fails to understand that (as Fedorov taught) heroes will become immortal gods only when they declare war upon death, instead of on mortals. Falconet's statue of Peter the Great a few centuries later would come closer to the notion of a Saint George crushing death. His rearing steed tramples the snake, or dragon of death.

43. Solov'ev, *Stikhotvoreniia*, p. 112.

44. The image of the discarded shell is borrowed from Fedorov (*Filo-

sofiia, 1: 83). The dire consequences of separating art from life are also explored in Oscar Wilde's *The Picture of Dorian Gray*, which is occasionally evoked in Merezhkovsky's *Leonardo da Vinci*. It is also very likely that Edgar Allan Poe's "The Oval Portrait" has left its traces in Merezhkovsky's novel, since Poe belongs to the cult figures of the Symbolist movement. Poe's story deals with an artist who "in pursuit of his pleasure and his dream ravages his bride in the act of painting her." When "his dream is completed, he finds that reality and art, the non-living representation, have exchanged places, and his wife is dead." For these quotes see Joan Delaney Grossman, *Edgar Allan Poe in Russia: A Study in Legend and Literary Influence* (Würzburg, 1973), p. 124.

45. But this detail only confirms that the living woman dies because the painted woman is immortalized: Looking at her portrait, da Vinci notices how well he succeeded in painting her throat. The dimple in it is so lifelike that the observer can almost feel the blood pulsating there. Yet his painting strikes da Vinci as "spectral" in its very lifelikeness, and the young woman on the canvas is "ancient in her immortal youth" (p. 496). He is, belatedly, realizing what he has done.

46. In one of his sketches for the Mona Lisa portrait, da Vinci endows her with certain masculine features, such as muscular arms and a flat bosom. This illustration, included in the novel (p. 396), may be there to show that the artist perceives her readiness to incorporate his masculinity. Yet he is not ready to absorb her femininity, in spite of his affinity with the feminine (he has effeminate features).

47. Walter Pater, *The Renaissance, Studies in Art and Poetry* (1893 text) (Berkeley, Calif., 1980), pp. 98–99.

48. Fedor Sologub, *Tvorimaia legenda* (Munich, 1972), pt. 3, *Dym i pepel*, p. 169. The other two volumes of the work are pt. 1, *Kapli krovi*, and pt. 2, *Koroleva Ortruda*. All further volume and page references to the trilogy are given in parentheses in text.

49. Mary and Paul Rowland see Lara as a Koré figure and explore her mythic-archetypal relation to her mother, Amalia Guichard, who is cast in the role of Demeter. See their *Pasternak's "Doctor Zhivago"* (London, 1967).

50. Boris Pasternak, *Doktor Zhivago* (Ann Arbor, Mich., 1967), p. 211. All further page references to this edition are given in parentheses in text.

51. Boris Pasternak, *A Tale*, in his *Proza 1915–1958*, ed. G. Struve and B. Filippov (Ann Arbor, Mich., 1961), p. 180.

52. For further discussions of resurrection symbolism in Pasternak's

work, see my papers "Zhivago as Fedorovian Soldier," *Russian Review*, 40, no. 3 (1981): 300–316; and "Bergsons Schoepferische Entwicklung und Pasternaks Doktor Schiwago," in E. Reissner, ed., *Literatur- und Sprachentwicklung in Osteuropa im 20. Jahrhundert* (Berlin, 1982), pp. 112–31.

Four / Lavrov: Andrei Bely

1. Vladislav Khodasevich, "Konets Renaty," in his *Nekropol'. Vospominaniia* (Brussels, 1939), p. 9.

2. *Alexander Blok i Andrei Bely. Perepiska* (Moscow, 1940), p. 7.

3. See Andrei Bely, *Nachalo veka* (Moscow-Leningrad, 1933), p. 21.

4. Andrei Bely, "Material k biografii (intimnyi), prednaznachennyi dlia izucheniia tol'ko posle smerti avtora" (1923). Central State Archive of Literature and Art (TsGALI), f. 53, op. 2, ed. khr. 3, l. 18.

5. Ibid., l. 26 ob. 6. Bely, *Nachalo veka*, p. 19.

7. Ibid., pp. 22–23. 8. Ibid., pp. 107–8.

9. See Andrei Bely, *Vospominaniia o Bloke, Epopeiia* (Moscow-Berlin), no. 1 (1922): 225.

10. Bely, *Nachalo veka*, p. 23.

11. Ibid., pp. 57, 54.

12. Bely, *Vospominaniia, Epopeiia*, p. 225.

13. Andrei Bely, *Vospominaniia ob Aleksandre Aleksandroviche Bloke*, *Zapiski mechtatelei* (St. Petersburg), no. 6 (1922): 113.

14. See Z. G. Mints, "Poniatie teksta i simvolistskaia estetika," in *Materialy vsesoiuznogo simpoziuma po vtorichnym modeliruiushim sistemam*, vol. 1, no. 5 (Tartu, 1974), pp. 134–41. A number of terms proposed by Mints will be used below, among them "tekst zhizni" ("life text") and "tekst iskusstva" ("art text").

15. Bely, *Vospominaniia, Epopeia*, p. 178.

16. Manuscript Division, Lenin Library, Moscow (hereafter GBL), f. 25, kart. 35, ed. khr. 46.

17. GBL, f. 167, kart. 1, ed. khr. 12.

18. Bely, "Material," l. 29.

19. See E. K. Metner, "Romantizm i Nitsshe," *Pridneprovskii krai*, no. 2310 (1904); signed "E."

20. TsGALI, f. 575, op. 1, ed. khr. 4. Compare the interpretation of the Russian Symbolists' "Nietzscheanism" in S. S. Averintsev, "Poeziia Viacheslava Ivanova," *Voprosy literatury*, no. 8 (1975): 152–53.

21. Bely, "Material," l. 15.

22. Sergei Solov'ev, "Pamiati Vladimira Solov'eva," written July 31, 1901, GBL, f. 25, kart. 26, ed. khr. 1.

23. Bely, *Vospominaniia, Zapiski*, pp. 24–25.

24. Bely, *Nachalo veka*, p. 54.

25. Andrei Bely, "Zolotoe runo," in his *Zoloto v lazuri* (Moscow, 1904), pp. 8–9.

26. GBL, f. 167, kart. 1, ed. khr. 15.

27. Bely, *Zoloto v lazuri*, pp. 197–210.

28. Bely, "Material," l. 41 ob.

29. GBL, f. 25, kart. 26, ed. khr. 13, l. 11.

30. Bely, "Material," l. 17.

31. Bely to E. K. Metner, first half of May 1904, GBL, f. 167, kart. 1, ed. khr. 35.

32. GBL, f. 25, kart. 21, ed. khr. 16.

33. GBL, f. 25, kart. 26, ed. khr. 2. Compare the July 6, 1904, letter of A. S. Chelishchev to Bely, which reflects the effort to transmit an inner condition by means of a psychological description of nature: "The shadows descended. Restless, sickly gloom, like unquiet dreams, came down on earth. In the distance beyond the forest the twilight is falling asleep, the golden sunset, as you say. The rosy gold of the sunset with a trembling glow dimmed, paled, died . . . The forest fell asleep . . . In a cluster of trees it was as if someone whispered in a quick, anxious whisper, as if he cast a spell with some kind of secret charms" (GBL f. 25, kart. 25, ed. khr. 6).

34. *Svobodnaia sovest'. Literaturno-filosofskii sbornik*, bk. 1 (Moscow, 1906), p. 98.

35. Ibid., pp. 100–101. Sergei Solov'ev's poems from the cycle "The Olive Trees of Galilee" ("Maslina Galilei," written chiefly in 1903–4) on Gospel and church themes, despite all of their historical coloration, contain meaning relevant to the Argonauts. (See S. Solov'ev, *Tsvety i ladan. Pervaia kniga stikhov* [Moscow, 1907], pp. 11–46.)

36. Bely to Metner, Dec. 11, 1902, GBL, f. 167, kart. 1, ed. khr. 5.

37. Andrei Bely, review in *Novyi put'*, no. 2 (1903): 171, 172.

38. Andrei Bely, "O teurgii," *Novyi put'*, no. 9 (1903): 109.

39. Andrei Bely, "Poeziia Valeriia Briusova," *Novyi put'*, no. 7 (1904): 138.

40. Andrei Bely, "Simvolizm kak miroponimanie," *Mir iskusstva*, no. 5 (1904): 179, 185.

41. Bely, *Vospominaniia, Zapiski*, p. 95.

42. Bely to Metner, Apr. 1, 1905, GBL, f. 167, kart. 1, ed. khr. 44.

43. Bely, *Vospominaniia, Epopeiia*, p. 225.

44. Bely gave a caricature of P. I. Astrov in *Nachalo veka* (pp. 357–63); the problems of the sessions were reflected in the letters of Astrov to Bely from that period (GBL, f. 25, kart. 8, ed. khr. 17).

45. Bely, *Vospominaniia, Epopeiia*, p. 157.

46. Andrei Bely, "Pochemu ia stal simvolistom i pochemu ia ne perestal im byt' vo vsekh fazakh moego ideinogo i khudozhestvennogo razvitiia" (1928). TsGALI, f. 53, op. 1, ed. khr. 74, l. 20 ob.

47. Bely to Blok, May 26, 1906, *Blok i Bely. Perepiska*, p. 177.

48. The project of a series of anthologies to be called *Argo*, conceived by Ellis, dates probably from 1906. Ellis composed a list of proposed members of an editorial committee and a constitution for Argo. The list included P. N. Batiushkov, Andrei Bely, Ellis, M. A. Ertel, K. P. Khristoforova, N. P. Kiselev, G. A. Rachinsky, M. I. Sizov, and S. M. Solov'ev. Also proposed was a "committee of five," to be made up of the editors of the sections of the projected anthologies (1. poetry, literature, esthetics; 2. philosophy; 3. science; 4. mysticism; 5. social issues. TsGALI, f. 575, op. 1, ed. khr. 15, l. 2). The constitution included the following points: "1. The basic task of the *Argo* anthologies is the synthesis of the five sections. 2. *Argo* will be published twice a year: at Christmas and at Easter. 3. Selection of materials is the responsibility of the editorial committee in the form of an 'editorial meeting.' 4. At general meetings the editors of sections shall choose by open ballot one of their number as chairman, who will conduct the proceedings as 'primus inter pares,'" etc. Ellis's project remained unrealized.

49. The years indicated are those of composition, in most cases considerably earlier than the years of publication.

50. "Spisok propavshikh ili unichtozhennykh avtorom rukopisei," compiled by Andrei Bely (1927), opens with the note: "Two cantos of the poem 'Child-Sun' ['Ditia-Solntse'] including more than 2,000 verses (iambs, blank verse, in lines of various lengths); the poem was intended to include three cantos; the third canto was unwritten; in its time the poem was recited to S. M. Solov'ev and A. A. Blok; it was lost in the spring of 1907." (GBL, f. 60, ed. khr. 31. See also Andrei Bely, *Mezhdu dvukh revoliutsii* [Leningrad, 1934], pp. 19–21.) Bely saw in this poem the "extinction" of the theme of the "symphonies" (1900–2). (See also Bely to R. V. Ivanov-Razumnik, Mar. 1–3, 1927, published in *Cahiers du monde russe et sovietique*, 15, no. 1–2 [1974]: 62–63.)

51. Bely to R. V. Ivanov-Razumnik, Jan. 21, 1931, TsGALI, f. 1782, op. 1, ed. khr. 22.

52. Bely, *Vospominaniia, Zapiski*, p. 9.

53. Bely, "Material," l. 16, 17.

54. Bely, *Vospominaniia, Zapiski*, p. 15.

55. Bely, "Material," l. 17.

56. GBL, f. 171, kart. 24, ed. khr. 1a. (Translator's note: The Russian word *zoria* refers simultaneously to "sunset" and "sunrise.")

57. Bely, "Material," ll. 28, 29.

58. Bely to R. V. Ivanov-Razumnik, Mar. 1–3, 1927, *Cahiers du monde russe*, p. 61.

59. Bely, "Material," l. 29.   60. Bely, *Zoloto v lazuri*, p. 16.

61. Bely, "Material," l. 39.   62. Ibid., l. 33.

63. Bely, *Vospominaniia, Zapiski*, p. 70.

64. Bely, "Material," l. 44 ob.

65. See below. For a more detailed account see S. S. Grechishkin and A. V. Lavrov, "Biograficheskie istochniki romana Briusova 'Ognennyi angel,'" *Wiener Slawistischer Almanach*, 1 (1978): 84–87. See also Joan Delaney Grossman's essay in this volume.

66. Bely, "Pochemu ia stal simvolistom," l. 18 ob.

67. Bely to R. V. Ivanov-Razumnik, Mar. 1–3, 1927, *Cahiers du monde russe*, p. 5.

68. Bely, "Material," l. 17 ob.

69. GBL, f. 171, kart. 24, ed. khr. 1a.

70. Bely, "Simvolizm kak miroponimanie," pp. 177–78.

71. Bely, *Nachalo veka*, p. 121.

72. Bely, "Material," l. 18 ob.

73. E. K. Metner, "Poeziia i kritika," *Pridneprovskii krai*, no. 2179 (1904); signed "E."

74. Valery Briusov, in *Vesy*, no. 4 (1904): 60–62.

75. Chronicle of the journal *Mir iskusstva*, no. 15 (1903): 163, signed "P.N."

76. Chronicle of the journal *Mir iskusstva*, no. 4 (1904): 164, signed "D.F."

77. GBL, f. 171, kart. 24, ed. khr. 1a.

78. M. K. Morozova, *Andrei Bely. Problemy tvorchestva. Stat'i. Vospominaniia. Publikatsii* (Moscow, 1988), p. 526.

79. Andrei Bely, "Svetovaia skazka," *Al'manakh "Grif"* (1904), pp. 11–12.

80. Bely to E. K. Metner, apparently written on Jan. 23, 1904, GBL, f. 167, kart. 1, ed. khr. 31.

81. Bely to E. K. Metner, written in Jan. 1903, GBL, f. 167, kart. 1, ed. khr. 7.

82. Bely, "Material," l. 18.

83. Bely to E. K. Metner, Feb. 14, 1903, GBL, f. 167, kart. 1, ed. khr. 9.

84. A. Bely, *Stikhotvoreniia i poemy* (Moscow-Leningrad, 1966), p. 418. Translation from Andrey Bely, *The First Encounter*, trans. Gerald Janeček, notes and commentary by Nina Berberova (Princeton, N.J., 1979), p. 33.

85. Bely, "Material," l. 18, 19 ob. It is noteworthy that the image of the sunset had great meaning in the work of Dostoevsky—one of the "rulers of thoughts" for Bely at that time. Sunset meditations and symbols in Dostoevsky transfer the described events to another register and endow them with a certain higher meaning. The experience of sunset there was of two kinds: "zakatnaia toska i gnet" and "zakatnoe osvobozhdenie mira." (See S. N. Durylin, "Ob odnom simvole u Dostoevskogo," in *Dostoevsky* [Moscow, 1928], pp. 163–68.) V. N. Toporov reveals in this a direct link to the mythopoetic tradition. (See his "Poetika Dostoevskogo i arkhaichnye skhemy mifologicheskogo myshleniia," in *Problemy poetiki i istorii literatury* [Saransk, 1973], pp. 96–97.)

86. Bely to E. K. Metner, Aug. 7, 1902, GBL, f. 167, kart. 1, ed. khr. 1. Bely drew many of those close to him into the discussion of sunsets. Characteristic is the postscript by M. S. Solov'ev added to a letter from his son, Sergei, to Bely, written in Gapsal' [Estonia], July 6, 1902: "A metameteorological observation: at Dedovo from 11 May to 11 June more and more often I was struck by the following: the background of the sunset was fine, completely May-like—rosy gold, but against that background was something not at all fine—an elongated inky-blue cloud with crimson edges. Generally, there was almost no May at all but instead something strange, more like July, but not July. In Gapsal' so far there have been few sunsets, and when they occurred, they were not fine, but orange-red." (GBL, f. 25, kart. 26, ed. khr. 2.)

87. Bely, "Material," l. 15.

88. Bely, *Vospominaniia, Epopeiia*, p. 174.

89. Bely, *Stikhotvoreniia i poemy*, p. 424; Janeček's translation, *First Encounter*, p. 47.

90. Valery Briusov, *Dnevniki 1891–1910* (Moscow, 1927), p. 129.

91. Bely to E. K. Metner, Mar. 15, 1903, GBL, f. 167, kart. 1, ed. khr. 11. Cf. Bely's poem "Mogilu ikh ukrasili venkami," dedicated to "the unforgettable memory of M. S. and O. M. Solov'ev" (Bely, *Zoloto v lazuri*, p. 216).

92. Bely, *Vospominaniia, Zapiski*, p. 57.

93. Briusov, *Dnevniki*, p. 134. Cf. T. Iu. Khmel'nitskaia, "Poeziia Andreiia Belogo," in Bely, *Stikhotvoreniia i poemy*, pp. 19–21.

94. Bely, *Nachalo veka*, p. 11.

95. Bely, "Neskol'ko slov dekadenta, obrashchennykh k liberalam i konservatoram," Chronicle of the journal *Mir iskusstva*, no. 7 (1903): 67.

See also Bely's assertion in a letter to Blok of July 14, 1903: "[R]ol' *iurodivogo*, anarkhista, dekadenta, shuta mne poslana svyshe" (*Blok i Bely. Perepiska*, p. 37).

96. Bely to E. K. Metner, Oct. 22, 1903, GBL, f. 167, kart. 1, ed. khr. 26.

97. GBL, f. 386, kart. 79, ed. khr. 5. The cards cited were sent to Briusov on Oct. 18, 1903.

98. TsGALI, f. 55, op. 1, ed. khr. 408.

99. On Oct. 20, 1903, Briusov sent his visiting cards to Bely in three envelopes addressed to "Boris Nikolaevich Bugaev" and respectively directed thus: "for transmittal to Vindalai Levulovich Belorog," "for transmittal to Ogyga Pellovich Kokhtik-Rrogikov," and "for transmittal to Pol' Ledoukovich Thathyvva" (GBL, f. 25, kart. 10, ed. khr. 9a).

100. Briusov, *Dnevniki*, p. 134.

101. Bely, "Pochemu ia stal simvolistom," l. 18 ob.

102. Andrei Bely, "Toska o vole," *Al'manakh "Grif"* (1905), pp. 9–19. In 1906 Bely planned a volume of poems under the title "Toska po vole." These poems were later distributed in his books *Pepel* and *Urna*. (*Literaturnoe nasledstvo*, vol. 85: *Valery Briusov* [Moscow, 1976], p. 392.)

103. Andrei Bely, "Na ulitse," *Al'manakh "Grif"* (1905), p. 10.

104. Andrei Bely, "O teurgii," *Novyi put'*, no. 9 (1903): 119.

105. GBL, f. 171, kart. 24, ed. khr. 1a.

106. Ibid., ed. khr. 1g.

107. Morozova, *Andrei Bely*, p. 528.

108. E. K. Metner to Viacheslav Ivanov, Dec. 12/25, 1912, GBL, f. 109.

109. Bely, *Vospominaniia, Epopeiia*, pp. 42, 45.

110. Bely, *Vospominaniia, Zapiski*, p. 56.

111. Ibid., pp. 103–4.

112. GBL, f. 25, kart. 30, ed. khr. 13.

113. GBL, f. 25, kart. 21, ed. khr. 17.

114. Boris Bugaev [Andrei Bely], "Formy iskusstva," *Mir iskusstva*, no. 12 (1902): 360.

115. Bely, *Zoloto v lazuri*, p. 18.

116. Ellis to E. K. Metner, Feb. 3, 1914, GBL, f. 167, kart. 8, ed. khr. 28.

117. D. S. Merezhkovsky to Bely, Sept. 30, 1904, GBL, f. 25, kart. 19, ed. khr. 9.

118. A. A. Kublitskaia-Piottukh to Bely, July 31, 1905, GBL, f. 25, kart. 18, ed. khr. 5.

119. GBL, f. 25, kart. 25, ed. khr. 31.

120. Bely, "Material," l. 16.

121. Khodasevich, *Nekropol'*, p. 16.

122. N. Valentinov, *Dva goda s simvolistami* (Stanford, Calif., 1969), p. 46.

123. K. Balmont to V. Briusov, Dec. 11, 1908, GBL, f. 386, kart. 76, ed. khr. 1.

Five / Grossman: Briusov and Petrovskaia

1. V. F. Khodasevich, "Konets Renaty," *Nekropol'* (Paris, 1976), pp. 7–25. The essay was dated "Versailles, 1928."

2. Khodasevich recalled that the first edition of Konstantin Bal'-mont's *Budem kak solntse* carried a dedication to another such figure, the little-remembered artist Modest Durnov, "sozdavshemu poemu iz svoei lichnosti" ("Konets Renaty," p. 9).

3. Ibid.

4. Khodasevich, who became acquainted with Nina Petrovskaia in 1902, is the chief, though scanty, source of information about her early biography. He reported that she completed the gymnasium and a dental course, adding that she preferred not to recall her earliest years and that she concealed her age, though he believed her to be about six years older than himself (ibid., p. 10). In this he was mistaken; he placed her birth "about 1880," whereas actually she was born in 1884. Thus in fact this extremely young woman had only a two-year advantage over one of whom she speaks offhandedly and sometimes unflatteringly in her memoir, regarding him as a combination of younger brother and devoted page. This originally unequal relationship, while it obviously changed with time, suggests reasons for the tone and sometimes the handling of facts in Khodasevich's recollections.

5. This is how she pictured those earliest years in the memoir she wrote in the vastly different milieu of postwar Berlin. Here, in personally desperate circumstances, she recalled her years with Briusov as a golden time of intense existence far above the common horde. By comparison almost all other participants in that culture appear in her memoir as lacking either in sincerity or in true understanding of the tasks and the possibilities open to Symbolism.

Petrovskaia's "Vospominaniia," first excerpted in *Valery Briusov*, vol.

85 of *Literaturnoe nasledstvo* (Moscow, 1976), pp. 775–89, appeared in a complete version in *Minuvshee*, vol. 8 (Paris, 1989), pp. 17–90, edited and with an introduction by Elda Garetto. Citations will refer to the latter edition.

6. Andrei Bely, *Nachalo veka*, ed. Alexander Lavrov (Moscow, 1990), p. 308.

7. Petrovskaia, "Vospominaniia," p. 18.

8. Khodasevich, "Konets Renaty," p. 13.

9. Ibid., p. 14.

10. Ibid., p. 15. Nina's unflattering description of Bal'mont and his relations with women readily confirms the surmise. (Petrovskaia, "Vospominaniia," pp. 39–40.)

11. In his diary some years earlier Briusov recorded the parallel role Bal'mont played in his formation. Briusov first met Bal'mont in September 1894 and for some time saw in him the embodiment of the Symbolist poet: "Bal'mont just dropped in, exultant, mad, Edgar [Poe]-like." (Valery Briusov, *Dnevniki 1891–1910* [Moscow, 1927], p. 23.) Their relationship did not always remain on this level, however, as I have described elsewhere. (Joan Delaney Grossman, *Valery Bryusov and the Riddle of Russian Decadence* [Berkeley, Calif., 1985]. See especially pp. 180–90.)

12. Petrovskaia, "Vospominaniia," pp. 39–40.

13. Petrovskaia summed it up: "Bal'mont was for me in my youth a kind of shore from which I soon pushed away. For me he was neither a theurge illuminated from on high, like Bely, nor a master worthy of obeisance and deep voluntary submission, like V. Briusov." ("Vospominaniia," p. 40.)

14. I am indebted for much valuable bibliographical and other information to the Ph.D. dissertation of Irena Szwede, "The Works of Stanislaw Przybyszewski and Their Reception in Russia at the Beginning of the XX Century" (Stanford University, 1970).

15. Petrovskaia, "Vospominaniia," p. 41.

16. Her interest in spiritualism was shared by many of her immediate Moscow circle, including her husband and of course Valery Briusov. (See Joan Delaney Grossman, "Alternate Beliefs: Spiritualism and Pantheism Among the Early Modernists," in *Christianity and the Eastern Slavs*, vol. 2: Robert P. Hughes and Irina Paperno, eds., *Russian Culture in Modern Times* [Berkeley, Calif., forthcoming].)

17. Years later, in his memoirs, Bely described the amorphous quality of Argonautism and its traces in the later careers of those associated with it. (Bely, *Nachalo veka*, "Argonavtizm," pp. 123–32.)

18. Andrei Bely, "Material k biografii," unpublished, quoted in Alexander Lavrov, "Kommentarii," in Bely, *Nachalo veka*, pp. 634–35. The fullest discussion of the tangled Bely-Petrovskaia-Briusov relationship is to be found in S. S. Grechishkin and A. V. Lavrov, "Biograficheskie istochniki romana Briusova 'Ognennyi angel,'" *Wiener Slawistischer Almanach*, vols. 1 and 2 (1978).

19. Bely, *Nachalo veka*, p. 635.

20. Bely, *Nachalo veka*, pp. 304–7. This volume of Bely's memoirs was completed in 1930, revised in 1932, and published in 1933. (Lavrov, "Kommentarii," p. 557.)

21. Bely, *Nachalo veka*, p. 308. The comparison with the heroine of Dostoevsky's novel *Idiot* implies the equally interesting comparison of Bely and *Idiot*'s hero, Prince Myshkin, a Christ figure.

22. Bely, *Nachalo veka*, p. 306.

23. Ibid., pp. 304–5.

24. The section in *Nachalo veka* devoted to describing Bely's relations with Nina Petrovskaia is entitled "'Orfei,' izvodiashchii iz ada." One of the sections in Briusov's book *Stefanos* (published at the end of 1905), which reflected the high phase of his relationship with Nina, was called "Iz ada izvedennye," and one of the most admired poems in that book is "Orfei i Evridika." (Valery Briusov, *Sobranie sochinenii v semi tomakh* [Moscow, 1973–75], 1: 385–87.) Concerning the application of this myth to aesthetic problems see Irina Paperno's essay in this volume.

25. Bely, *Nachalo veka*, p. 311.

26. Ibid., p. 307.

27. Bely, "Material k biografii," quoted in Lavrov, "Kommentarii," pp. 635–36.

28. Bely explained his delays, withdrawals, and returns by the difficulty in clarifying for himself what was happening and the equal difficulty of persuading Petrovskaia to accept his interpretation. ("Material k biografii," quoted in Lavrov, "Kommentarii," p. 636.)

29. Petrovskaia, "Vospominaniia," p. 29.

30. Briusov's wife, Ioanna Matveevna, a former governess in the Briusov household, was totally outside the Symbolist milieu. She lived painfully through many such episodes, though Briusov's relationship with Petrovskaia was the longest. Briusov's need for her and his secure home endured through it all, much to Petrovskaia's chagrin. Petrovskaia's husband, Sergei Sokolov-Krechetov, on the other hand, was an active player in the culture and by this time had found another mate in the actress Lidiia Ryndina, whom he ultimately married. Ryndina pub-

lished reminiscences of those days later in emigration: Lidiia Ryndina, "Ushedshee," *Mosty*, no. 8 (1966): 295–312.

31. Bely, *Nachalo veka*, p. 308.

32. Petrovskaia, "Vospominaniia," p. 56. Their correspondence naturally offers much information. In addition to that published in *Valery Briusov*, a large number of unpublished letters are to be found in archival funds in the Lenin Library (GBL), the Central State Archive of Literature and Art (TsGALI), and the Institute of World Literature (IMLI).

33. Stanislaw Przybyszewski's early professional ambitions were first for architecture, then for medicine and psychology, and his literary enthusiasms were mixed. He recalled his reading in the autumn of 1889 as including "Nietzsche, Zola, Dostoevsky, Huysmans, Maupassant" (quoted in Maxime Herman, *Un sataniste polonais: Stanislas Przybyszewski* [Paris, 1939], p. 69). Przybyszewski's writing is heavily loaded with comparisons taken from the natural sciences, but, as Herman notes, the role he assigns to the "hero" in the advancement of the species puts him closer to romanticism than to naturalism.

34. Stanislaw Przybyszewski, "Shopen i Nitsshe," in his *Polnoe sobranie sochinenii* (Moscow, 1905–11), vol. 5 (1909), pp. 9–53. This essay was first published separately and then together with his study of the Swedish writer Ola Hansson, who had introduced him to the writings of Nietzsche (*Zur Psychologie des Individuums*, 2 vols. [Berlin, 1892], vol. 1: *Chopin und Nietzsche*). The contemporary Russian translations of Przybyszewski's Polish or German originals are used as the basis for the English translations since they are the versions Nina Petrovskaia and her circle read, along with most Russians of that time. Two multivolume Russian translations of Przybyszewski's works appeared between 1900 and 1910: one was published in two four-volume Scorpio editions and the other in the ten-volume *Polnoe sobranie sochinenii*, published by V. M. Sablin. A fuller publication history is to be found in Szwede, "Works of Przybyszewski," pp. 192–94, 213–16, 222–25, 241.

35. Przybyszewski, "Shopen i Nitsshe," p. 12.

36. Ibid., p. 39.

37. Ibid., p. 43.

38. Ibid., p. 40.

39. Cited in Herman, *Sataniste polonais*, p. 116.

40. "V nachale byl pol." Reference here is to the Russian translation entitled *Requiem Aeternam*, in Przybyszewski, *Polnoe sobranie* (Sablin), 7: 67. Originally published as *Totenmesse* (Berlin: Fontane, 1893). "Sex" here is sometimes translated as "lust."

41. The name "Certain" was taken from the title (*Certains*) of a collection of articles by J.-K. Huysmans dealing with artists so far little known to the public. Przybyszewski at that time was under the influence of Huysmans. (Herman, *Sataniste polonais*, p. 161 n. 2.)

42. "Obratnaia metamorfoza mozhet nachat'sia." Przybyszewski, *Requiem Aeternam*, p. 119.

43. See Olga Matich, "Androgyny and the Russian Religious Renaissance," in A. Mlikotin, ed., *Western Philosophical Systems in Russian Literature* (Los Angeles, 1979), pp. 164–75. Przybyszewski's acquaintance with the Cabala was perhaps less thorough than that of Vladimir Solov'ev. See the latter's article "Kabbala," in *Entsiklopedicheskii slovar'*, bk. 26 (St. Petersburg, 1894), pp. 782–84.

44. Matich, "Androgyny," p. 170.

45. "Os' nashei zhizni eto—liubov' i smert'." Stanislaw Przybyszewski, *Syny zemli*, *Vesy*, no. 5 (1904): 1. The original Polish version, *Synowie ziemi*, appeared in Lwow the same year. A new Russian collected edition of Przybyszewski's works in four volumes was published in 1904 by the Symbolist publishing house Scorpio, in which Briusov played a major role. Printing this short introduction in *Vesy*, also published by Scorpio and edited by Briusov, was of course a familiar strategy.

46. Ibid., p. 2.

47. Ibid., p. 3. Przybyszewski does not here use the term "androgyne," already associated with his name in other contexts (see below).

48. Even at this stage Przybyszewski's ideas were overtaking those of the Argonauts in her consciousness. Two stories by Nina Petrovskaia published in the January 1904 *Al'manakh "Grif"* are of interest in this regard. The first of them, "Poslednaia noch'," dedicated to Bely, is redolent of Argonautism. (See Grechishkin and Lavrov, "Biograficheskie," 1: 84.) But it is also not without a touch of Przybyszewski. The (male) narrator concludes a day and night of waiting for the coming of Christ by shooting himself, crying out: "I am coming!" This is the refrain of Przybyszewski's "Gorod smerti" (see below). The other, "Tsvetok ivanovoi nochi," ends with a murder and an easily recognizable Przybyszewskian flourish: "Love and death are eternal!"

49. Briusov, *Dnevniki*, 136.

50. Solov'ev's "Koldun-Kamen'" recounted an ancient belief, common to the mythology of some northern tribes, that the giant mossy boulders marking the Finnish landscape were wizards who, for some primeval crime, had been changed into stone, and who would come alive once a century to wreak havoc in nature. (Vladimir Solov'ev, *Stikhotvore-*

niia i shutochnye p'esy [Leningrad, 1974], pp. 102–3.) F. I. Buslaev wrote, in his *Russkii bogatyrskii epos* (Voronezh, 1987), that the mythology of Finnish and northern Germanic tribes presented some of their divinities as titanic figures easily mistaken for natural features and presented some natural features—cliffs, mountains—as the skeletons of ancient giants. See the Russian "starshii bogatyr'" Sviatogor, whose legendary origin Buslaev (p. 45) linked to the same myths.

51. Solov'ev, *Stikhotvoreniia*, pp. 105–6, 107, 112–13.

52. "Temnogo khaosa svetlaia doch'!" Solov'ev, "Na Saime zimoi," *Stikhotvoreniia*, p. 107.

53. Andrei Bely, *Vospominaniia ob A. A. Bloke* (Munich, 1969), p. 164.

54. In the first edition of *Stephanos* "Na Saime" is a cycle of seven poems forming part of the book's first section, "Vecherovye pesni." In later editions, beginning with Valery Briusov, *Puti i pereput'ia II* (Moscow, 1908), an eighth poem was added and the cycle was elevated to an independent section.

55. Briusov, "Menia iskavshego bezumii," *Sobranie sochinenii*, 1: 378; Valery Briusov, *Stephanos* (Moscow, 1906), p. 27.

56. Briusov, "Zheltym sholkom [*sic*], zheltym sholkom," "V dali, blagostno sverkaiushchii," and "Mokh, da veresk, da granity," *Stephanos*, pp. 28–29.

57. "Ia upoen—mne nichego ne nado! / O tol'ko b dlilsia etot iasnyi son," Briusov, *Stephanos*, p. 30.

58. In her memoir Nina wrote: "Darkness. I know and love it." Describing her experience she concludes: "Everything contradicts the most elementary physical laws, and therefore it is sweetly terrible and one wants it to endure, like the last, already conscious, stage of some kind of drug, when one cannot distinguish between vision and waking." ("Vospominaniia," p. 63.)

59. Briusov, "My v lodke vdoem" and "Goluboe, goluboe," *Stephanos*, pp. 30–31.

60. TsGALI, f. 376, op. 1, ed. khr. 4.

61. Letters of Briusov to Nina Petrovskaia, *Valery Briusov*, p. 791.

62. Przybyszewski, *Syny zemli*, p. 3.

63. Nina Petrovskaia, review of Stanislav Pszybyszewski's *Zaupokoinaia messa*, in *Pereval*, no. 1 (1906): 49.

64. Petrovskaia, review of *Zaupokoinaia messa*, p. 50.

65. From notes of D. M. Maximov, Institute of Russian Literature (IRLI), f. 39, ed. khr. 833. Liudmila Vilkina, a minor poetess and the wife of Nikolai Minsky (Vilenkin), was Briusov's current romantic inter-

est. I have treated this matter in *Bryusov and Russian Decadence*, chap. 9, "The Year 1905 and *Stephanos*."

66. Valery Briusov, "Strast'," *Vesy*, no. 8 (1904): 25.

67. Przybyszewski, *Syny zemli*, p. 3.

68. Two examples, early and late respectively, both plays, are Valery Briusov, *Zemlia*. (*Stseny budushchikh vremen*) (1905), in his *Polnoe sobranie sochinenii i perevodov* (St. Petersburg, 1913–14), vol. 15, and idem, *Diktator. Tragediia v piati deistviiakh i semi stsenakh iz budushchikh vremen* (1921), *Sovremennaia dramaturgiia*, no. 4 (1986), published by S. I. Gindin.

69. See particularly Valery Briusov, "Istiny," in his *Sobranie sochinenii* 6: 55–61. This sentiment is elaborated in letters and in his diary (*Dnevniki*, p. 61). See Grossman, *Bryusov and Russian Decadence*, chap. 7, "The Third Watch."

70. Briusov, *Sobranie sochinenii*, 1: 354.

71. Quoted in Briusov, *Dnevniki*, p. 61.

72. Briusov, "Istiny," p. 57.

73. In September 1901 Sergei Poliakov, the proprietor of the publishing house Scorpio and coeditor with Briusov, brought to him "one Semenov" (M. N. Semenov), a translator of Przybyszewski, to whom, Briusov later claimed, he hardly spoke (*Dnevniki*, p. 106). Briusov likewise referred slightingly to a fellow Russian tourist in Italy (May–June 1902) who talked incessantly about Przybyszewski (*Dnevniki*, p. 121). However, these disclaimers can in no way be taken as definitive.

74. "Strast'" should also be read as a companion piece to Briusov's much more famous essay considered programmatic for Symbolism, "Kliuchi tain," published in *Vesy*, no. 1 (1904): 3–21, also found in Briusov, *Sobranie sochienii*, 6: 78–93.

75. ". . . se fondre totalement dans l'être aimé, s'unir a lui de manière a récréer l'être dans sa primitive unité, l'Androgyne." (Herman, *Sataniste polonais*, p. 252.)

76. Petrovskaia, "Vospominaniia," p. 72.

77. Ibid. She recalled that twice, much later, he invited her to die with him. "Ia ne mogu sebe prostit', chto v 1909 godu ne soglasilas' na eto."

78. Briusov to Petrovskaia, Aug. 29, 1905, TsGALI, f. 376, op. 1, ed. khr. 4.

79. Petrovskaia, "Vospominaniia," p. 55.

80. Ibid., p. 56.

81. Stanislaw Przybyszewski, *V chas chuda* and "Gorod smerti," in his *Polnoe sobranie* (Sablin), vol. 1 (1905), pp. 139–226. This poem in prose

initially appeared in sections in the Cracow journal *Życie* in 1899 under successive titles: *Androgyne, W godzinie cudu,* and *Fragment.* The title *Androgyne* created various problems. The finished version was printed in Warsaw under the title *W godzinie cudu,* imposed by the Russian censors. (Herman, *Sataniste polonais,* p. 427 n. 1, p. 428 n. 1.)

82. Przybyszewski, "Gorod smerti," p. 225.

83. Briusov to Petrovskaia, Aug. 29, 1905, TsGALI, f. 376, op. 1, ed. khr. 4.

84. TsGALI, f. 56, op. 1, ed. khr. 95. Unfortunately most of the very large number of letters from Nina Petrovskaia to Briusov in TsGALI and in the Manuscript Division of the Lenin Library have been unavailable to me. However, the numerous Briusov letters to her, in TsGALI, GBL, and IMLI tell much about the relationship.

85. TsGALI, f. 376, op. 1, ed. khr. 4.

86. At the same time, the Russo-Japanese War was coming to a humiliating close for Russia, and Briusov poured his strong nationalist feelings into a series of poems that cheered on the rising revolutionary wave in the fall of 1905. This was a short-lived theme in his poetry. See Grossman, *Bryusov and Russian Decadence,* chap. 9, "The Year 1905 and *Stephanos,*" and chap. 10, "The Death of a Poet?"

87. Briusov to Petrovskaia, the night between June 13 and 14, 1906, *Valery Briusov,* p. 791. Briusov then accuses her of hiding the fact that she has herself already moved away from these ideals. If indeed Przybyszewski's ideas lie behind these names, Petrovskaia's writings at the time (see below) do not bear out Briusov's suspicion. However, further context, particularly others of Nina's letters, may cast a different light.

88. Briusov to Petrovskaia, June 5, 1906, ibid., p. 790.

89. Briusov to Petrovskaia, June 10, 1906, ibid.

90. Briusov, *Sobranie sochinenii,* 1: 604–5. Alexander Blok's first book, *Stikhi o Prekrasnoi Dame* (1903), was apparently indebted to Briusov for this as well as other inspirations. (See Joan Delaney Grossman, "Blok, Brjusov, and the Prekrasnaja Dama," in Walter N. Vickery and Bogdan B. Sagatov, eds., *Aleksandr Blok Centennial Conference* [Columbus, Ohio, 1984], p. 165.)

91. See Grossman, *Bryusov and Russian Decadence,* chap. 9.

92. Bely, *Nachalo veka,* pp. 311–12, 636–37. The section also contains the poem mythologizing the struggle between the two men and Briusov's alleged threats to Bely: "Balderu Loki." The myth of Orpheus and Eurydice had significance in another direction for Symbolism and particularly for Bely as a metaphor for one type of creativity, in which

fantastic images are drawn from the artist's soul into the world of reality. (See Irina Paperno's essay in this volume.)

93. Briusov, *Sobranie sochinenii*, 1: 396. Briusov's note identified Astarte as the goddess of love, to whom the morning star was dedicated (1: 628).

94. Ibid., 1: 396.

95. One poem from the cycle "Mgnoveniia" was omitted from the 1973–75 *Sobranie sochinenii*. It begins: "Muki sladostrastiia/Iskrivili guby." Briusov sent two others, "Molniia" and "V zastenke," to Liudmila Vilkina, presumably to revise the lament he had sent to her earlier about his failure to experience passion. "Molniia" he called "a photograph of my soul today" (Briusov, *Sobranie sochinenii*, 1: 627.)

96. Briusov, *Sobranie sochinenii*, 1: 400–401.

97. Ibid., 1: 406–7, 628.

98. This poem was later considerably revised, lengthened, and placed much less prominently, within a new short section "Mgnoveniia" (Briusov, *Sobranie sochinenii*, 1: 410–11). This fact suggests the special intention of its placement in the 1906 edition.

99. Petrovskaia, review of Scorpio translation of *Zapokoinaia messa* [*Totenmesse*], p. 50.

100. Nina Petrovskaia, review of *Dlia schast'ia*, in *Zolotoe runo*, no. 2 (1906): 111.

101. Ibid., pp. 112–13.

102. Nina Petrovskaia, *Sanctus Amor* (Moscow, 1908). The title came from Andrei Bely's 1903 poem "Predan'e," earlier called "Sanctus Amor," which reflected an early stage of his relations with Nina Petrovskaia (Grechishkin and Lavrov, "Biograficheskie," 1: 85). Vladislav Khodasevich dedicated a 1908 poem to Petrovskaia under that name (ibid., p. 102). Valery Briusov wrote a variation on Bely's poem, also called "Predan'e," which he composed and revised between November 1904 and January 1906 (Briusov, *Sobranie sochinenii*, 3: 290–92).

103. These are "Lozh'," "Rab," and "Severnaia skazka."

104. Nina Petrovskaia, "Brodiaga," in her *Sanctus Amor*, pp. 56–69. In the climactic scene the heroine describes herself as a "dukhovnaia brodiaga." The same words are used by Certain to describe himself in the Russian translation of *Totenmesse*.

105. Petrovskaia, "Brodiaga," pp. 59, 61–62.

106. Grechishkin and Lavrov, "Biograficheskie," 2: 83.

107. Quoted ibid., pp. 83–84. *Ognennyi angel* was published serially in *Vesy* in 1907, nos. 1–3, 5–12, and 1908 nos. 2, 3, 5–8. It came out

in 1908 in book form and in 1909 in a corrected edition with Briusov's explanatory notes.

108. Quoted in Grechishkin and Lavrov, "Biograficheskie," 2: 84.

109. In Khodasevich, *Nekropol'*, p. 21.

110. Briusov, *Sobranie sochinenii*, 4: 13.

111. Ibid., p. 302.

112. Grechishkin and Lavrov, "Biograficheskie," 2: 84. Briusov's letters to Nina, only a small number of which have so far been printed (in *Valery Briusov*), often approximate the cadence of his best lyrical prose. The narrative they contain, when published, will fill out yet more of Briusov's own biography and the story of this ill-fated relationship.

113. *Valery Briusov*, p. 790.

114. Briusov to Petrovskaia in Paris, Nov. 8/21, 1908, TsGALI, f. 376, op. 1, ed. khr. 4. This section is omitted from the letter as printed in *Valery Briusov*, pp. 793–94.

115. Briusov to Petrovskaia, "Dec. 1908/Jan. 1909," TsGALI, f. 376, op. 1, ed. khr. 4.

116. *Valery Briusov*, p. 785.

117. Przybyszewski, *Syny zemli*, p. 2.

118. See a discussion of this question in Joan Delaney Grossman, "Blok, Brjusov, and the Prekrasnaja Dama."

119. For an analysis of Briusov's position, see Joan Delaney Grossman, "Briusov's Defense of Poetry and the Crisis of Symbolism," in J. D. Clayton, ed., *Issues in Russian Literature Before 1917* (Columbus, Ohio, 1989), pp. 196–204.

Six / Wachtel: Viacheslav Ivanov

1. The work of Olga Deschartes, Ivanov's longtime friend and posthumous editor, represents a noteworthy exception to this tendency. Her "Vvedenie," the lengthy introduction to Viacheslav Ivanov's *Sobranie sochinenii* (Brussels, 1971–), 1: 7–227, consistently draws parallels between the biography and the literary work. Though an invaluable aid to understanding Ivanov's legacy, this essay nevertheless betrays its author's emotional attachment to her subject. The present study offers a different approach to many of the same issues.

2. Ivanov, *Sobranie sochinenii*, 2: 599. In this essay, all translations (from Russian, German, and Latin) are my own.

3. This notion comes most directly from Vladimir Solov'ev. Cf. James

West, *Russian Symbolism: A Study of Vyacheslav Ivanov and Russian Symbolist Aesthetics* (London, 1970), p. 172.

4. Vladimir Solov'ev, *Sochineniia v dvukh tomakh* (Moscow, 1990), 1: 744. Ivanov repeatedly attributes this concept, which has its origins in religious discourse, to Solov'ev (e.g., Ivanov, *Sobranie sochinenii*, 2: 538, 3: 305).

5. Ivanov, *Sobranie sochinenii*, 2: 538–39.

6. In this respect, Ivanov differs from Bely. Cf. J. D. Elsworth, *Andrey Bely: A Critical Study of the Novels* (Cambridge, Eng., 1983), p. 34: "In Ivanov's view the artist's task is to reveal the hidden, but real essence of things; in Bely's the artist, in common with other creative humans, creates an order that is not present in raw nature."

7. Ivanov first uses this phrase in his discussion of medieval art (*Sobranie sochinenii*, 2: 542–43). However, further usage (e.g., 2: 572, 3: 182–83, 4: 256) makes clear that he applied the term to any artistic movement that discovered the "true" reality hidden beneath the phenomenal world.

8. Ivanov made no apologies for his numerous coinages, asserting that "every new movement demands its own terminology" (ibid., 3: 87).

9. Ibid., 2: 598–99.

10. Such usage reflects the practice of the time. Even in Novalis's own writings, "magical idealism" is never explicitly defined. The phrase appears only in the "Fragments," which, in Ivanov's day, were published in such corrupt form that no reader could possibly have discerned the coherent philosophical system that modern scholars have reconstructed.

11. Ivanov, *Sobranie sochinenii*, 4: 740, emphasis in the original.

12. The fact that Novalis's beloved was named "Sophie" provided Ivanov with a felicitous link to Solov'ev's cult of Sophia. See ibid.

13. In 1912, a critic lamented the fact that this myth had achieved widespread acceptance. "It was mainly due to Tieck [i.e., Ludwig Tieck, Novalis's friend, publisher, and biographer] that a 'romantische Legende' about Novalis was formed and spread. The poet was considered a gloomy, melancholy mystic, a poetic dreamer, reveling in remote spiritual realms of fancy, a ghost-seer and visionary enthusiast, brooding over his loss, living only for his grief. . . . There is certainly a bit of truth in this characterization of Novalis, but unfortunately this has become the entire truth." J. F. Haussmann, "German Estimates of Novalis from 1800–1850," *Modern Philology*, 9, no. 3 (1912): 403.

14. A letter of 1810, written by the minor poet Justinus Kerner, exemplifies the widespread desire to disregard the "unromantic" aspects

of Novalis's life: "It has a strange and disturbing effect, when one imagines Novalis as a civil servant or an assessor of salt-mines. It's horrible!! I had imagined Novalis's life very differently. Also, that young lady Charpentier [i.e., the second fiancée] so disturbs the poesy." Cited by Hans-Joachim Mähl in the Afterword to Novalis, *Werke in einem Band* (Munich, 1984), p. 655.

15. Ivanov, *Sobranie sochinenii*, 4: 740. Sergei Auslender, in a review of Ivanov's lecture, notes: "the Romantics made Novalis's biography into a 'sweet saint's life.'" Yet this does not deter Auslender from continuing this very tradition. Accordingly, after Sophie's death, "[Novalis] lived another four years, having firmly told himself that he would die not from poison or a bullet, but from the firm desire not to live." Sergei Auslender, "Goluboi tsvetok," *Apollon*, no. 3 (1909): 41–42.

16. Five years later, in his essay on Novalis, Ivanov gave a far less romanticized account of the biography. See Ivanov, *Sobranie sochinenii*, 4: 268. In this respect (as in many others) he was clearly influenced by Professor F. A. Braun, whose essay on Novalis appeared in F. D. Batiushkov, ed., *Istoriia zapadnoi literatury* (Moscow, 1912), 1: 289–332.

17. Victor Zhirmunsky, *Religioznoe otrechenie v istorii romantizma* (Moscow, 1919), p. 7. Zhirmunsky, a Germanist intimately familiar with contemporary Russian literature, unabashedly projected his knowledge of Russian Symbolism onto his reading of German romanticism. When Zhirmunsky states in his introduction (p. 7), "Romantic poetry does not want to be 'only art,'" he consciously paraphrases Ivanov's already cited slogan: "Symbolism did not want to be and could not be 'only art'" (Ivanov, *Sobranie sochinenii*, 2: 599). An even more explicit example of this phenomenon occurs when Zhirmunsky (p. 99) places a passage from Alexander Blok as an epigraph to a section devoted to Clemens Brentano's *Godwi*.

18. For the history of composition and publication, see Ivanov, *Sobranie sochinenii*, 3: 862. The fact that Ivanov would excise a passage from a letter and publish it in a journal exemplifies the conflation of the literary and the biographical so characteristic of Russian Symbolism.

19. Ibid., p. 646. The original is in German:

Vor etwa dreissig Jahren war's: einige Sterne wurden eben erst am dämmernden Himmel sichtbar, als wir aus einer Bergschlucht herausfuhren an den Küstenstrich des Schwarzen Meeres. Da vernahm ich, mitten unterm Geplauder meiner Reisegefährtinnen, wie einen leisen Ruf aus meiner verborgenen Stille—oder war es ein seelisches Echo des fernen

Wellenschlags?—etliche lateinische Worte, so unerwartet, dass ich ihren Sinn zunächst nicht erfassen konnte. Umso bedeutsamer erschien er mir bei immer tieferer Meditation: wohnte ja dem auch schon früher irgendwie Gedachten, das jene Worte mir mit sanftem Nachdruck einprägten, eine so lichte Augenscheinlichkeit inne, dass sie auf mich wie eine neu gewonnene reale Erkenntnis wirkten. "Quod non est debet esse; quod est debet fieri; quod fit erit"—so hiess es. ("Was nicht ist, soll sein; und was ist, werden; und das Werdende wird sein.")

Der Gewohnheit getreu, das Tiefbewegende rhythmisch zu gestalten, habe ich den Versuch gemacht, mein heimliches Kleinod in den goldenen Reif eines Distichons einzufassen:

> Quod non est, Pater esse iubet fierique creatum,
> Spem iusso fieri Spiritus afflat: "eris."

Ivanov does *not* translate his distich: "What is not, Father will order to be and be created, / The Spirit breathes hope to what was ordered to be: 'you will be.'"

20. Ivanov went to the Crimea for the first time in the summer of 1908, as a guest of the Gertsyk family. See Evgeniia Gertsyk, *Vospominaniia* (Paris, 1973), pp. 53–54. Her version corroborates Ivanov's less precise statement ("about thirty years ago"), since he wrote the text in August of 1939 (see Olga Deschartes, "Vyacheslav Ivanov," *Oxford Slavonic Papers*, no. 5 [1954]: 41).

21. In the original text, a morphological detail accentuates Ivanov's special status: he is the only male in the group (he calls his companions "Reisegefährt*innen*").

22. Ivanov, *Sobranie sochinenii*, 1: 606. "Blazhen, kto slyshit pesn', i slyshit otzvuk." The entire poem is based on an elaborate set of echoes—motivic, aural, and intertextual (most obviously, to Pushkin's 1831 "Echo").

23. This notion had been present, although not fully elaborated, in Ivanov's early essays. See "Athena's Spear" (written in 1904) in Ivanov, *Sobranie sochinenii*, 1: 727.

24. Ibid., 2: 606, emphasis in the original.

25. The notion of a "polyphonic" echo may seem difficult to reconcile with Ivanov's theurgic ideal of maximum receptivity. It should be emphasized that this echo is never an expression of subjective will. According to Ivanov's own imagery, a Symbolist work causes "an awakening of certain overtones clearly sensed by us." The audience does not *actively*

add anything; the harmony arises independently within the listener. (See ibid., 2: 608.)

26. My emphasis. Cf. "Thoughts on Symbolism," where Ivanov again avoids identifying the source by describing the echo within the listener as "resembling at times a primordial remembrance . . . at times a distant, vague presentiment, at times the trembling of someone's familiar and desired approach" (ibid.).

27. Ivanov had spent nine semesters studying ancient history and classical philology at the University of Berlin. In his "Autobiographical Letter," he recalled participating in seminars that were conducted in Latin. (Ivanov, *Sobranie sochinenii*, 2: 17.) He wrote his 132-page dissertation in Latin: *De societatibus vectigalium publicorum populi romani* (St. Petersburg, 1910); it was published almost fifteen years after its completion.

28. The phrase is from Deschartes, "Vyacheslav Ivanov," p. 41.

29. The interplay of Latin (spoken by Sophia) and Russian (the language of "the flesh") is thematized in the distich "Rosa Sophia" (Ivanov, *Sobranie sochinenii*, 2: 502). In structure and message, these mystical verses bear a striking resemblance to the Latin distich in "An Echo."

30. For a detailed account of Mintslova's connection to Russian Symbolism, see Maria Carlson, "Ivanov-Belyj-Minclova: The Mystical Triangle," in Fausto Malcovati, ed., *Cultura e memoria: Atti del terzo Simposio Internazionale didicato a Vjačeslav Ivanov* (Florence, 1988), 1: 63–79.

31. Manuscript division of the Lenin Library in Moscow (hereafter referred to by the Russian abbreviation GBL), f. 109, kart. 30, ed. khr. 2.

32. Gertsyk, *Vospominaniia*, pp. 48–49.

33. Ivanov notes month and day, but not year. Mintslova's letters, which have survived in full, lead me to believe that the year was 1908. While I refer to Ivanov's texts as letters, they are actually drafts. The final versions, if sent at all, presumably disappeared with Mintslova.

34.   Separated for a short time
             Joined together for a long time
             In God's honor
             What has suffered the earth
             Will come here exhausted by life
             For days of consecration.

35. GBL f. 109, kart. 10, ed. khr. 20.

36. Part of the problem is of course the very notion of "the reader." Ivanov envisioned only one—Mintslova, who, to judge from her "other-

worldly" responses, did not recognize any artifice whatsoever. In a letter of January 21, 1908 (night), Mintslova wrote: "I received your registered letter. *All* of your visions are so harmonious, clear, and unconditional, that it is difficult to speak about them, and only words of Thanks are possible here, words of Great joy.—All of them, these visions, say *one thing*—that She Herself wants to lead you, and that with every day your powers grow" (GBL, f. 109, kart. 30, ed. khr. 2, l. 92). Similar passages can be found in virtually all of the letters Mintslova wrote to Ivanov at this time.

37. Ivanov's letter of January 16 makes clear that the idea of midnight prayers came from Mintslova: "Dear teacher, today at 12 o'clock midnight I prayed, as you ordered" (GBL, f. 109, kart. 10, ed. khr. 20).

38. Since the text of the letter switches to Russian after the Latin poem, one can assume that Lidiia also reverts to Russian in the discussion that ensues. The initial contact, however, is forged by means of Latin.

39. Deschartes, "Vvedenie," p. 130.

40. Ivanov, *Sobranie sochinenii*, 2: 395. The only difference is that the pronoun *quidquid* ("whatever") is altered to read *quisquis* ("whoever"), with the participial endings changed to reflect this (*perpessum* to *perpessus, fessum* to *fessus*). The minor emendation, reflected in Deschartes's version, is noteworthy insofar as it reveals yet another inconsistency. Deschartes emphasizes that Ivanov, when he incorporated these verses in *Cor Ardens*, made no changes whatsoever; see Deschartes, "Vvedenie," p. 131.

41. Ivanov, *Sobranie sochinenii*, 2: 787. Kuzmin was living in "the Tower" at this point. In his diaries, Ivanov frequently comments on Kuzmin's musical performances.

42. See Viacheslav Ivanov, *Ellinskaia religiia stradaiushchego boga, Novyi put'*, no. 2 (1904): 62. "The Ninth Symphony, finally, after so many centuries of oblivion, realizes in spirit the Dionysian dithyramb."

43. See, for example, "Prayer of Morning," in *Messale dell' Assemblea Cristiana* (Torino, 1973), p. 1491. R. E. Pomirchy, in his notes to the Soviet "Biblioteka poeta" edition of Ivanov, incorrectly states that the phrase occurs in the "Pater Noster."

44. Ivanov, *Sobranie sochinenii*, 2: 424.

45. Ibid., p. 537.

46. The biblical passage describes the "journey to Emmaus," when, after his resurrection, Christ meets and speaks with two apostles. "And they said one to another, Did not our heart burn within us [in Latin,

nonne cor nostrum ardens erat in nobis], while he talked with us by the way, and while he opened to us the scriptures?"

47. Ivanov, *Sobranie sochinenii*, 2: 772.

48. For a thorough discussion of the biblical and Dantesque uses of this image, see Pamela Davidson, *The Poetic Imagination of Vyacheslav Ivanov* (Cambridge, Eng., 1989), pp. 195–200.

49. GBL, f. 109, kart. 8, ed. khr. 25. In 1989, I was refused access to these documents. I am therefore extremely indebted to K. M. Azadovsky, who generously took the time to examine them and take notes for me. In 1991, I received access and was able to confirm his discoveries.

50. For a discussion of these translations, see Efim Etkind, "Poeziia Novalisa: 'Mifologicheskii perevod' Viacheslava Ivanova," in Malcovati, *Cultura e memoria*, 2: 171–85; Dimitri Ivanov's commentary in Ivanov, *Sobranie sochinenii*, 4: 724–37; and Michael Wachtel, "Goethe and Novalis in the Life and Work of Vyacheslav Ivanov" (Ph.D. diss., Harvard University, 1990), pp. 114–240.

51. The 1906–7 experiments in "the Tower" (e.g., the Hafiz tavern, the relationships with Sabashnikova and Gorodetsky) also reveal attempts to organize life in accordance with literary and/or theoretical ideals. See N. Bogomolov, "'My—dva grozoi zazhzhennye stvola'. Erotika v russkoi poezii—ot simvolistov do oberiutov," *Literaturnoe obozrenie*, no. 11 [1991]: 59–61; Davidson, *Poetic Imagination*, pp. 110–20; and Matich's contribution to this book.

Seven / Gutkin: Symbolist Aesthetic Utopia

I wish to acknowledge, with much gratitude, the Academic Senate grant of the University of California at Los Angeles which provided partial financial support for my contribution to this volume.

1. See, for instance, A. Kruchenykh and V. Khlebnikov, "Slovo kak takovoe" ("The Word as Such"), which contains the most overt attack on Symbolism. The manifesto is printed in Vladimir Markov, ed., *Manifesty i programmy russkih futuristov* (Munich, 1967); see especially p. 56.

2. Quoted in David Elliott, *New Worlds: Russian Art and Society, 1900–1937* (New York, 1986), p. 15. The text for *Victory over the Sun* was written by Alexei Kruchenykh, with the exception of the Prologue, which was by Victor Khlebnikov; Kazimir Malevich designed costumes and sets; Mikhail Matiushin wrote the music. Solar symbolism, prominent among

Symbolists in general, was mythologized by the Argonauts; see the study by Alexander Lavrov in this volume.

3. Il'ia Zdanevich and Mikhail Larionov, "Why We Are Painting Ourselves," quoted in translation by John Bowlt, *Russian Art of the Avant-garde: Theory and Criticism. 1902–1934*, 2nd ed. (New York, 1988), p. 81.

4. Quoted in Elliott, *New Worlds*, p. 15.

5. The First All-Russian Congress of Singers of the Future took place in July 1913 at Matiushin's summer cottage; apparently there were only three participants—the host, Malevich, and Kruchenykh.

6. Quoted in Elliott, *New Worlds*, p. 15.

7. Victor Khlebnikov, "Prolog. Chernotvorskie vestuchki," in *Pobeda nad solntsem: Opera A. Kruchenykh, Muzyka M. Matiushina* (Petersburg, 1913), p. 1.

8. [Iz al'manakha "Sadok sudei"], in Markov, *Manifesty i programmy*, p. 52.

9. Kruchenykh and Khlebnikov, "Slovo kak takovoe," p. 56.

10. [Iz al'manakha "Sadok sudei"], p. 52.

11. Benedikt Livshits, *Polutoroglazyi strelets*, in his *Stikhotvoreniia. Perevody. Vospominaniia* (Leningrad, 1989), p. 417.

12. Ibid., p. 392.

13. For a discussion of "millenarian" conceptions of history see Rolf Gruner, *Philosophies of History: A Critical Essay* (Aldershot, Eng., 1985).

14. In the essays of the learned Andrei Bely, especially in those dominated by futurological themes (such as "Theater and Contemporary Drama" ["Teatr i sovremennaia drama"] or "The Window onto the Future" ["Okno v budushchee"]), one finds references, used interchangeably, to Nietzsche, Solov'ev, Marx, and Engels. It is likely that Maiakovsky never perused anything by Nietzsche, Marx, or Fedorov, yet one can discern something very similar to Bely's cross-referential spectrum in his poems, particularly in those of 1915–18. For example, in *The Cloud in Trousers* (*Oblako v shtanakh*, 1915), the poet portrays himself as a "loud-lipped Zarathustra" of the downtrodden proletarian masses. In *War and World* (*Voina i mir*, 1916), he paints the current World War as an apocalypse, and then in its aftermath envisions the coming millenarian world wherein, among other things, death will be abolished and the dead resurrected ("iz mogil'nykh kurganov, / miasom obrastut khoronennye kosti").

15. On god-building see chap. 4 in George F. Kline, *Religious and Anti-Religious Thought in Russia* (Chicago, 1968). See also Zenovia Sochor, *Revolution and Culture* (Ithaca, N.Y., 1988).

16. In the 1960's and early 1970's there was a revival of Bogdanov's organizational ideas, which were interpreted as precursory to the growing fields of cybernetics and structuralism. See, for instance, the introduction to A. Bogdanov, *Essays in Tektology*, translated from the Russian by George Gorelik (Seaside, Calif., 1980). See also Ilmari Susiluoto, *The Origins and Development of Systems Thinking in the Soviet Union: Political and Philosophical Controversies from Bogdanov and Bukharin to Present-day Re-evaluations* (Helsinki, 1982).

17. Bogdanov addressed this task comprehensively in *Techtology: The Universal Organizational Science (Vseobshchaia organizatsionnaia nauka (tektologiia)*, written during 1912 (vol. 1) and 1917 (vol. 2), and published in a three-volume edition in 1922.

18. A. Bogdanov, *Filosophiia zhivogo opyta* (Moscow, 1911), p. 253.

19. See chaps. 5 and 6 in Bogdanov, *Essays in Tektology*.

20. Trained in psychology and medicine, Bogdanov had a personal commitment to the realization of this task as the head of the Institute for Blood Transfusion, created in Moscow in 1926. Bogdanov's death, in 1928, came as a result of a transfusion experiment that he conducted on himself.

21. Bogdanov, *Filosophiia zhivogo opyta*, p. 252.

22. A. Bogdanov, *Kul'turnye zadachi nashego vremeni* (Moscow, 1911), pp. 7, 11.

23. Ibid., p. 14.

24. See the chapter entitled "Nauka budushchego" in Bogdanov, *Filosophiia zhivogo opyta*.

25. On *Proletkul't* see Lynn Mally, *Culture of the Future: The Proletcult Movement in Revolutionary Russia* (Berkeley, Calif., 1990).

26. For information on N.O.T. see chap. 4 in Richard Stites's *Revolutionary Dreams: Utopian Vision and Experimental Life in the Russian Revolution* (Oxford, 1989).

27. Quoted in Halina Stephan, *"Lef" and the Left Front of the Arts* (Munich, 1981), p. 9.

28. Leon Trotsky, *Literatura i revoliutsiia* (Moscow, 1923), pp. 184–88. Hereafter, the translations are mine, based on Rose Strunsky's translation in Trotsky, *Literature and Revolution*, 2nd ed. (Ann Arbor, Mich., 1966).

29. I refer here to Maiakovsky's early poem (1913) "A vy mogli by?" (Vladimir Maiakovsky, *Polnoe sobranie sochinenii v trinadtsati tomakh* (Moscow, 1955–61), vol. 1, p. 40). See the Appendix at the end of the present volume for the Russian text of the poem.

30. Trotsky, *Literatura i revoliutsiia*, p. 187.

31. Ibid., p. 188.   32. Ibid.

33. Ibid.   34. Ibid., p. 189.

35. Ibid., p. 190.

36. When Trotsky offhandedly mentioned new gigantic canals, oases in the desert, and the reversing of the course of rivers, he put his finger on a number of aspirations and even actual projects that later became a part of the party's "Programs for the Building of Communism." As an example, one may cite the construction of the Baltic–White Sea canal and other canals in the 1930's, or mention that the project to divert the flow of the major Siberian rivers in order to irrigate the desert was officially abandoned only in August 1986, with the beginning of Gorbachev's *perestroika*.

37. Stites, in *Revolutionary Dreams*, gives a comprehensive review of these trends.

38. For a discussion of the term "Left Art," see the Introduction to Stephan's *"Lef" and the Left Front of the Arts*.

39. Both Constructivism and Production Art have been the subject of many studies in recent decades. Christina Lodder's *Russian Constructivism* (New Haven, Conn., 1983) and Anatolii Mazaev's *Kontseptsiia "proizvodstvennogo iskusstva" 20-kh godov* (Moscow, 1975) present the most comprehensive treatments of the two movements respectively.

40. Maiakovsky, *Polnoe sobranie sochinenii*, 2: 18–19.

41. V. Tatlin, with T. Shapiro, I. Meerzon, and P. Vinogradov, "The Work Ahead of Us" ("Nasha predstoiashchaia rabota," 1921). Quoted in translation by Bowlt, *Russian Art of the Avant-garde*, p. 206.

42. The idea apparently belongs to Kazimir Malevich, in whose Suprematist project of the early 1920's the ideal city of the future was conceived as a system of floating skyscrapers. It had a substantial following throughout the decade. Among other examples one could name the model "Flying City" (1928) by Georgy Krutikov and the design of a flying city by I. Iuzefovich dated 1927–28.

43. B. A. [Boris Arvatov], "Oveshchestvlennaia utopiia," *Lef*, no. 1 (Mar. 1923): 64, emphases in the original. Glass and light metals, such as aluminum, are materials that make one think of the Crystal Palace, a pavilion that was built in 1851 near London for what may be called the proto–World Exposition and that inspired Nikolai Chernyshevsky's vision of the future ideal city.

44. Ibid.

45. Photographs of Galaktionov's "Folding bed" and Sobolev's de-

sign for a bed that could be easily converted into an armchair from this exhibit were published in *Lef*, no. 3 (July 1923): 54–55.

46. *Lef*'s critic dubbed these experiments "the concept of mobile thing." Varst [Varvara Stepanova], "Rabota konstruktivistskoi molodezhi," ibid., p. 56.

47. On polemic about the bed see Olga Matich, "Sueta vokrug krovati: Utopicheskaia organizatsiia byta i russkii avangard," *Literaturnoe obozrenie*, no. 11 (1991): 80–84.

48. Alexandra Ekster and Vera Mukhina may be added to the list of artists who worked on clothes design for mass production.

49. "Iunoshe, obdumyvaiushchemu zhit'e, reshaiushchemu—sdelat' by zhizn' s kogo, skazhu ne zadumyvaias'—'Delai ee s tovarishcha Dzerzhinskogo.'" Maiakovsky, "Khorosho!," in *Polnoe sobranie sochinenii*, 8: 319.

50. Reproduced in Elliott, *New Worlds*, p. 93.

51. Vladimir Papernyi, *Kul'tura dva* (Ann Arbor, Mich., 1985), p. 122; see the photograph of the apartment on p. 313.

52. "[B]io-mekhanicheskii teatr povel bor'bu s psikhologizmom . . . , kul'tiviruia navyki, neobhodimye cheloveku proizvodstva." Nikolai Chuzhak, "Pod znakom zhiznestroeniia. Opyt osoznaniia iskusstva dnia," *Lef*, no. 1 (Mar. 1923): 32, emphasis in the original in boldface.

53. Tret'iakov's expression shows a casual mixture of Viacheslav Ivanov's key notions with the more current ideas of Bogdanov on "organizational art." S. T. [Sergei Tret'iakov], "Vsevolod Meierkhol'd," *Lef*, no. 2 (May 1923): 169.

54. If Meyerhold's production of Blok's *The Puppet Show* (*Balaganchik*) in 1906 marked the debut of Russian modernist theater, his staging of Maiakovsky's *The Bathhouse* (*Bania*) in 1930 may be considered its closing act.

55. Viacheslav Ivanov, *Sobranie sochinenii* (Brussels, 1971–), 2: 95. See also Andrei Bely, "Teatr i sovremennaia drama," first published in Georgy Chulkov, ed., *Teatr. Kniga o novom teatre* (St. Petersburg, 1908), and later reprinted in Bely's *Arabeski* (Moscow, 1911). For a discussion of varying Symbolist attitudes toward theater see Bernice Glatzer Rosenthal, "Theater as Church: The Vision of the Mystical Anarchists," *Russian History / Histoire russe*, 4, pt. 2 (1977): 122–41.

56. On Meyerhold's biomechanics see Marjorie Hoover, *Meyerhold: The Art of Conscious Theater* (Amherst, Mass., 1974), p. 92. See also N. Moranjak-Bamburac, "'Teatral'nyi Oktiabr'—istoriia dvizheniia," *Russian Literature* (Holland), 19 (1986): 32–33, and M. Kolesnikov, "Con-

structivist Theater and Ballet as Laboratories for the New Man," forthcoming in the proceedings of the conference "The Russian Avantgarde," held at the University of Southern California, Los Angeles, November 1990.

57. V. E. Meierkhol'd, [Otzyv o knige A. IA. Tairova "Zapiski rezhissera"], in his *Stat'i. Pis'ma. Rechi. Besedy*, vol. 2 (Moscow, 1968), p. 43, Meyerhold's emphases.

58. See Moranjak-Bamburac, "Teatral'nyi Oktiabr," pp. 32–33.

59. That is to say, these are the only articles discovered by scholars so far. On Chuzhak see Hans Günther, "Zhiznestroenie," *Russian Literature* (Holland), 20 (1986): 41–48.

60. For this analysis I had at my disposal the reprinted version of "K estetike marksizma," which appeared in a collection of Chuzhak's prerevolutionary essays, *K dialektike iskusstva. Ot realizma do iskusstva kak odnoi iz proizvodstvennykh form* (*Toward a Dialectics of Art: From Realism to Art as a Form of Production*) (Chita, 1921), pp. 23–34. The collection consists primarily of reprints of his prerevolutionary critical essays advocating, for the most part, Symbolist and Futurist literary experiments. All the quotations below are from this edition.

61. Nikolai Chuzhak, "Literatura zhiznestroeniia," *Novyi Lef*, no. 10 (Oct. 1928): 12–17, and no. 11 (Nov. 1928): 15–19.

62. *Literatura fakta. Pervyi sbornik rabotnikov lefa*, ed. N. Chuzhak (Munich, 1972).

63. Chuzhak, "K estetike marksizma," p. 25.

64. Ibid., p. 33.

65. See Belyi, *Arabeski*, pp. 32–35.

66. "Izobrazit' [zhizn'] . . . ne prosto kak 'ob"ektivnuiu real'nost',' a izobrazit' deistvitel'nost' v ee revoliutsionnom razvitii." The formula—which first appeared in an essay by Ivan Gronsky in *Literaturnaia gazeta* on May 20, 1932, with a slightly different wording—received its final codification in the opening speech of Andrei Zhdanov at the First Congress of Soviet Writers, in 1934. See *Pervyi vsesoiuznyi s"ezd sovetskikh pisatelei. Stenograficheskii otchet* (Moscow, 1934), p. 4.

67. Chuzhak, "K estetike marksizma," pp. 24 and 25, Chuzhak's emphases.

68. Ibid., p. 25, Chuzhak's emphasis. In Solv'ev's text all the words in the phrase are italicized. See "Obshchii smysl iskusstva," in Vladimir Solov'ev, *Sochineniia v dvukh tomakh* (Moscow, 1988), 2: 399.

69. Chuzhak, "K estetike marksizma," p. 25.

70. Nikolai Chuzhak, "Kakoe zhe iskusstvo blizhe proletariatu?," in his *K dialektike iskusstva*, p. 42.

71. Nikolai Chuzhak, "Vvedenie," in his *K dialektike iskusstva*, p. 6.

72. Chuzhak was a member of *Inkhuk* (Russian acronym for the Institute of Artistic Culture, which functioned in 1921–24) and, as mentioned, an editorial member of *Lef*, the journal that served as the forum
of the Left Art movement.

73. First section of "Pod znakom zhiznestroeniia," entitled "Early
Search" ("Rannie poiski"), consists largely of quotations from Chuzhak's
previous work (see pp. 14–22). Evidently, Chuzhak's penchant for quoting himself, an uncanny stylistic procedure, served to demonstrate that
his ideas emerged independently but coincided with those of the "most
revolutionary and truly creative" groups in the center (p. 20), as well
as to show life-building aesthetics as historically predetermined—i.e., as
having sprung up independently and inevitably in autonomous minds
and distant locales.

74. Specifically, the quotation from "Toward Marxist Aesthetics"
cited earlier (see no. 64) is repeated verbatim but for the words "takov
ternistyi, no radostnyi put' geniia" ("such is the thorny, but joyful, path
of the genius"), which are replaced by "such is the path of art" ("vot put'
iskusstva"). Chuzhak, "Pod znakom zhiznestroeniia," p. 17.

75. Günther suggests the influence of Bogdanov, pointing to the
semantic synonymy between "techtology," as Bogdanov called his "universal organizational science," and Chuzhak's term "life-*building*" (Günther, "Zhiznestroenie," p. 45). It is equally possible that Chuzhak's term
reflects the pathos of construction that dominated the Soviet culture in
the 1920's. "Building of new life" (*stroitel'stvo novoi zhizni*) and, eventually,
"building socialism" (and then communism), became clichés that permeated every form of expression—from popular songs to newspapers
and to party programs.

76. Chuzhak, "Pod znakom zhiznestroeniia," p. 20. (The quote is repeated from Chuzhak's essay "Kakoe zhe iskusstvo blizhe proletariatu?,"
p. 51). The metaphor of Pygmalion and Galatea is borrowed from Symbolist discourse, where it served as the primary trope for the expression
of "life-creating" ideas (see the essay by Irene Masing-Delic in this collection). Although Chuzhak uses the metaphor in a different context,
its core meaning remains intact—namely, the idea of bringing a "dead
form" to life. It is clear from Chuzhak's general line of argument that
the Futurists' experimentation would be but an empty form had they
not been linked, by historical divination, to the proletarian cause.

77. Chuzhak, "Pod znakom zhiznestroeniia," p. 21. He alludes to
concrete projects and text, such as Meyerhold's biomechanics and Maiakovsky's metaphor of artist as wood carver (see p. 179).

78. Ibid., p. 13.

79. Ibid., p. 32. It is difficult to agree with Günther, who says that in this second stage of Chuzhak's career as theorist, the term "life-building" exists only as a theoretical postulate with no corresponding aesthetic practice (Günther, "Zhiznestroenie," p. 41). In fact, the main purpose of Chuzhak's essay was to validate such trends as Constructivism and Production Art as current examples of "life-building."

80. *"Tvorchestvo novykh ideologicheskikh ili matrial'nykh tsennostei—vot edinstvenno nadezhnyi kriterii, s kotorym dialektik podkhodit k khudozhestvu."* Chuzhak, "Pod znakom zhiznestroeniia," p. 37, Chuzhak's emphasis.

81. "Osoznaniiu rukovodiashchei filosofii iskusstva, *kak odnogo iz metodov zhiznestroeniia*—dolzhny byt' posviashcheny nashi usiliia." Ibid., p. 33, Chuzhak's emphasis.

82. Tret'iakov, "Otkuda i kuda (Perspektivy futurizma)," *Lef*, no. 1 (Mar. 1923): 192–203.

83. Ibid., pp. 198 and 202.

84. Ibid., pp. 201–2.

85. Ibid., pp. 200–201.

86. "Isskusstvo v zhizn', k polnomu rastvoreniiu v nei!" Ibid., p. 197.

87. "Novyi chelovek v deistvitel'nosti, v ezhednevnykh postupkakh, v stroe svoei zhizni material'noi i psikhicheskoi—vot chto dolzhen budet prodemonstrirovat' futurism." Ibid., p. 203.

88. Until recently, in existing interpretations of the theoretical origins of socialist realist aesthetics, both Western and Soviet, emphasis has inevitably been placed upon Marxist theories—political, economic, and literary—and on the role of party policy in creating socialist realism. See, for example, the comprehensive study by Herman Ermolaev, *Soviet Literary Theories (1917–1934): The Genesis of Socialist Realism* (Berkeley, Calif., 1963). In the past decade some attempts were made to view socialist realism as an autonomous cultural phenomenon and to reconsider the role of the avant-garde in relation to socialist realism. Among them should be mentioned Katerina Clark's *The Soviet Novel: History as Ritual*, 2nd ed. (Chicago, 1985); Vladimir Papernyi's *Kul'tura 2* (Ann Arbor, Mich., 1985); and Boris Groys's *Gesumtkunstwerk Stalin: Die gespaltente Kultur in der Sowjetunion* (Munich, Vienna, 1988), English translation, *The Total Art of Stalinism: Avant Garde, Aesthetic Dictatorship, and Beyond*, trans. Charles Rougle (Princeton, N.J., 1992). See also the essay by Boris Groys, "Stalinism kak esteticheskii fenomen," *Sintaksis*, no. 17 (1987): 98–110.

89. *Sovetskaia literatura na novom etape. Stenogramma pervogo plenuma orgkomiteta Soiuza sovetskikh pisatelei* (Moscow, 1933), pp. 144–45.

90. Vladimir Papernyi was the first to point out the paradoxical fact that socialist realism both rejected and realized life-building ideas of the avant-garde. Papernyi, *Kul'tura 2*, p. 218. Boris Groys further attempted to sort out what was taken and what rejected by the Stalinist aesthetic ideology from the avant-garde. See chap. 2 in his *Total Art of Stalinism*.

91. Groys, *Total Art of Stalinism*, p. 35.

92. Maxim Gorky, "Doklad na pervom s"ezde pisatelei," in *Pervyi vsesoiuznyi s"ezd sovetskikh pisatelei*, p. 15.

93. Hence also the generic peculiarities of the socialist realist novel which Katerina Clark defined aptly as "modal schizophrenia." Clark, *The Soviet Novel*, p. 36.

94. *Pervyi vsesoiuznyi s"ezd sovetskikh pisatelei*. p. 4.

95. N. Valentinov, *Dva goda s simvolistami* (Stanford, Calif., 1969), p. 127.

Index

In this index an "f" after a number indicates a separate reference on the next page, and an "ff" indicates separate references on the next two pages. A continuous discussion over two or more pages is indicated by a span of page numbers, e.g., "57–59." *Passim* is used for a cluster of references in close but not consecutive sequence.

Index   283

Library of Congress Cataloguing-in-Publication Data

Creating life : the aesthetic utopia of Russian modernism /
edited by Irina Paperno and Joan Delaney Grossman
p. cm.
Includes index.
ISBN 0-8047-2288-9 (alk. paper)
1. Russian literature—19th century—History and criticism.
2. Russian literature—20th century—History and criticism.
3. Symbolism (Literary movement)—Russia.
4. Modernism (Literature)—
Russia.   I. Paperno, Irina.   II. Grossman, Joan Delaney.
PG3015.5.S9C74   1994
891'.709—dc20   93-27948   CIP
∞ This book is printed on acid-free paper.